Beckett On and On . . .

Beckett On and On . . .

Edited by
Lois Oppenheim
and Marius Buning

Madison • Teaneck
Fairleigh Dickinson University Press
London: Associated University Presses

© 1996 by Associated University Presses, Inc.

All rights reserved. Authorization to photocopy items for internal or personal use, or the internal or personal use of specific clients, is granted by the copyright owner, provided that a base fee of $10.00, plus eight cents per page per copy is paid directly to the Copyright Clearance Center, 222 Rosewood Drive, Danvers, Massachusetts 01923.
[0-8386-3623-3/96 $10.00 + 8¢ pp, pc.]

Associated University Presses
440 Forsgate Drive
Cranbury, N.J. 08512

Associated University Presses
25 Sicilian Avenue
London WC1A 2QH, England

Associated University Presses
P.O. Box 338, Port Credit
Mississauga, Ontario
Canada L5G 4L8

The paper used in this publication meets the requirements
of the American National Standard for Permanence of Paper
for Printed Library Materials Z39.48-1984

Library of Congress Cataloging-in-Publication Data

Beckett on and on— / edited by Lois Oppenheim and Marius Buning.
    p. cm.
  Papers presented to the Second International Samuel Beckett Conference, held in The Hague, Apr. 22, 1992.
  Includes index.
  ISBN 0-8386-3623-3 (alk. paper)
  1. Beckett, Samuel, 1906– —Criticism and interpretation--Congresses. I. Oppenheim, Lois. II. Buning, Marius. III. International Beckett Symposium (2nd : 1992 : The Hague)
PR6003.E282Z57186 1996
848'.91409—dc20   95-20868
                                                                               CIP

PRINTED IN THE UNITED STATES OF AMERICA

Contents

Introduction / 7
    LOIS OPPENHEIM

Part 1. Gender and Genre

"Fuck Life": *Rockaby,* Sex, and the Body / 19
    LESLIE HILL

Beckett's Model of Masculinity: Male Hysteria in
    Not I / 27
    ANDREAS BJØRNERUD

Gender in Beckett's Music Machine / 36
    MARY BRYDEN

Beckett's Irish Rhythm Embodied in His Polyphony / 44
    JOHANNEKE VAN SLOOTEN

A Short Statement with Long Shadows: *Watt*'s Arsene
    and His Kind(s) / 61
    JOHN PILLING

Beckett's Trilogy and the Limits of Autobiography / 69
    FRANK MATTON

Mourning, Schopenhauer, and Beckett's Art of
    Shadows / 83
    ANGELA MOORJANI

Re-Mythologizing Beckett: The Metaphors of Metafiction
    in *How It Is* / 102
    WANDA BALZANO

Entering Beckett's Postmodern Space / 111
    ELIZABETH KLAVER

Part 2. Textuality and Theatricality

"My Life Natural Order More or Less in the Present More or Less": Textual Immanence as the Textual Impossible in Beckett's Works / 127
CARLA LOCATELLI

Rehearsals for the End of Time: Indeterminacy and Performance in Beckett / 148
GERRY MCCARTHY

The Proper Handling of Beckett's Plays / 160
ROBERT SCANLAN

Au Contraire: The Question of Beckett's Bilingual Text / 164
DAVID J. GORDON

"A Voice from Elsewhere": Impossible Survivals and the Annihilating Power of Language in Beckett's Fiction / 178
HARRY VANDERVLIST

Dramatizing Silence: Beckett's Shorter Plays / 187
DOROTHEE OSTMEIER

Undoing and Doing: Allegories of Writing in the *Trilogy* / 199
LI-LING TSENG

Beckett's Dramatic Vision and Classical Taoism / 212
KIRILL O. THOMPSON

Special Features of Beckett Performances in Japan / 226
MARIKO HORI TANAKA

The Syntax of Closure: Beckett's Late Drama / 240
HERSH ZEIFMAN

Notes on Contributors / 255
Index / 259

Introduction

LOIS OPPENHEIM

In April 1992, "Beckett in the 1990s," the Second International Samuel Beckett Conference, was held in The Hague. This symposium was closely associated with the Samuel Beckett Festival, a two-week-long event in which an unprecedented number of actors, directors, and composers came together to celebrate in performance Beckett's work in the theater. The festival featured some of the world's best-known Beckett theater artists (including Barry McGovern, Walter Asmus, and Pierre Chabert), while the academic conference included well over a hundred speakers, drawn from six continents, in thirty panel and paper sessions, including a plenary session with Beckett's American, English, German, and Dutch publishers. Following six years after the first international Beckett conference at the University of Stirling in Scotland, it was the largest symposium devoted to Beckett studies around the world to date.

From the outstanding contributions to the conference, Marius Buning and I have culled two publications: One, under the title "Beckett in the 1990s," appeared in 1993 as a special issue of the annual bilingual journal *Samuel Beckett Today/Aujourd'hui*, with forty somewhat shorter articles, in French and English, on a great variety of topics presented more or less in accordance with the chronology of Beckett's work. The other is the present companion volume, which testifies to the diversity of interest in Beckett studies by presenting fewer but, for the most part, expanded essays arranged along thematic lines.

This collection is divided into two major sections. Part 1 is devoted to considerations of *gender* and *genre*—subjects of considerable interest to Beckett scholars at the present time, and subjects intimately linked by the interplay, characteristic of Beckett's work, between boundary and its undoing.

The depiction of gender in Beckett has only recently come to the foreground with the publication of Linda Ben-Zvi's casebook *Women in Beckett*. Earlier studies had focused on those works in which women appear, but none posed the question of gender—its specificity (or lack thereof) and significance in Beckett—systematically or comprehensively.

As Ben-Zvi notes in the introduction to that work, "The metaphysical human condition Beckett describes is not gender-specific. All characters exist in a grey umbra, where 'perhaps' is the most surety they can muster; all struggle with the vagaries of memory, time, and the perception of self."[1] Beckett's work, however, is remarkable for *simultaneously* depicting the world—our world, one in which gender plays an all too often determining role—as we live it as men and women. Ben-Zvi's demonstration is convincing:

> "Astride of a grave" describes a metaphysical situation, but by choosing to omit the female from the description of birth, Beckett—or his character in *Godot*—makes a gendered comment. Time may affect both sexes, but the pressures on females to retain youth and beauty make their confrontations with the mirror more threatening and more devastating—and Beckett shows this. Even the phrase "this bitch of an earth," describing the scene of procreation and temporal decay, does not sidestep gender, since it indicates the coalescence of nature and the female, both denigrated by the phrase, spoken in a play in which no woman appears.[2]

Beckett's opposition to the cross-casting of his plays is well-documented. His refusal to authorize all-female stagings of *Waiting for Godot*, for example, reflected not a mere stubborn determination to have his plays played as written, but a profound awareness of fundamental difference in male and female experience—that of his characters and that of his spectators. Perception never takes place outside of the referential field that delimits subjectivity and Beckett's work requires, both for authenticity of character portrayal and that of audience reception, the faithful adherence to his determination of gender.

Yet not all his characters are gender defined. We have only to consider the four players in *Quad* or those of *What Where*, for example, to know the force sexual indeterminacy wields on the Beckett stage. In the fiction as well, the image of androgyny (the narrator of the story *Enough* comes immediately to mind) is a powerful consequence of the ambiguity of gender specification. The confusion surrounding the question of gender is often in Beckett a matter of precedence, voice (as a "thought overheard, an imaginary audition," to quote Enoch Brater)[3] having priority over anatomy. But male/female boundaries also fade before the more implicit existential and ontological struggles of simply being *human*, struggles that are the sine qua non of any Beckett text: Both in the exploration of solitude, preeminent in Beckett's work, and that of its ironic counterpart, the primordial condition of Being as being-with (or alongside) others, the laws of gender are inoperative. Indeed, it is precisely this indivisibility of Being that provides the foundation for Beckett's privileging of language, of the narrative voice that must continue saying "words, as long as there are any."[4]

Those essays dealing with gender explore the full range of interest in what I have termed elsewhere the dialectic of anonymity and individuation,[5] the neutralization versus inscription of difference. Leslie Hill uncovers in Beckett a structure, common to the plays and the narratives, that gives rise to "a series of unstable binary oppositions or contrasts." Focusing primarily on *Rockaby*, Hill demonstrates a profound interrelation between the absence of "any verifiable identity, . . . even an identity rooted in gender and sexuality," and the persistent rocking, "the limbo-like movement of a constant 'going to and fro' between self and other, voice and body, male and female. . . ."

Andreas Bjørnerud's essay investigates femininity in *Not I* and its relation to Beckett's figuring of masculinity. Within the framework of an evaluation of feminist readings of the play, he explores conflicting interpretations in an effort to determine the nature, "progressive or not," of the playwright's rendering of the feminine in this work.

It is the evolution of gender inscription in Beckett that is used by Mary Bryden to demonstrate both a metaphorical function of music and the significance of sound (or its absence), melody, and rhythm for the ultimate dissolution of gender as bipolar determinant in the later work. Indeed, for Bryden, the progression of the relation of the musical dynamic to the oppositional notion of gender may be seen as a result of the progression from prose to drama, a point reminiscent of Enoch Brater's thinking that Beckett's late theater (more experiential than experimental) goes beyond genre, in a fusion of the poetic and dramatic, to reach a kind of fluidity incompatible with the oppositional categories of literary tradition.

Beckett's "voices" textualize and retextualize what Brater terms "silent monologues," utterances seemingly overheard and (mis)interpreted for, as Brater tells us, "*hearing is inventing.*" "Every interpretation is a simulation," moreover, "like a musical phrase written in one key transposed up or down for another."[6] Hence the claim that "Genre is under stress,"[7] with the breakdown of conventional boundaries resulting in the textual transcendence of both gender and genre. Similarly, for Johanneke van Slooten, the multiplicity of monologues—sometimes the mere splitting of a single voice into several—constitutes a "polyphonic colloquy" that renders the text musically eloquent. Genre is transcended precisely in the rhythm (demonstrably Irish), pitch, and melodic movement of the text, as is gender in the anonymity of the speaking subject.

With John Pilling and Frank Matton, inquiry into the interrelation of gender and genre gives way to an investigation of rhetorical (Pilling) and autofictive (Matton) extensions of generic distinction. Pilling uncovers formal characteristics of the textual whole prefigured in Arsene's "statement" in *Watt* and rigorously circumscribes a kind of retentive and protective movement, the one "backward in time to a period when kinds of things, and all the varieties of genus and species, could be confidently assigned their names and their places in a well-defined and well-ordered hierarchy," the other forward "into an ethos where, before long, there will be nothing but 'nameless images' and 'imageless names.'"

So, too, Matton seeks a temporal—albeit autobiographical—connection in fundamental structures of language, but his analysis points above all to the insufficiency of the structure of representation itself upon which autobiography, as the expression of identity, depends. His analysis of Beckett's trilogy, therefore, leads to a convincing dismantling of the "laws of genre" wherein the relation of autobiography to fiction is thrown into question and a "fundamental discontinuity between the narrator and 'his' texts" is exposed.

The remaining three essays in this section probe the relation of gender and genre within the broader aesthetic frameworks of the nonrepresentational (Moorjani), the metafictive (Balzano), and the postmodern (Klaver). Moorjani seeks in mystic and philosophic thought sources of the "ungendered shadows" of Beckett's late works in an effort to illustrate the aesthetic ramifications of representation conceived beyond the gender dichotomy, within the neutrality or anonymity of the creative process. Balzano, on the other hand, focuses on a single work, *How It Is*, to demonstrate the infinite repetitions, reflections, or rebounds that provoke a shift from *what* to *how* (from fictive to metafictive) the work, in its transgression of the very notion of genre itself, means. Shift is again the operative notion in Klaver's essay, which invokes theories of postmodernism to define the semiotization of space in Beckett that precludes both "perceptual, psychological, or epistemological depth" and "totalization, delimitation, [and] cataloguing," the requisites, in short, of genre classification.

In part 2 of the book contributors look at *textuality* and *theatricality* as both dichotomous and interdependent components of Beckett's writing. Locatelli offers a cogent argument for the development of new habits of reading and strategies for understanding that acknowledge difference while not resorting to the objectivation of the Other in differentiation. She succeeds in revealing precisely what it is in Beckett's texts that prevents their reduction to artifacts and require their appreciation as, at once, contextual and self-contextual mobile events whose uncertain textual boundaries result in their characteristic open-endness.

Indeterminacy is also the inspiration for McCarthy's discussion, but here the focus is on interpretation and directorial "vision" for the specific purposes of rehearsal and performance rather than the act of reading. McCarthy, like Scanlan in the essay that follows, endeavors to come to terms with the meaning of directorial fidelity and the role, in particular, of the Beckett director, and the richness of his analysis lies in the recognition of this role in relation to the psychic sensibility of the performer. As for Locatelli, in her consideration of the author and reader, the Beckett imagination—both the forms that it breeds and the primacy of the dramatic tensions it sets into motion—demands, according to McCarthy, a dialogic interplay between actor, director, and spectator. And it is openness or indeterminacy rather than objective or determinate motives that is the measure of performance success.

The question of the director's faithfulness to Beckett's text is of singular importance. As I have claimed elsewhere,[8] perhaps even more now than before Beckett's death in 1989 the meaning of directorial integrity and the preservation of the integrity of the playwright's work is of the essence. Beckett wrote with a distinct view of what was to be seen and heard on the stage, and while the exactitude of his scenic indications is well documented, the question of directorial integrity is not limited to a faithful adherence to them. Rather, it is the degree of sensitivity to the interrelation of ambiguity and precision (that required, for example, by the silences so prominent in Beckett's work) that is to be evaluated.

Several recent productions in the United States and Europe, as well as in Japan and elsewhere, have fostered considerable debate among directors and scholars alike. Disturbing legal and aesthetic questions have been raised by all-female casts performing *Waiting for Godot*, by the replacing of the recorded voice in *Rockaby* by onstage speech, by the rewriting of the ending of *Catastrophe*, the staging of *Godot* with multiple couples and without the second act, and the substitution of a wheelchair for Winnie's mound in *Happy Days*. The American Repertory Theatre's interpretation of *Endgame* (which relocated the play to the tunnel of a subway), the Comédie Française's production of the same play (with its pink decor, musical score and mannequins), and Mike Nichols's staging of *Godot* at New York's Lincoln Center remain highly controversial.

Robert Scanlan's essay on directorial integrity—on the "proper" handling of Beckett's plays—departs significantly from the notion of openness and indeterminacy as defined by Locatelli and McCarthy. Not only does he argue for the complete and utter respect of the parameters set by the playwright but he offers a compelling view of plays, and Beckett's plays included, as "formal artifacts," the very view that Locatelli just as compellingly attempts to dispel. For Scanlan, "Beckett's formal plays are completely analogous to 'solved' equations in mathematics: there is no meaning whatsoever to errors in mathematical problems. Changing the theatrical parameters of his plays makes nonsense of his 'situation' of the problem of being on the stage." Deviation from the constraints in question is tampering with the essence of the art, and this, says Scanlan, "matters."

Language provides the framework for the following three essays, those by Gordon, Vandervlist, and Ostmeier. Gordon discusses Beckett's bilingualism (his self-translations), variations in his texts (which range from nuance to free translation, insertions, and deletions) and the question of a definitive or authoritative version of a given work. The questions of "author-based" criteria versus "reader-based" criteria, of the superiority of the original over a published form, and of the significance of authorial intention illustrate the difficulties inherent in assessing both the stability of textual meaning and the meaning of textuality itself.

The relation of speaker to speech, the obligatory though impossible figuration of self in language, has long been recognized as the generative force of Beckett's writing, the "I"/"Not I" conundrum forever constituting "the drama in the text" (to borrow a title from Brater). Vandervlist and Ostmeier reevaluate this tension between the authenticity of expression and the impossibility of the writer's task—the tension, in sum, between language and silence—in view of recent criticism and their essays complement each other in Vandervlist's centering of the discussion around Beckett's fiction and Ostmeier's doing so around the shorter plays.

The interrelation of textuality and theatricality moves to the cultural horizon of East/West influences with the contributions of Tseng (on Beckett and the Western intellectual Cartesian tradition), Thompson (on parallels between Beckett's dramatic vision and classical Taoism), and Tanaka (on adaptations of Beckett's theater for a Japanese audience). All three critics address, though on different fronts, questions of appropriation and identity (of author, character, reader/spectator) and draw attention to the increasing necessity for a rigorous reconsideration of the cultural criteria that have habitually determined the direction of literary history.

Notwithstanding the impressive cases made by several of the contributors for indeterminacy or openness as the primary means of access to the "irreducible relation of reality and textuality, of ontology and figurality" (to cite Locatelli) in Beckett's oeuvre, closure makes a strong comeback in the book's final essay by Hersh Zeifman. In a moving testimony to the simultaneous pull of Beckett's work on the aesthetic and personal levels, Zeifman traces the denial of closure through several of the early plays to its attainment in the late drama—a trajectory reflected in "the shift from 'Little is left to tell,' the opening words of *Ohio Impromptu*, to 'Nothing is left to tell,' the words that bring that play to a close." The movement outlined by the critic from a repeated defiance of closure in circularity toward the achievement of closure in the playwright's late work, it should be noted, is the very same itinerary followed by the critical analysis: Just beyond the close of the circle, wherein a personal memory evoked at the start of the essay by Beckett's *Rockaby* is revisited, it is a final acceptance—a "[making] peace with fate"—that brings the volume to an end.

Together the essays of *Beckett On and On . . .* reflect a significant geographic diversity of Beckett scholars—contributors come from eight countries in Europe, North America, and Asia—as well as the breadth of Beckett's appeal to and the linguistic and semiotic difficulties imposed upon Beckett readers and spectators of differing cultural backgrounds. Such is the power of Beckett's aesthetic undoing of the boundaries of gender and genre, textuality and theatricality, that his work will continue to fascinate, to mediate, to go on . . .

Notes

1. Linda Ben-Zvi, *Women in Beckett* (Urbana and Chicago: University of Illinois Press, 1990), p. ix.
2. Ibid., p. x.
3. Enoch Brater, *The Drama in the Text: Beckett's Late Fiction* (New York: Oxford University Press, 1994), p. 62.
4. Samuel Beckett, *The Unnamable* (New York: Grove Press, 1958), p. 179.
5. See, for example, my "Anonymity and Individuation: The Interrelation of Two Linguistic Functions in *Not I* and *Rockaby*," in Robin J. Davis and Lance St. J. Butler, eds., *"Make Sense Who May"* (Totowa, N.J.: Barnes & Noble, 1988), pp. 36–45, and "Anonymity and Individuality in the Nouveau Roman," *LittéRéalité* 1, no. 1 (1989): 59–67.
6. Brater, *Drama in the Text,* pp. 61; 61–62.
7. Enoch Brater, *Beyond Minimalism* (New York: Oxford University Press, 1987), p. 3.
8. See my introduction to *Directing Beckett* (Ann Arbor: University of Michigan Press, 1994).

Beckett On and On . . .

Part 1
Gender and Genre

"Fuck Life":
Rockaby, Sex, and the Body

LESLIE HILL

Fuck life," declares Voice in the closing lines of Beckett's 1981 play, *Rockaby.*[1] The manner is uncharacteristically earthy and explicit, and, perhaps for this reason alone, the words, allegedly spoken by a "prematurely old" (*CSP* 273), lace-clad woman, are no doubt apt to shock. But the phrase itself, as the play ends, proves, like many others in Beckett's work, to be instantly self-disabling. It invokes copulation as a gesture of violence, destruction, and death, only to remind us that in copulation life itself also begins. So what at first seems to resemble an emblematic effacement of sexuality and bodily difference yields to an unexpected reaffirmation of that difference. In the process, instead of an erotically charged and valued event, life turns rather—as Beckett's French version of the play emphasizes—into a bodily fiasco, whose more appropriate fate would be to have been flushed down the toilet from the outset: "aux gogues la vie," in the words of Voice's French-speaking counterpart in *Berceuse* (*B* 52). (And there are echoes here of Moran's wry description of his own predicament as akin to that of "the turd waiting for the flush" (*T* 163), or of the woman in *Not I* "pouring it out" in the "nearest lavatory" (*CSP* 222).

The principle at work here—as well as the bodily terms in which it is couched—is, I would suggest, a familiar one. Beckett's plays and prose narratives are all structured, virtually without exception, according to a series of unstable binary oppositions or contrasts. No sooner is a distinction articulated in the writing—like the apparent difference between "fucking" and "living"—than it is dismantled and comically canceled out. Extremes meet, meaning is paralyzed, and, as here, what once spoke of procreation tends instead merely to reenact the ever-present threat of anal catastrophe. Distinctions in language dissolve into what one might call an undifferentiated "mush" (and I cite the word in memory of the fate of the captured hedgehog in *Company* [*C* 41]). But as meaning is erased in this way, linguistic difference reemerges; as it does so, however, the effect is not to consolidate or reassure meaning but to create within meaning a sense of puzzlement or panic. "Fuck life," then, is a phrase that, although—or rather because—it refuses ultimately to convey any stable message, nevertheless oscillates uncontrollably between the possibility of speech that it enacts and the impossibility of finally making sense that it enshrines. Its status, in this way, is more nearly akin to that of a bodily signature or inscription that, though meaning almost nothing, survives as a spasm of performative, theatrical intensity. Language as enactment or bodily rhythm is thus affirmed in Beckett's writing as an enigmatic excess that perpetually outlives the many local disasters and fiascos of meaning on which at the very same time it is itself also necessarily dependent.

This process with respect to Beckett's writing is one I have described at greater length elsewhere.[2] In this article what I want to do is briefly to rehearse some of its main emphases in relation to *Rockaby*. In the play, as elsewhere in Beckett, it is not difficult to find an extensive series of unstable binary contrasts. Most prominent among these figures of precarious and unsettled differentiation is the figure of the rocking chair itself, which, as readers will know, has many familiar antecedents in Beckett's work, beginning with the rocker employed by Murphy in his moments of trancelike abdication from a world of irresolvable antagonisms. In *Rockaby*, too, as in that earlier novel, the figure of the rocker serves not so much to resolve the dilemmas to which it is a response as offer a heightened and intensified version of them. Rocking, here, works as a kind of metatextual shorthand for the oscillating uncertainties created by the instability of structural oppositions in Beckett's play; it is a graphic embodiment of the continual oscillation between extremes that Beckett thematizes here—as he does elsewhere—as a ceaseless coming and going, or "going to and fro" (*CSP* 275) between light and dark. If the rocker is a figure of endless and uncontrollable movement, it leads its occupant—as it once did Murphy—to the stillness found only at the core of ceaseless motion. If it comforts, it does so only by returning the body on the rocker to the endless round of indeterminacy from which it might seem initially to have wanted to escape. Thus, if the rocker is a cradle, it also represents a coffin; if the arms of the rocker reenact the embrace of the mother, they also announce or recall her death as well as that of the sitter; and if they refer to the possibility of that unnamed other of whom Voice speaks, they also remind the audience that, like the bicycle in *Molloy*, they are merely a mechanical, prosthetic extension of the speaker's own body.

But if rocking, in this way, exemplifies how life and death in Beckett are part of a circular process in which beginning and ending are never separate or distinct, this ought not to suggest that living, or dying, is a process dedicated to preserving some underlying continuity or identity belonging to the self or the body. So, while Voice in *Rockaby* may imply that the character "she" is a reincarnation of her own mother (whose rocker she inherits), what this primarily serves to emphasize is the enigmatic and unspoken moment of procreation, the result of copulation with an unnamed other (the "fucking," so to speak, to which the body on stage owes its "life," and death). But this sexual encounter with another, though necessary, is left in suspense within the story that *Rockaby* narrates, with the paradoxical result that the question of sexual difference that is here put to one side in the text is constantly in the process of recurring within it. Sexual difference, here, however, is treated not as an encounter between opposites but is instead dissolved into a series of asymmetrical doublings and replications, with the result that narrative in the play dramatizes neither birth nor death themselves but the impossibility of ever locating an origin—temporal or ontological—to the movement of rocking by which the play figures the process both of living and of dying. So if death therefore, in the play, is a species of birth, and birth a manner of death, this would seem to be because sexuality is always already the crux of a failed encounter, already an indication of the impossibility of making sense of life and death (which is what, in its own way, the verdict "Fuck life" seems to suggest).

Central to the plot of *Rockaby* is the female character's desire for a companion. The drama of the play turns on this possibility—or impossibility—of there being, as Voice puts it, "another creature like herself" (*CSP* 275). Voice adds to this the qualification: "a little like" (*CSP* 275), and this restriction raises a key issue with respect both to this other and to the body visible on stage: for what is this body "like," and what would the other also have to be "like" to be this other for whom "she" is searching? Refusing to answer these questions, what the play does instead is to enact a complex series of aporias with respect to the relationship between otherness and sameness that the play foregrounds in this way. Is this other, for instance, going to be male or female, other or same? What might this imply about the gender or identity of W, who is ostensibly a "woman" and certainly dressed as such, though Beckett takes care (as he does in *Mercier et Camier*) to obscure her body by swathing it in lacy frills and fancy clothing? But what does this clothing mask and thereby conceal, or even reveal?

Beckett's text offers no reliable answers to any of these questions; and it is thus, at the very least, open to argument as to what sex or gender this body on stage in fact belongs, assuming that the relationship between a body and its sex is indeed one of appurtenance (and in turn, as though to underscore these uncertainties, the French text of *Berceuse*, when referring to the other, hesitates purposefully between "un autre" in the masculine and "une autre âme vivante" in the feminine [*B* 43]). Despite the desire that "she" has for this other, according to Voice, there is no evidence of any process of mutual recognition taking place between them, and therefore no dialectic of reciprocity that might allow the identity of either "she" or this other to be reliably positioned. Their relationship, to the extent that there is one, is based not on difference and reciprocity but on repetition, duplication, and undecidable coincidence: thus the other, were he or she to exist, might be found looking out some window, "going to and fro," "a little like" the protagonist in the story (but, by that same token, undecidably different from "her"). Similarly, though they seem to converge metaphorically, it is far from evident that the female character referred to in Voice's account is the same as W, the body the audience sees before it, or that Voice and W, in turn, are, in any meaningful sense of the words, either the "same" or "different." Throughout Beckett's play, one is confronted not with a series of stable characters, voices, or bodies, but rather an irredeemable proliferation of doubles or simulacra, with the result that relations of sameness are constantly undermined by difference, and relations of difference are thrown off balance by apparent similarity.

These disturbed relations between similarity and difference in the play already have a potent emblem in the shape of the relationship between the two letters—*V* and *W*—that Beckett uses to refer to the speaking voice and the rocking body. In the same way that the one is a truncated, half-sized version of the other, so the other is an excessive and redoubled instance of the one. While the two letters seem to share a common origin, to the point of being indistinguishable in some languages, they also give rise elsewhere to radically diverse pronunciations, and to confuse them can often seriously compromise meaning (as well as challenge, at least in British English, received assumptions regarding sexual identity or gender affiliation). In this way, then, there is a clue that the relationship between V and W in the play may not be a simple case either of straightforward identity or opposition. Admittedly, in his stage directions, Beckett specifies that the two share the same voice. But this neatly eludes the question of whether they are indeed the same person. After all, the narrator of *L'Innommable* spends long pages claiming—undecidably—that the voice speaking "his" text is not in fact his own; and one could likewise claim that though V and W speak with the "same" voice, they do not necessarily share the "same" "body." In much the same manner, the movement by which W, V, the character "she" to whom Voice refers, "her" mother, and the other for whom "she" is searching all become confused is proof not of some underlying identity between these different figures but rather of a profound loss of identity, as a result of which each of these potential part-persons is bereft of any autonomy and consequently merges into each of the others.

But despite the similarities between them, it is also clear that the differences between each of these figures are irreducible. W and V, for instance, are far from simply being the "same." For one thing, one of them keeps talking while the other remains largely silent, constantly being rocked "to and fro" (and in this respect their relationship is perhaps most reminiscent of the sexually differentiated pair of Winnie and Willie in *Happy Days*). In turn, this uncertainty about the relationship between them generates a sequence of other enigmas and it becomes in fact impossible to tell, among other things, whether, say, V is a displaced, travestied version of W, or whether V is the sought-after other herself for whom "she" is looking, or whether V is perhaps not W's mother (which would make *Rockaby* itself into a repetition or double of *Footfalls*). As a result, it would be precipitate even to decide upon the gender identity of the body Beckett puts on stage and names as W (thereby seeming to suggest "she" is a "woman"). After all, elsewhere in Beckett, the appellation *W* turns out to be no more than an inverted *M,* and if the figure of W is at all like anything from Beckett's previous work, it is the sight of Murphy sitting on—that is, "off"—his rocker, or Molloy waking up to sit in an armchair, dressed in a flimsy nightshirt as though he, too, were a "woman" (*M* 56–57).

Instead of any verifiable identity, then, even an identity rooted in gender and sexuality, what the spectator is given, in *Rockaby*, is an oscillating motion of indeterminacy affecting both a body and the words of an unnamed voice. The rhythmic repetition of the one echoes and mimics the self-defeating paradoxes of the other; what the play dramatizes is the limbolike movement of a constant "going to and fro" between self and other, voice and body, male and female, without any of these poles or positions ever being properly secured. Beckett specifies, of course, that the body seen on stage is that of a woman and that it is her voice that the audience is able to hear. This marking of sex is crucial, it seems to me, for it demonstrates convincingly that, in Beckett's work, there is no escape beyond gender into asexual selfhood. To mark W as a woman defies a humanist interpretation of the play; it shows that, as far as Beckett is concerned, there is no universal self that stands (or sits!) beyond gender or difference, and thus no appeal in Beckett's writing to any form of undifferentiated or predicated being that might be enlisted on the side of ungendered, so-called gender-neutral humanism. W is not Everyman, nor even Everywoman. At the same time, however, the mention of "woman in chair" by the stage directions (*CSP* 275) is radically unstable, for there is no unifying identity that lies behind or within the doubles or versions of self scripted throughout the play, only an oscillating chair that only ever stops in order to be rocked off again, propelled by a motion that has no beginning nor end because it is itself—like Mr. Knott in *Watt*—forever a constant process of beginning and ending. Sexual difference in the play is similarly a process of differentiation without beginning nor end; it is movement without stability or fixity, but equally it is a process that cannot be eluded or wished away, however much Beckett's protagonist may wish to "fuck life" and all its attendant fiascos.

The question arises here, of course, as it did several times during the conference in The Hague, as to whether it is legitimate, contrary to what may be stated in Beckett's published texts, to have certain roles in Beckett's late plays done by women rather than by men, or vice versa. As far as *Rockaby* is concerned, written as it is for a "woman" (*CSP* 275), one might argue that what is clearly crucial, if the play is to succeed, is that the relationship between the body seen on stage and the "she" of Voice's story, founded as it is, simultaneously, on similarity and difference, convergence yet incompatibility, needs to remain both undecided and undecidable. It is no doubt possible, in principle, for this effect to be achieved while using a male rather than a female actor, provided that the audience is not given the opportunity of seeing the relationship between the male actor and the female role as a stable, univocal one, and it is most likely to avoid the facility of any static binary reading of this sort that Beckett insists that the voices of V and W are the "same." It is probably also the case that, in practice, in most contemporary Western theatrical contexts, actors tend to be perceived as either male or female; and if gender affiliation is unclear or ambiguous, audiences will tend to see this purely as a comic device, unless it is viewed as belonging to some alternative—exotic—theatrical tradition. This is one reason why having a male actor do *Rockaby* would probably end up reducing the play's ambiguities rather than increasing them and for that reason is a tactic that might well be rejected. One can object, however, as does Cobi Bordewijk apropos of some of the various all-female productions of *Waiting for Godot* that have been attempted over the years, that an actor and the role he or she is playing are in fact functionally and formally distinct.[3] If this is true, it would follow that to use a male actor in *Rockaby* would not, in itself, change the character of W into a man and would thus, in principle, remain faithful to the letter of Beckett's text. Such a production, though, would remain crucially dependent on the audience's ability to differentiate reliably between the actor's body and the role he or she is embodying, at the very moment when it would seem that in Beckett's later plays, as elsewhere in contemporary theatrical practice, it is precisely this kind of stable, formal distinction that is under serious threat.

In a number of cases, of course, Beckett refuses to specify gender, preferring to leave the sex of some characters—like that of the Auditor in the stage version of *Not I*, or the four players in *Quad*—"undeterminable" (*CSP* 216) or "indifferent" (*CSP* 293), leaving one to wonder whether such instances, rather than being exceptional, are not rather symptomatic of a more general state of precariousness attaching to sex and gender identity in the whole of Beckett's writing. Increasingly, Beckett's later plays, when they experiment with theatrical and other forms, are seeking to redefine performance in nonanthropomorphic terms (and this, at bottom, is probably the main reason for Beckett's sustained interest in the use of technology on stage and in the development of radio and television drama). *Rockaby*, like *Not I* and the late television pieces, is a play that hovers—undecidably—on the crucial borderline between what is still and what is no longer consistent with theater as an anthropomorphic medium. For that reason, for the play to succeed as a dramatic spectacle, it is no doubt crucial in *Rockaby* that W be perceived as existing on the very brink—the extreme limit—of what is recognizable or understandable as gendered humanity. W is thus at that margin where it is no longer possible to pretend to be sexually undifferentiated, but equally well where it is no longer clear, or even fathomable, what terms like "human," or "female," or "male" might indeed mean; in any case, such questions can no longer be adequately addressed by any of the usual binary paradigms that seem to govern the politics of sexual identity.

What the audience sees on stage in *Rockaby*, then, is not a body for whom gender is irrelevant, but, more radically, a body that cannot be captured within the oppositional logic of sexual identification or definition. Figured in the indeterminacy of the rocker's movement, it is a body that escapes the paradigm of binary closure in order to dramatize its own irreducible singularity as a differentiated but nevertheless indescribable flesh; and in the process it leaves its mark in the theater in the form of a verbal orgasm, or act of excretion, or masturbation—at any rate as a performance in which it is clear that the body in question is always already at least double. In this way, to the extent that it escapes nomination and is forever oscillating between extremes in the absence of any stable identity, I would contend that the sitting body of *Rockaby* cannot be described satisfactorily as either a male or a female body. Indeed, in order for Beckett's play to carry out its own promise to "fuck life," it would seem that the body on stage would in fact have to belong to both sexes, but only to the extent that it would, by that token, also belong to neither, and continue to oscillate "to and fro," as though in indefinite suspension, on the very margins or limits of what may be recognizable as human. *Rockaby* refuses to offer its audience a reassuring vision of humanity at leisure, but testifies instead to the catastrophic event that differentiates each singular body from all other such bodies and that, by separating the bodies of humans from themselves and from whatever they happen to be "like," leaves the moment of birth, and thus of death, perpetually and enigmatically in abeyance. Theater, here in Beckett's work, as it rocks towards the end of the century, tends therefore towards a savage de-anthropomorphization of stage, body, voice, and gender.

Notes

1. In this paper I shall be referring to the following works by Beckett: *Molloy* (Paris: Minuit, 1951), henceforth M; *Molloy, Malone Dies, The Unnamable* (London: Calder & Boyars, 1959), henceforth T; *Company* (London: John Calder, 1980), henceforth C; *Berceuse,* in *Catastrophe et autres dramaticules* (Paris: Minuit, 1983), henceforth B; and *Collected Shorter Plays* (London: Faber & Faber, 1984), henceforth CSP. All references will be to these editions and will be given directly in the text, preceded by the abbreviation indicated.

2. See Leslie Hill, *Beckett's Fiction: In Different Words* (Cambridge: Cambridge University Press, 1990).

3. See Cobi Bordewijk, "The Integrity of the Playtext: Disputed Performances of *Waiting for Godot,*" *Samuel Beckett Today/Aujourd'hui* 1 (1992): 143–54.

Beckett's Model of Masculinity: Male Hysteria in *Not I*

ANDREAS BJØRNERUD

THE question underlying this paper is how to evaluate Beckett's work with respect to feminism. To suggest an answer to that question, I have chosen to concentrate on the play *Not I*, to examine both the way in which that play figures femininity and the implications of such a figuring for Beckett's model of masculinity. Where does Beckett's work stand in relation to patriarchal masculinity? Is it critical? Is it critical in a way that might be taken as progressive from a feminist perspective? In the context of such questions, my reasons for focusing on *Not I*, apart from the obvious constraints of space, are twofold. First, it is an exemplary work: exemplary both in general of Beckett's constant preoccupation with the speaking subject, with the possibility of saying "I," and, in particular, exemplary of Beckett's attitude to the feminine, insofar as it is one of his most powerful representations of a woman. Indeed, Linda Ben-Zvi has suggested that *Not I* is ur-Beckett, the image that underlies all other Beckett works: a mouth, unable to stop, unable to get "It" right or "I" acknowledged, attempting to talk itself—in this case, herself—into sense (Ben-Zvi, *Women in Beckett,* p. 243). Second, this play has itself already been the object of critical interpretations that conflict precisely on the question of whether its depiction of the feminine can be taken as progressive or not, that is, the question central to this paper. Thus, by working through these contradictory interpretations, I hope to suggest answers to the questions with which I have begun: how does Beckett figure femininity, what does this imply for his relation to masculinity, and where does that place him with respect to feminism?

To take the positive interpretation first, Peter Gidal's reading of *Not I* is unequivocally feminist: "*Not I* instantiates the loss of male power-positions, and instantiates the power of a woman's speech and gesture" (Gidal, *Understanding Beckett,* p. 43). Gidal takes the woman's speech to be challenging patriarchy's unequal binary of sexual difference. The key term for this reading in Gidal is hysteria (p. 98). It is by understanding the voice and the mouth of the play as belonging to a female hysteric that Gidal is enabled to come to his feminist conclusion. Two points need to be clarified. In what sense is hysteria a feminist position, and, of course, in what sense is the woman of *Not I* a hysteric? The second point can be dealt with after a consideration of what is meant by hysteria.

As Elizabeth Grosz explains (*Sexual Subversions,* pp. 132–39), there are, for Freud, typically three paths to femininity. On the "normal" path, the young girl accepts the father's negative definition of the mother as castrated; she therefore ceases to desire the mother but instead identifies with her in order to desire the father. That is, she devalues herself and her mother in order to submit passively and desiringly to the father, thus conforming to the ideal norm of femininity within patriarchy. On a second path, however, the young girl may reject her castration and continue to perceive herself as phallic: in this case, the girl may identify with the father insofar as she takes herself as phallic (the "masculinity complex") and continue in a homosexual desire for the mother. The third path is that of frigidity, which, for Grosz, leads to hysteria and which is unable to come down firmly on either side of the phallic/castrated divide. Thus the hysteric accomplishes the first step on the normal path to femininity—she takes herself as castrated, accepting a negative definition of herself and her mother—but she nonetheless does not take the second step, which is desire for the father. She does not take the step that within the psychoanalytic schema is famously so difficult for the woman to take, or rather to make her take, since unlike with the boy there is precisely no castration threat to channel the paths of her identification and desire. The hysteric finds herself in the tragic position of having renounced the mother but still refusing the father. The mother as object of desire is lost and replaced by a negative identification; the hysteric identifies with the passivity and compliance of castration, but she is frigid, without desire for the father, and caught in the melancholic's position of a continual mourning for a lost object that generates an insistent self-reproach and self-contempt.

Slavoj Zizek makes the same point but with a different emphasis:

> the resistance, the hesitation of the subject fully to assume his [*sic*] symbolic mandate [. . .] defines the position of a hysteric: what is a hysteric if not an "I" who resists full identification with the mandate [. . .] what is hysterical theatre if not a staging of this resistance? This is the ultimate domain of doubt and certainty: a certainty that "I" am my symbolic mandate, a doubt if "I" really am that. (Zizek, *For They Know Not,* p. 156)

The hysteric is certain she is castrated, but she is not certain of the object of her desire. Who is she castrated for? What does the other want of her? Her frigidity and melancholia are an effect both of her passive assumption of the symbolic mandate of femininity and of her self-debilitating refusal of that mandate.

With such an understanding of hysteria, one can see why it is central to Gidal's interpretation of the play. The woman of *Not I* passively accepts the call to come "out . . . into this world," accepts that she must "keep on," though "not knowing what . . . what she was [. . .] what she was trying . . . what to try . . . no matter . . . keep on . . ." (due to the brevity of the text, page references will not be given). She accepts she has a position; moreover, she accepts that hers is a position of subjection, that there is a command she has to fulfill, a position for herself she has to find, but "she did not know . . . what position she was in." In her inability to connect, to find an "I," she finds her "feeling so dulled." Fallen into a loveless world, she both complies with her condition and resists it insofar as she cannot recognize herself in it, cannot invest it with affect. Frigid, fallen, and melancholy, she cannot suffer, but she knows, passively, that she ought to be suffering.

In short, Gidal's characterization of the woman as a hysteric seems to me apt, but what is altogether more questionable is his feminist reading of that hysteria. For even if one can see the feminist potential in hysteria, it nonetheless seems hard to argue for it as a feminist position. The hysteric clearly resists the patriarchal mandate for femininity, for she cannot be the desired feminine norm. However, her mode of resistance is properly tragic inasmuch as she takes patriarchy's negative evaluation of her as a given. She cannot desire the father, but she has renounced the mother. The impossibility of an empowering identification on the basis of a positive conception of the mother is part of her condition. This condition is therefore certainly available for a sympathetic recuperation by a feminist critical praxis, but it is hardly a role model. Hysteria is a pathology whose conditions it is in the interests of feminism to uncover, but hopefully it will be a misfortune to look back on and not a future utopia.

With this, it would seem that one is moving from an interpretation of *Not I* as feminist to one that would hold that the play is a vehicle of patriarchal discourse such that, to quote John Lutterbie:

> It defines a community of subjects from which she is excluded, and I am not. It limits a discourse in which she appears but in which she cannot participate. It reinforces my belief that I can exercise the power of agency within a dominant, if not hegemonic, male structure. ("Tender Mercies," p. 105)

On this reading, the woman, unable to be an active speaking subject herself, confirms the male spectator in his agency by virtue of her exclusion. Her pitiful and broken speech, her desire to please, would consolidate a masculine hegemony. The theoretical premises for such a reading are all too familiar and at first sight seem very appropriate to the formal structure of the play. As Kaja Silverman puts it:

> her exclusion from symbolic power and privilege is articulated as a passive relation to classic cinema's scopic and auditory regimes—as an incapacity for looking, speaking, or listening authoritatively [. . .] the female subject's gaze is depicted as partial, flawed, unreliable [. . .] although her own look seldom hits its mark, woman is always on display before the male gaze. [. . .] Woman's words are shown to be even less her own than are her "looks." They are scripted for her, extracted from her by an external agency, or uttered by her in a trancelike state. Her voice also reveals a remarkable facility for self-disparagement and self-incrimination. [. . .] The female subject [. . .] makes possible the male subject's identification with the symbolic father, and his imaginary alignment with creative vision, speech and hearing [. . .] her obligatory receptivity to the male gaze is what establishes its superiority, just as her obedience to the male voice is what "proves" its power. (*The Acoustic Mirror*, pp. 31–32)

Silverman is talking about the cinematic apparatus, but clearly what she is saying can be generalized to visual and auditory reception in the theater. The woman in *Not I*, a stumbling voice tied to a mouth, caught up in an inadequate performance of a confession she cannot make sense of, would be an extreme example of the objectified woman confirming the male gaze. The tying down of the woman within the diegesis to the physical and the incompetent would confirm the extradiegetic and transcendent authority of her male spectator: the woman as confused, dark, emotional, nonintellectual babble to the male's rational mind, her castrated body confirming his phallic ideality, her tormented mouth writhing, spitting, stumbling under his untroubled gaze.

There would thus seem to be two readings of the play available within this psychoanalytic paradigm, the second subsuming the first. The woman as hysteric is unable to assume the subjectivity held out to her by patriarchy, but she is nonetheless still subjected and so her hesitation is recuperated into a confirmation of the patriarchal hegemony. By this account, her failure, her "not I," would consolidate his "I," his continuing success. Beckett's man would be the conventional patriarchal male. Such a conclusion, however, seems unsatisfactory on two counts. On the one hand, in the general context of Beckett's work, the failure of the male protagonist to assume his "I" with any confidence is so familiar it is almost a given; on the other hand, with respect to this play in particular, the assumption that the spectatorial gaze is untroubled seems altogether misguided. The play, and its televisual successor, offers no overall cognitive assurance. The eye is no more able to follow the contortions of the lips than the ear is able to make sense of the rushed delivery of the broken sentences. Further, it is literally impossible for eye and ear to combine and sum up the whole. Reception is here necessarily fragmented and disjoined, a condition exacerbated either by the difficulty in seeing the object of representation in the theater or by the excessive magnification of that object on the screen. It therefore makes no sense to speak of the male gaze here as if it were unproblematically in control. Moreover, this interpretation would seem to be confirmed by the prior description of the female hysteric as refusing desire for the phallus. The hysteric is passive, but her desire is failed from a normative perspective and therefore she cannot be said to confirm the male in his possession of the phallus as the "normal" female, the castrated object of the male gaze, is habitually taken to do. The phallus is not reassured by the hysteric, since it is not her object of desire.

But is this to say that we have returned to the initial feminist reading of the play, namely, that the hysteric disturbs and challenges patriarchal certainties and, in particular, the certainties of a representation that is an objectification and specularization of woman? This would seem plausible, but there is still the problem of aligning hysteria with feminism. Or to put the problem another way, there is a disturbance of representation, but there is also its undeniable corollary: that even if representation is disturbed, the woman is still the object of representation. The hysteric is defiant but passive. She disturbs the old order but is not in a position to renew it. She remains an object, although an unsettling one.

But then, perhaps, this is the issue: her remaining an object. And perhaps a more productive line of inquiry at this point would be not the woman but the man. What is his relation to the hysteric, his investment in her?

To begin at the beginning, hysteria is after all not just *a* psychoanalytic category but *the* psychoanalytic category. It was by listening to their hysterical patients that Freud and Breuer developed psychoanalysis (a theory whose father may be uncertain—Freud or Breuer?—but whose mother seems sure: Anna O). It was the "happy event" of Anna O.'s speech (Bowlby, "A Happy Event," p. 10), that ultimately unlocked, for Freud, the other space of the unconscious, which allowed her so-called disease to be seen as an effect of the repression of, and ensuing difficult relation to, fantasy. What is dramatized here is the unusual position of the male. The doctor treating and curing his prostrate(d) female patient would seem the very epitome of the knowing male eye and ear transcending the woman's inability to be conscious of her disease. The woman trapped in her body, her symptom, is raised to health and the light by her analyst/teacher. Yet in watching her, and above all listening to her, what has happened to the doctor? He has discovered that her illness has nothing to do with her body but with her mind, that ultimately her femininity is an effect not of biology but of culture, and further, that that which unconsciously affects her mind affects his also. In short, he discovers himself in her, discovers his lack in hers.

Historically, this has led to the often discussed and very ambivalent relations between feminism and Freudian psychoanalysis. Does Freud imprison women within his theory, or does his very failure to do so productively open up psychic spaces for femininity/feminism, as well as demonstrating the instability of the masculinity that habitually opposes them? Leaving aside, however, the complexities of such a history and politics, what is interesting here is the way in which the hysteric unsettles the male who looks and listens with attention. Quite simply, the male discovers that men can be hysterics too.

Consider again the hysteric's "path." Typically the young girl who, like the boy, desires her mother, discovers herself and her mother to be castrated. A negative identification is established, but her desire remains open. The mother as object of desire is lost but not replaced, leaving the hysteric in the posture of the melancholic, desiring a lost object that has now become a hated, because lost, part of the self. What her fall into self-recrimination presumes is a once blissful relation to the mother, now lost: that oneness of the child and the phallic mother prior to the paternal intervention that is the assertion of her castration. Now consider the boy's position: he too desires the mother, but upon the threat of castration, he defers that desire, defers to the father, in order to have the phallus. However, the unwelcome truth of his situation is that the father's promise is always already broken: the desired mother is lost upon acceptance of the father's law. The boy's motive for identifying with the father is his presumption that the father possesses the phallus he desires to be to the mother—he desires the oneness of the phallic mother—but the condition of his identification with the father is that he relinquish the mother to the father. The boy's desire will never be satisfied; his having the phallus is an illusion. This is certainly an illusion he will seek to maintain, seeking the ideal woman who will desire him as the father who has the phallus. This ideal woman by her lack will confirm his plenitude, but the melancholy truth underlying such plenitude is that his desire is open, directed toward that which is lost. In this he meets the hysteric.

In her account of male hysteria, Barbara Creed speaks of phallic panic. If this is the case in the female hysteric, who panics in the face of the phallus, who does not know where to position herself in relation to it, who refuses it, it may also be the case in the male who feels the possibility of its lack, who senses that he may not have the phallus, that it may be illusion, who is subject, in short, to castration anxiety. Creed's description of the male hysteric, unable to sustain the phallic illusion of masculinity, engaged in a repetitive and failed representation of his masculine identity, moreover, stresses the parallel to the female hysteric's anxious relation to identity. However, there is a crucial asymmetry: the male is falling into castration, the female is fallen. This is a question of identification: the male is coming to perceive himself as not identified with a positive phallic father but with a negative castrated mother, whereas the female has only had the one negative identification. This asymmetry in identification results in a different targeting of aggression: the woman's aggression is partly self-directed, partly a refusal of the father; the man's, to the contrary, is partly self-directed, partly a refusal of the mother. Even a very brief look at the relation of the male Beckett protagonist to the woman, to the mother, makes this clear.

Indeed, Molloy's relation to his mother at the very threshold of the *Trilogy* is almost paradigmatic. The trajectory of Molloy's narrative quest is motivated by his search for his absent mother; she is the object of his desire, and in this, Molloy follows the typical masculine oedipal trajectory: the mother is forbidden but desired. But, in contrast to a typical masculinity, Molloy is plainly unable to sustain his belief that he has the phallus, that he ever will have the mother. He has lost his faith in the paternal guarantee, fears he lacks the phallus, fears he is castrated, and as a consequence the mother returns not as desired but as castrated. The mother as she is present in the text is memorably disgusting. More broadly, the mother as lost beloved is elegiacally mourned in Beckett's work, but the mother, as present woman, is energetically repulsed and repulsive. The woman as absent represents the possibility of having the phallus, but the woman as present represents the possibility of castration.

I have left the framework of *Not I*, but the pattern is quite clear there also. The female hysteric of the diegesis presumes her own castration and the absence of the phallus that would supply her with an identity, an "I." As representation that escapes her frame, she disturbs the male spectator, the male gaze that would contain her in order to assert himself, but precisely she disturbs that gaze as threat, as castrating threat—something that is almost painfully clear in the television version, where Mouth literalizes the vagina dentata. In other words, the female hysteric intimates to the male spectator, the gaze to which she is still always subjected, that her refusal of the phallus that is the dissatisfaction of her desire is also his lack of the phallus, his dissatisfied desire. By so doing, she provokes in him a hysterical crisis, a phallic panic, but although this brings him closer to her, its condition is his perception of her as threatening and repulsive. The lesson of the female hysteric is an unwelcome one.

In conclusion, I think this brings us closer to an understanding of the dynamics of gender and identity in the play, and closer too to a resolution of its contradictory interpretations. Thus, on the one hand, *Not I* might seem an extreme example of the female object confirming the superiority of the male gaze "which projects male lack onto female characters in the guise of anatomical deficiency and discursive inadequacy" (Silverman, *The Acoustic Mirror,* p. 1). Of course, the very mechanism of projection and the need for its continued repetition asserts the actuality of male lack, an actuality that the female hysteric makes clear in her refusal to desire the phallus. This, on the other hand, should not lead one to claim that because *Not I* challenges the male gaze, it is to be taken as a work informed by feminism. The female hysteric is nonfeminist insofar as she presumes a negative evaluation of herself and the mother, whose positive phallic side is lost to her. It is this loss of the phallic mother, the final impossibility of his having the phallus, of his securing of his masculine subjectivity, that she demonstrates to the male, provoking in him a hysteria parallel to her own.

However, if the female hysteric is passively nonfeminist, the male hysteric is actively antifeminist, since he is thereby shifted from a positive paternal identification to a negative maternal identification that he takes as threatening and destructive of his identity. It is this model of masculinity that finally seems most consistent with both Beckett's work in general, where the only good woman is a lost one and any present woman is a menace, and with *Not I* in particular, where the disturbance of a masculine subjectivity is portrayed across and through a threatening and negative evaluation of femininity. Significantly, the father throughout Beckett, though but a shadow of himself, is almost invariably a positive figure and the object of a nostalgic regret, while the mother, perhaps most powerfully in this play, is abject in her oppressive presence.

Finally, Beckett's work lays the blame for the collapse of a patriarchal subjectivity not on the father's deceitful promise but on the mother for returning him to her castration. Curiously, the mother is blamed for her own castration, when, without the father's pretension to the phallus, the horror of that castration could not exist.

Works Cited

Beckett, Samuel. *Not I*. In *Collected Shorter Plays*. London: Faber & Faber, 1984.

———. *The Trilogy*. London: John Calder, 1976.

Ben-Zvi, L., ed. *Women in Beckett*. Urbana and Chicago: Illinois University Press, 1990.

Bowlby, R. "A Happy Event." *Paragraph* 14, no. 1 (1991): 10–19.

Creed, B. "Phallic Panic: Male Hysteria and Dead Ringers." *Screen* 31, no. 2 (1990): 125–46.

Gidal, P. *Understanding Beckett*. London: Macmillan, 1986.

Grosz, E. *Sexual Subversions: Three French Feminists*. Sydney: Allen & Unwin, 1989.

Lutterbie, J. H. "'Tender Mercies': Subjectivity and Subjection in Samuel Beckett's *Not I*." In *The World of Samuel Beckett*, edited by J. H. Smith, 86–106. London and Baltimore: Johns Hopkins University Press, 1991.

Silverman, K. *The Acoustic Mirror: The Female Voice in Psychoanalysis and Cinema*. Indianapolis: Indiana University Press, 1988.

Zizek, S. *For They Know Not What They Do: Enjoyment as a Political Factor*. London: Verso, 1991.

Gender in Beckett's Music Machine

MARY BRYDEN

It is noticeable that actors and directors who have entered deeply into the Beckettian enterprise often stress above all its musical imperative. Walter Asmus, in an interview with Jonathan Kalb, described his own production of *Godot:* "I saw almost every performance every night, and they were always different. It started to become music."[1] The late Peggy Ashcroft, in an interview with Katharine Worth, voiced her perception in similar style. Speaking of Beckett the director, she stated: "The emphasis was really musical in his approach."[2] Similarly, in response to John O'Mahony's question "What guidelines do you employ in the performance of Beckett's work?" Pierre Chabert replied: "You must feel the rhythm of the punctuation and the commas. It's just like musical notation."[3] Indeed, Beckett's approach was often, it seems, explicitly musical, and Walter Asmus describes how, at one point in rehearsals for the 1978 production of *Play*, Beckett even experimented for a time with working with a piano, to concentrate upon the musicality of the delivery. The experiment was finally renounced, yet Asmus commends the aspiration that prompted it: "You get a longing to experience it as mere music, not in terms of tones but in terms of feelings, or relationships between people" (Kalb, *Beckett in Performance,* p. 183).

This perception is far from being an artificially or authorially induced one. Moreover, it is one that appears recurrently in the mouths of both male and female actors. This point is apposite, for there is a pervasive cliché within our Western culture that has to do with male as designer or owner, and female as interpreter or presenter of that product. This gender stereotype is not, I would suggest, applicable to interpreters of Beckett's work, and if Billie Whitelaw often refers to herself as a musical instrument played by Beckett, David Warrilow does so with equal conviction. In an interview with Jonathan Kalb, he states that "the action in performing a Beckett play is making the instrument resonate," and that "What works is finding what musicians have called the "right tone" [. . .] I then have to trust that it'll work for somebody else—that if I get it right, if I sing it "on key," "in tune," it's going to vibrate properly for somebody else" (ibid., pp. 229, 224).

This paper does not, however, merely assert that participation in the Beckettian music machine—particularly with regard to the theatrical moment—is automatically a fully democratic and gender-inclusive process. It aims to go further and explore how the evolution of the gender referent in all of Beckett's work can not only recruit very fruitfully the musical metaphor but can in a sense be drawn or subsumed into a musical dynamic.

It is clear, I think, that the inscription of gender undergoes a fascinating evolution in the course of Beckett's writing career. In the early fiction there is, of course, a markedly oppositional character in the designation of male and female specificities. When Murphy declares that "Women are all the same bloody same,"[4] he is also saying that they are all the "same bloody different"—different, or deviant, in relation to that maleness which a patriarchal frame of reference has constructed as centrality or as norm.

This opposition is echoed or underlined by another important dualism that manifests itself within Beckett's early fiction: namely, the difficult reconciliation of mind and body. In those early male narrators/protagonists, like Murphy, who struggle to piece together an identity from what they construe as the separate compartments of mind and body, women are a destabilizing factor. In arousing physical desire in the male, they wield the power to arrest his bodily attention, thus wresting from him the option of intellectual autonomy. Women then become the scapegoats for the anxiety and insecurity experienced by these early males when struggling to subject the troubling lurches of appetite to the reins of the mind. Yet, even when physically absent from Celia and installed as an employee within an institution whose ministrations address the mental equilibrium, Murphy finds it impossible to displace physical desire by intellectual: "It continued to divide him, as witness his deplorable susceptibility to Celia, ginger, and so on. The means of clinching it were lacking" (*Murphy*, p. 102).

Within this context, music serves occasionally in Beckett's early writing as a metaphor for sexual interaction or gratification. Thus, when Murphy is with Celia, "their nights were still that: serenade, nocturne and albada" (*Murphy*, p. 46). When long separated from Celia, Murphy determines just before his premature demise "to face the music, MUSIC, MUSIC, back to Brewery Road, to Celia, serenade, nocturne, albada" (*Murphy*, p. 141). The succession of musical terms here denotes that this is no perfunctory liaison, for serenade (evening music) gives way to nocturne (music suggesting the romantic beauty of night) and thence to albada (morning music, often linked with the parting of lovers at dawn).

Similarly, in *Dream of Fair to Middling Women*, Belacqua's erotic liaisons are experienced not as a grabbed snack but as a "banquet of music."[5] It is a banquet, moreover, to which many women may contribute. Speaking of the Syra-Cusa, the narrator conjectures: "We could chain her up with the Smeraldina-Rima and the little Alba, our capital divas, and make it look like a sonata, with recurrence of themes, key signatures, plagal finale and all" (*Dream*, p. 49).

Nevertheless, it is also the case within Beckett's early fiction that musical sound may be seen as providing solace for the woman-haunted male; indeed, the entry of Woman into such a domain is bitterly resented. The narrator of *The Unnamable* reflects with dread at one point upon the possible auditory torture that a woman soprano might inflict upon him: "What can be worse than this, a woman's voice perhaps, I hadn't thought of that, they might engage a soprano."[6] Similarly, Dougald McMillan describes the "nude piano player covering his genitals with white sheet music" at the end of *Watt* as "a man seeking refuge in the absolute of music."[7]

However, to regard music as fulfilling the function of hospitable woman-proof enclosure for the male of the early fiction is also to imply that it provides a space in which the posited alterity of womanhood can be set aside. Moreover, as Beckett's work proceeds, such male/female bipolarities begin to be unsettled, such that the territorial segregation associated with male and female in much of the early work is subjected to dispersal. The later work thus begins to manifest—to use a term central to the analysis of the French theorists Gilles Deleuze and Félix Guattari—a much more "deterritorialized" space:[8] a space that is stripped of all claim to patrimony or hierarchy, whether linguistic, sexual, or geographic. This dissolution of the tendency towards a gender-based apartheid is not so much a function of pressure towards integration as of an intense recognition of the mutuality attendant upon the imposition, in Beckettian terms, of the life sentence: a simultaneous death sentence, apprehended with intensity by male and female alike.

The identification of this progression may appear to rely upon an unduly linear, chronological analysis. I hope to counteract this a little later in positing the view that it is a change of genre—from prose to drama—that catalyzes the change. Nevertheless, to return to the musical referent, these remarks are intended to provide not a coda to a climactic progression but, rather, a 'da capo'. (And here I define a 'da capo' as an invitation or direction to recapitulation: to go back to the beginning of a work or section of a work and begin again).

As early as *Proust*, Beckett was writing of "the beautiful convention of the 'da capo' as a testimony to the intimate and ineffable nature of an art that is perfectly intelligible and perfectly inexplicable."[9] Indeed, his analysis of Proust's work assigns to music in its entirety a role that "synthesises the moments of privilege and runs parallel to them" (*Proust*, pp. 92–93). Thus Beckett observes that Swann, of Proust's *A la recherche du temps perdu*, "identifies the 'little phrase' of the Sonata with Odette, spatialises what is extraspatial, establishes it as the national anthem of his love," whereas "The narrator [. . .] sees in the red phrase of the Septuor, trumpeting its victory in the last movement like a Mantegna archangel clothed in scarlet, the ideal and immaterial statement of the essence of a unique beauty, a unique world, the invariable world and beauty of Vinteuil" (*Proust*, p. 93).

I referred earlier to the French philosophers Deleuze and Guattari, and one might note here the remarkable complementarity of their analysis with that of Beckett. In volume 2 of their monumental work *Capitalism and Schizophrenia* (quoted here from the English translation of the French original), they state: "The little phrase from Vinteuil's sonata is associated with Swann's love, the character of Odette, and the landscape of the Bois de Boulogne for a long time, until it turns back on itself, opens onto itself, revealing until then unheard-of potentialities, entering into other connections, setting love adrift in the direction of other assemblages."[10]

This recurrent musical phrase is an example of what Beckett refers to as the 'da capo' *(Proust*, p. 92) and Deleuze and Guattari refer to as the *ritournelle* or refrain.[11] (Indeed, the English musical term "ritornello" is occasionally used as a synonym of the 'da capo'). Just as Beckett affirms that Swann "spatialises what is extraspatial" upon hearing the "little phrase" (*Proust,* p. 93), Deleuze and Guattari draw attention to the refrain as "a prism, a crystal of space-time" (*A Thousand Plateaus*, p. 348).

That "privilege" synthesized by music, to which Beckett refers, is not bonded to, or bounded by, human taxonomies such as gender or age. Deleuze and Guattari, instancing Messaien, concur: "Music is not the privilege of human beings: the universe, the cosmos, is made of refrains; the question in music is that of a power of deterritorialization permeating nature, animals, the elements, and deserts as much as human beings," such that the musicality of a moment is also its deterritorialized flow: "Music dispatches molecular flows" (*A Thousand Plateaus*, p. 309). Thus, although codes and coordinates within musical systems are symptoms of molarity (a term Deleuze and Guattari recruit to designate the fixed or static, the antithesis of "molecularity"), these *points fixes* are also preconditions for the transforming power of molecularity: "This dualist system of the sexes that reappears on the level of the voice, this molar and punctual distribution, serves as a foundation for new molecular flows that then intersect, conjugate, are swept up in a kind of instrumentation and orchestration that tend to be part of the creation itself" (*A Thousand Plateaus*, p. 308). Within that molecularity, male/female affiliations are not dissolved: indeed, opera—referred to resoundingly in Beckett's *Proust* as "a hideous corruption of this most immaterial of all the arts" (*Proust*, p. 92)—is structured upon assumptions of gender-related vocal differentiations. However, such dualisms can be, as Deleuze and Guattari point out, caught up by the musical flow and accommodated by an energy that subsumes segregation: "Voices may be reterritorialized on the distribution of the two sexes, but the continuous sound flow still passes between them as in a difference of potential" (*A Thousand Plateaus*, p. 308).

Given the presence of these potentialities of sound and rhythm, essentialist definitions can be fragmented, for each performance of music is different, organic. Even if recorded, its transmission relies upon variables of air, atmosphere, acoustics, and the senses/aural capacities of the listener. In Beckett's later work, music functions no longer as a metaphor for coition or for woman-free sanctuary. Rather, it becomes the current into which the multiple tributaries of desire may pour. It is no longer a state or a destination. Instead, it is a developing flow of multigendered energies. Hélène Cixous describes this provisional dynamic well at the outset of her text *La Venue à l'écriture*: "Un désir cherchait sa demeure. J'étais ce désir. J'étais la question."[12]

Within musical sound in its widest sense, then, gender as site of oppositional challenge loses its position. As Deleuze and Guattari maintain, in accordance with the analysis already explored: "Being a man *or* a woman no longer exists in music" (*A Thousand Plateaus*, p. 304). The italicized "or" is important here. Gender is not said to be eluded or demoted by music: only gender apprehended as polarity/molarity is destabilized by that molecular flux. The differing character of Beckett's later work might thus be associated with the extension of voice potency and of musicality so that it no longer represents an optional haven, but, rather, a constant that inhabits the intensities of male and female desire. Within this work, sound (or its withdrawal), rhythm, fitful melody, and refrain are often the expression or accompaniment of circumstance.

Moreover, it is the advent of the drama that, as this study has suggested, catalyzes the change from "phallogocentrism" to gender fluidity. Within the dramatic moment, women and men are both "en-voiced" within a multilayered acoustic imperative. The voices of women and men acquire a potent rhythm that shares (indeed, often constitutes) a musical dynamic. It may be akin to the musical intermezzo that is always between positions, as Deleuze and Guattari describe: "The only way to get outside the dualisms is to be between, to pass between, the intermezzo" (*A Thousand Plateaus*, p. 277). What is clear is that this musical dynamic often absorbs bipolarities within its own precedent course. Perhaps it is not inapposite to recall in this connection the text Beckett supplied to Morton Feldman specifically to be set to music. The 1976 text, entitled "Neither," exemplifies a transient subjectivity—"From impenetrable self to impenetrable unself by way of neither"[13]—which Feldman respected in his polyrhythmic setting. The antipathies of the narrator of *The Unnamable* towards women sopranos notwithstanding, the piece is scored for soprano solo and full orchestra. Notably, however, the voice is interspersed and modulated by what a contemporary reviewer called "the shifting orchestral texture,"[14] to be superseded eventually by instrumentation alone. The pulsating movement thus achieved by Feldman fully exemplifies that "passing between" of which Deleuze and Guattari speak. As Feldman himself observes: "You"re back and forth, back and forth."[15]

Billie Whitelaw has described this ebb and flow in a similar way. Speaking of playing Winnie in *Happy Days*, she talks of it as "something for movement and voice like piano and voice, and the movement was very technically worked in and flowed absolutely like *perpetual mobile* [*sic*]" (Ben-Zvi, *Women in Beckett,* p. 5). Indeed, in the same interview with Linda Ben-Zvi, Whitelaw sidelines the organizational issues of gender and age within the Beckettian context by asserting: "I just don't think of Beckett in terms of gender or age" (p. 4), and goes on to say: "I do think of the parts in terms of music" (p. 6).

Music as understood here, then, is not restricted to orchestral notation but includes human sounds, cries and whispers, or occasionally louder screams, perhaps approximating to what George Steiner has called "the inchoate scream out of the blackened mouth in the Beckett parable."[16] Such sounds and cries are, as *How It Is* observes, sexually impartial: "good a fellow-creature more or less but man woman girl or boy cries have neither certain cries sex nor age."[17]

It is notable in this regard that Hélène Cixous, in a short and remarkable essay on Beckett, has focused precisely upon this sexual multiplicity inhabiting and structuring a Beckett text. Within the dramatized chorus of voices that she includes in the second part of her essay comes the authorial voice (that of Beckett), which explains: "Tout se passe ici toujours dans un site étrange, à la fois schématique, symbolique et cependant réel, aux proportions très grandes et cependant réduites. On peut tout y mettre. C'est un site agité, corporel, anonyme, bon conducteur."[18] In illustration, a voice later proclaims: "Autrefois je fus déjà garçon et fille, buisson, oiseau, muet poisson dans la mer" ("Une Passion," p. 404).

This fluidity of identity, this suspension of taxonomies, may find a natural home within the dynamics of musical sound. Indeed, in her essay "Tancredi Continues," Cixous demonstrates how Rossini's use of a woman's voice for the role of Tancred in his opera *Tancredi* releases a flow of energies "from one pleasure to the other whose sex is not revealed. It is a question of the grace of genders, instead of the law of genders, it is a question of dancing."[19] One might note in this connection the remark made by Beckett to Lawrence Shainberg to the effect that music is "the highest art form" because "it's never condemned to explicitness."[20] Indeed, as Hélène Cixous also proposes in her essay on Tancred, the space proper to artistic/musical creation is one that permits liberation from the structuration imposed by gender conceived as bipolarity. Thus, although music as conceived by the central male narrator or protagonist of Beckett's early fiction is a signifier of sexuality, or, conversely, a refuge for the male dictator of differentiation, it becomes in Beckett's drama, and in his later writing as a whole, the very (text/sex)uality, or the vessel in which gender may ferment.

Music cannot achieve this fermentation by itself. But it may provide the necessary fluidity for the fragmentation and release of space that has been too rigidly appropriated by gender stereotypes. This is not to preclude the positing of gender as agenda, but it may unsettle the notion of gender as a predetermining key signature in Beckett's writing and create a space in which gender-as-opposition becomes dysfunctional.

NOTES

1. J. Kalb, *Beckett in Performance* (Cambridge: Cambridge University Press, 1989), p. 183.
2. L. Ben-Zvi, ed., *Women in Beckett: Performance and Critical Perspectives* (Urbana: University of Illinois Press, 1990), p. 12.
3. See "Beckett Comes Home," *Plays International,* January 1992, p. 26.
4. S. Beckett, *Murphy* (London: John Calder, 1977), p. 25.
5. S. Beckett, *Dream of Fair to Middling Women* (Dublin: Black Cat Press, 1992), p. 40.
6. S. Beckett, *The Unnamable,* in *The Beckett Trilogy* (London: Picador, 1979), p. 335.
7. D. McMillan, "*Echo's Bones*: Starting Point for Beckett," in E. Morot-Sir, H. Harper, and D. McMillan, eds., *Samuel Beckett: The Art of Rhetoric,* North Carolina Studies in the

Romance Languages and Literatures (Chapel Hill: University of North Carolina Press, 1976), p. 184.

8. Deleuze and Guattari use the concept extensively in their work, but see notably their *Capitalism and Schizophrenia,* vol. 2: *A Thousand Plateaus*, trans. B. Massumi (London: Athlone Press, 1988).

9. S. Beckett, *Proust,* in *Proust and Three Dialogues with Georges Duthuit* (London: Calder & Boyars, 1965), p. 92.

10. *A Thousand Plateaus*, p. 349. Like Beckett, Deleuze has written a monograph on Proust: *Proust et les signes*, deuxième éd. augmentée (Paris: Presses Universitaires de France, 1970).

11. Deleuze and Guattari develop their concept of the *ritournelle* at length, notably in chapter 11 of *A Thousand Plateaus*, pp. 310–50.

12. H. Cixous, "La Venue à l'écriture," in *Entre l'écriture* (Paris: Des femmes, 1986), p. 9.

13. *Neither* was first performed in 1977 at the Rome Opera; the text was first published in *Journal of Beckett Studies* 4 (Spring 1979): vii, and is republished in *As The Story Was Told: Uncollected and Late Prose* (London: John Calder, 1990), pp. 108–9.

14. See the article "Beckett as Librettist," *Music and Musicians*, May 1977, pp. 5–6.

15. Feldman is cited within ibid., p. 6.

16. G. Steiner, "A Note on Absolute Tragedy," *Literature and Theology* 4, no. 2 (July 1990): 152.

17. S. Beckett, *How It Is* (London: John Calder, 1964), p. 60.

18. H. Cixous, "Une Passion: l'un peu moins que rien," in T. Bishop and R. Federman, eds., *Cahier de l'Herne: Samuel Beckett* (Paris: Editions de l'Herne, 1976), p. 402.

19. H. Cixous, "Tancredi Continues," trans. A. Liddle and S. Sellers, in S. Sellers, ed., *Writing Differences: Readings from the Seminar of Hélène Cixous* (Milton Keynes, U.K.: Open University Press, 1988), p. 38.

20. L. Shainberg, "Exorcising Beckett," *Paris Review* 29, no. 104 (Fall 1987): 116.

Beckett's Irish Rhythm Embodied in His Polyphony

JOHANNEKE VAN SLOOTEN

"A voice comes to one in the dark. Imagine."

WITH an opening sentence such as this, Beckett turns the reader into a listener: the voice is presented as "company," directly addressing the reader as a witness. With the request to imagine the voice rising from the dark, the reader becomes directly involved with the story. It is a stimulus to join thinking and listening. The narrator as well as the "deviser of the voice and of its hearer and of himself, deviser of himself for company," introduces himself via this intermediary.

In many of Beckett's plays characters are called or asked compelling questions as a starting signal. Sometimes the voice as a character has the ability to split into several voices talking independently, at cross-purposes or commenting on each other in a polyphonic colloquy. Through this multiplicity and through breath, rhythm, pitch, and timbre rendered audible, the voices are imbued with musicality and develop separate existences as melodic movements. Both the visual effect of the verbal configurations and the way they sound confront the reader with the musical eloquence of the text.

Music was important to Beckett from an early age. His mother loved to sing and sang many songs with him. He was a technically capable pianist, albeit with a heavy, somewhat percussive touch. At one time he was even an amateur performer on the flute. He actively participated in extensive music-making, singing and dancing, both at home and during visits to friends. This typically Irish custom familiarized him with many Irish songs and ballads that he would later hear in pubs and in the Dublin Musical Society, where poets and singers performed. In the 1930s, when he lived in Paris, these cultural "music evenings," an important aspect of Anglo-Irish intellectual life, would find a sequel in James Joyce's home in the French capital. Joyce was a connoisseur of the Irish ballad, an enthusiastic singer who accompanied himself on the piano and even liked to dance to Irish music when he got the chance.

The influence of Beckett's early musical experiences in his country of origin left many traces in his work. After having moved to France, he often visited Ireland while his mother was still alive. He returned to Dublin time and again with the same intensity as Proust visited Combray. And in the same fashion. In his later works he returned to his country of origin with increasing frequency—to the Dublin Mountains (in "Love and Lethe," "Walking out," and *Stirrings Still*), along the seashore of Dublin Bay where he and his father used to ramble for hours on end. The atmosphere in plays like *Embers* is frequently determined by the sea and the wind, which hold a firm grip on daily life on this island pulsating in "a mighty systole." So, too, in his prose similarly symbolically heavy details can be found. For example, the moon shines as the only spot of light in the darkness of being, or shines its old rays over decaying life. Beckett uses the same imagery and spherical elements that occur in the Irish art of chanting stories since times immemorial.

Glimpses of the influence of Irish music and its fundamental characteristic of oral transmission can be caught throughout the text. He uses the whole range of musical elements for the emotional coloring and painting of the atmospheric moods. Here, not only the visible traces are meant as expressed in allusions and quotes, patronyms, place-names, historical and literary references, or explicit examples of the Anglo-Irish dialect such as in *More Pricks than Kicks*, "A Wet Night," and *All That Fall*, but also the typical turns of thought, turns of phrase, cadences of speech, and the way of storytelling. The Irishness in Beckett's work seems part of its vital core; he himself sees it as constituting the "condensing spiral of need" in any work of art.

He quoted Irish ballads less frequently than Joyce, although his work was profoundly affected by this oral Irish tradition. That he studied this tradition in depth is proved by his translation into French of fragments from Joyce's *Finnegans Wake* (like the Anna Livia Plurabelle segment) that include dozens of musical allusions of this kind. Furthermore, Joyce gave him the supervision of the complete translation, which proves that Beckett was equipped with an extensive acquaintance with folklore, early Irish (mythic) art, and literature. He also published an essay on *Finnegans Wake* that is universally acknowledged as the best article on the subject. This emphasizes his knowledge of the peculiar value that Irish myths possess.

The following exploration of the correspondences between distinctive features of the Irish ballads and their performance and Beckett's works written in English, especially his theatrical works, will reveal the musicality of Beckett's use of language. This may have consequences for reading his work.

The Irish Rhythm

The distinctive personal sound produced by Beckett, acting as a musical improviser using to the full all poetic freedom that language offers him within a predesigned structure, is heard throughout his work, although there are marked differences in musicality between the works which he originally wrote in English and those he wrote in French.

Colloquial language is essential both for Beckett and in the tradition of chanting stories and commenting on the Irish ballads. It is a combination of contemplating, thinking aloud, and performing of a story, in other words an interaction of listening and being listened to. This "Sean Nós" tradition drew upon elements from medieval bardic poetry, which was the preserve of the scholarly elite. These forms are as complete and sophisticated as classical or European art music and important enough to be mentioned in an Irish mythological account.

The other characteristic of this traditional music is anonymity, which gives the performer the opportunity to indulge himself in variations and ornamentation. The songwriter is a performer and composer at the same time. "Sean Nós" singing is rooted in the Irish language, and its fortunes as an art form were historically affected by the encroachment of English as the spoken language in Ireland. The most distinctive feature of Beckett's work is its creation of characters who are laughable and horrible at the same time, like Hamm, Clov, Watt, Arsene, Estragon, and many others. These grotesque, macabre figures have usually been regarded as a modern decadent element in Beckett's work, but they are also closely akin to the stark, archaic figures found in ancient Irish art, in its carvings, manuscript illustrations, mythic tales, and in "Sean Nós."

Beckett, who acts as a sort of prompter whispering words in the ears of his anonymous voices and, supported by breath, providing them with sound and rhythm, gives Molloy the words: "Speaking is inventing like a ballad singer will say: 'Singing is improvisatory composing.'" In the long run Beckett's extensive texts ask for internal variation on the same theme, just like the "long songs" of twenty verses or more call for. In the course of the beseeching repetitions that are typical to both story forms, events are dealt with which come from the vortex of daily life and that are consequently interwoven in daily language.

Because "talking" and storytelling is the main activity in both Beckett's dramatic works and his prose, his style is engrafted onto colloquial speech to a large extent. This must also be the origin of what is often called Beckett's "Irish rhythm," the phenomenon that even his most austere texts, with their idiosyncratic syntax, still sound like Irish music.

In my search for the origins of the musicality of Beckett's language, I was struck by the remarkable correspondences that can be found between Beckett's specific language characteristics on the one hand, and the typical idiom and grammar of Anglo-Irish speech, which can be heard in songs and ballads, on the other.

In that rhythm characteristic of Irishmen speaking and singing in English, several gaps in the sentence structure occur, caused by the omission of copulas and auxiliaries, and of some nouns and syllables. Personal pronouns are often omitted, while verbs are frequently unconjugated ("That's what it be to be"). In Irish-English, a curious use of the personal pronoun is employed that can be seen in the following examples: "He interrupted me and I writing my letters" instead of "as I was writing." "I found Phil there too and he playing his fiddle for the company." This, although very incorrect English, is a classic idiom in Irish, from which it has been imported as it stands into English. Thus: "Do chonnairc me Tomas agus e n'a schuihe coisna teine" is in English: "I saw Thomas and he sitting beside the fire . . . and I be in bed at the time." The same structure can be found in "And we far away on the billow" and in Beckett, who also frequently uses it: "Talking to yourself who else out loud imaginary conversations there was childhood for you ten or eleven on a stone." The pronoun "I" is sometimes replaced by "myself" with retroactive force later in the sentence. ("Looking about the fair for myself.") Asceticism is also achieved by the use of "if" or by rhetorical questions used as an answer. Equally in Beckett's texts, the linguistic jumps resulting from these omissions appear to make the text more abstract, to "pare it down." Musical logic permits the omission of notes from a melodic phrase if this is based on a tonal chord. Similarly, words can be omitted from a sentences due to implicit grammatical logic. Thus the omission of subject or object creates a gap, a moment of loss, which, however, is not a grammatical void.

In many cases Beckett's words are in English, but the syntax is Irish. When the Irish adopted, or were forced to adopt, the English language, they discovered that one of its defects was its lack of a habitual present tense of the verb "to be." They rectified this by simply translating their own *bíonn sé* (he does be). Educated Irish people, unless they are being ironic, avoid its use, because it is considered uneducated speech.

Other features of Anglo-Irish speech are the repetitive use of words or sentences; the transformations, division, contraction, shortening, and lengthening of words; and the minimalization of the number of different words per sentence, but also exaggeration through redundance. Anglo-Irish speech did not only form the basis for Beckett's linguistic talent, as appears from the many Irish references and his use of words, proverbs, and expressions from this dialect (such as "I'd give my eyes to be listening to him"), he was also fascinated by linguistic experiment. As he grew older, producing his progressively austere texts, he increasingly reverted to the language of his childhood.

About Music

Beckett liked to see his work compared to music, and rightly so, for he frequently employed vocal techniques and sound effects: the sound of vowels and consonants and the alternately winded, syncopated, and pounding rhythms shaped his texts. For concrete musical quotations he uses fragments from Schubert *(Nacht und Träume),* Beethoven (Fifth Piano Trio), and Irish songs and ballads, but also snatches of music, such as barrel organ tunes and street cries, as well as his own compositions, complete with score, such as the chorus for soprano, alto, tenor, and bass in his novel *Watt*. In this most Irish novel of his, Watt hears a croaking choir of three frogs. Their part-singing is noted down in a graphic score. There is a lot of singing, and the narrator of his legend describes the musical effect of these fairy voices as "a wild strain of unearthly melody." Then there is the duet of the piano tuner, which changes Watt's life completely. From that moment onwards he starts to invert words and sentences, which is quite demanding for the audience. In his novel *Murphy*, Beckett gives proof of his technical and theoretical knowledge of music. He uses, in the intimate situations in which Watt finds himself, a cuckoo clock sounding from afar and the echo of the street cry "Quid pro quo! Quid pro quo!" in order to create a difference between his inner world and the big world outside. And in *All That Fall*, his first radio play, a whole gamut of sound effects is used, such as rural sounds, sheep, a bird, cock crows, and, finally, Schubert's *Death and the Maiden*.

The composer Morton Feldman, with whom he closely cooperated on a number of occasions, stated that Beckett wrote highly musical texts, that he repeatedly read his texts aloud and even sang them in order to discover and test the right rhythm and the "fundamental sounds." For his plays this procedure was even more imperative than for his prose and poetry, because the actor who is to perform the text cannot avoid making his own interpretations, and Beckett wanted to prevent various kinds of errors that the actor might produce. That is why, when rehearsing and directing his own plays, Beckett kept timing the rests and the duration of words, keeping the rhythm firmly under control, with the precision of a metronome. As a conductor of his own plays he wanted to ensure that the modulations, the transitions towards silence, and the shifts in sound coloring as laid down in his "scores" were accurately realized.

In his trilogy he lets his "writers," Malone and Molloy, write in musical forms. This happens according to the speaking mode, and thus both write in a highly auditive way to make the gesture of language visible and audible. The language's movement becomes moving. Most of the dramatis personae have their own characteristic sounds, according to which they are identifiable. For example, Maddy Rooney has to "sound fat," whereas her husband has to "sound blind." Furthermore, it must be audible whether someone either comes or leaves the stage. The anonymous voices come out of the dark and they owe their theatrical existence only to their sound. Without their precisely specified voices they literally are not there. Music is particularly present in the rendering of all the side effects; sometimes it is as sound setting, sometimes to illustrate the protagonists' moods. In *Stirrings Still*, for example, the clock strikes the hour. The strokes are in an order associated with death. Once in a while the strokes sound clear, as if carried by the wind; at other times they can barely be heard in the quiet air. Distant cries alternate sometimes from afar, sometimes loud and clear. In several plays the music itself is even given its autonomous voice and becomes an additional cast member playing an autonomous part, such as in *Rough for Theatre I*, *Words and Music*, *Cascando,* and *Ghost Trio*.

Heterophony

A number of composers, including Marcel Mihalovici, Luciano Berio, and Morton Feldman, have been attracted to Beckett's texts because of their musical nature. Berio used fragments from *The Unnamable* in his *Sinfonia*, the text of which is treated in a way that is analogous to the musical development. It is a very complex, rampant text that provides a parallel stream to the music. Berio said, "One of the most important proliferations of the Beckett text (though not the only one) is the sequence of verbal signs which describe, sometimes metaphorically, sometimes explicitly, the various stages of the harmonic voyage, musically marked and punctuated by the quotations. This part of *Sinfonia* is both the center and the macroscopic model of the entire work."

Feldman composed the opera *Neither* on a libretto by Beckett and also wrote the music for *Words and Music*. He expressed great enthusiasm about their collaboration, the exploitation of the many variations in vocal technique, and the metaphor of colloquy. Feldman calls this cooperation of the independent characters "words" and "music" Beckett's "heterophony, the simultaneous sounding of a melodic theme and a variation on it." In his texts every poetic line is directly related to the sounding equivalent. The text itself is the carrier of the musical qualities. Beckett made the friction between text and music into the main subject of works such as the radio plays *Cascando* and *Words and Music*. This friction arises as soon as the text assumes a self-willed stance towards the music. Beckett aimed for a cross-fertilization, a fusion of literary and musical elements, of rationality and feeling. Both radio plays came into being in cooperation with musicians. They are considered to be part of his most moving works. That is hardly surprising if one takes into account that for Beckett music was always synonymous with emotion. In *Words and Music*, the intellect operates as if cut off from feeling, producing meaningless utterances. Music or feeling triumphs over words, the haughty intellect. Music is also associated with love and passion.

When the Irish singer speaks of love, this will be lyrically and with irony, the characteristic Irish black humor. In most ballads, like in Beckett's novels, things go wrong when love as passion is concerned. In the song "Love is pleasing" we are warned against the quick rotting of love. A father wants to murder his son in order to prevent his child of running away with a whore. Usually love causes deep suffering, as in the lamentation "lament love song."

Cascando was first meant to be called "Calando," a musical term meaning diminishing in tone (equivalent to diminuendo or decrescendo). It was written as a commission from the composer Marcel Mihalovici, who composed the music of *Krapp's Last Tape*. He describes Beckett as a remarkable musician: "he possesses an astonishing musical intuition, that I often used in my composition and moreover he has a very sure opinion in music." Mihalovici comments on *Cascando:* "It was not a matter of musical commentary on the text but of creating, by musical means, a third character, so to speak, who sometimes intervenes alone, sometimes along with the narrator without however merely being the accompaniment for him."

Music is the art through which we are able to express joy and sadness, pain and fear, but also through which the spark of humor can leap from the text. The musical qualities reveal the unspeakable that is hiding behind the words. At a certain moment in *Words and Music* when Music is given an increasingly lingual quality, "Words" has the stage direction "Trying to sing this." These singing exercises finally lead to a true "song." Anglo-Irish speech is strongly linked to song, and Beckett's text and music also become closely interwoven in a synchronism of voices and moods. The composers who tackle his texts either feel the inclination to comply with them completely or the obligation to strongly respond to them. The use of the Anglo-Irish dialect does not only allow Beckett to escape some of the limitations of standard English but also gives him the opportunity to multiply the meaning of the text. In addition he lets several voices sound simultaneously so that the heterophonic character of the sentences is multiplied into a polyphonic composition.

At first sight, the pessimistic novel *How It Is* seems a monologue of a creature crawling through a sea of mud that will pull him down as soon as his efforts to stay afloat weaken. He occasionally comes across others crawling through the same mud. Sometimes sexual contact is made, while the mind thinks faster and faster; the creature gasps for breath and breaks down in panic as it asks itself if its screams are heard. The voice wonders if the answers he hears are real voices or not. But the voices are in his head, ear whisperings with counter voices playing around the main voice. Seemingly monotonous texts turn out to include more voices than they at first appeared to do. This polyphony can be created by the constant shifting of the pronoun from one character to another, connecting them either in parallel or in series. At any given time, at least two characters are involved: the voice that talks to us and the voice that is audible to the first voice, which talks for him, has to repeat him, arouses, puts into perspective, tackles, or endorses.

The Unnamable, the last part of the trilogy, starts with a voice asking a series of questions. This voice is not that of Molloy or Malone, or a derivation of Moran. Probably all characters are encompassed in his voice. They are his creation and he has invented their stories, which he is listening to. It is easy for the voice to change roles, to situate himself as subject or as another figure. The three voices A, B, and C in the theatrical piece *That Time* are three character variations of one and the same voice. One narrator tells three stories, each of them from a different point of view, as if he was three "others": one telling from the perspective of childhood, one of being middle aged, and one as an old pensioner. The threefold source and context are combined so as to let them, tuned to each other, speak from one mouth.

His novel *Watt* contains a song by the Magrew ladies: "Many voices, each mingling and blending with each other so strangely that they seemed to be one, though all singing different strains." In traditional ballad singing, a kind of polyphony is achieved in the same way as in *That Time*, namely through the presentation by a single singer of several characters, each with his own story line. A fascinating form of heterophonic singing is the parallel singing of two voices, where one is a fast echo of the other. This way of singing is often practiced by Irish women who continually work until old age at perfecting their technique. All developments of the melody, even the smallest ornamentations and modulations, progress in a paired movement. This manner of singing demands an enormous amount of concentration and in particular a refined listening. One beloved song, titled "Thinking," deals with eternal thinking, especially thinking aloud and being listened to.

Listeners

In many of Beckett's works the action takes place in a minimal sound world, described and stage-managed in great detail, in which the auditive involvement of the reader (and in some cases the spectator) is reinforced by the presence of a listener. Beckett draws our attention to the spectacle, as if announcing: "Come and listen." And simultaneously, he becomes a subject of the story he is listening to.

Thus in *Not I* there is a shadowy figure on the left side of the stage who in his role of "bystander" allows himself to be flooded by the torrent of words issuing from the woman's mouth. In *Ohio Impromptu*, reading and listening are ostensibly divided by distributing these activities among two identical figures sitting at a table. The audience finds itself with three possibilities of identification. It can project itself in the role of the Reader, who in an oral recital tells of a love affair that has ended in death. The audience can also recognize its alter ego in the Listener. In *Embers*, Henry listens to the waves of the sea breaking upon the shingle, to the beating of horses' hooves that he himself announces, to a piano lesson involving much yelling, and to the invisible conversation partners that he invokes, some of whom have already died. We hear Henry's child Addie at her music lesson, struggling with "Chopin's fifth waltz in A Flat Major." By the sound effect of the beating of the sea, sometimes loud, sometimes scarcely audible, the shingle on which Henry is sitting becomes more visualized than audible, even though it is a radio play. Henry likes to sit by the stretch of sea where his father perished. Powerless to escape its sound, he is always trying to evoke his father's presence to talk to him, yet he is afraid to ask the one question that would reveal the truth about his death. Was his drowning a suicide, prompted by his disappointment in his only son? Henry listens to his deceased father's voice, which he knows how to arouse in his own head. In the ballads as well, the sea is sung about in all kinds of ways. The sea has both a visual function and acts like a ubiquitous sound source, as in *Henry Joy*. In *Joe Hill* a deceased father is being called and is given a speaking voice. In that sense the father is drawn into the conversation by his son, who is able to ask his father compelling questions.

Like in *Not I,* there is a juxtaposition of speaking to and listening. In *That Time* our concentration is drawn from a speaking mouth to the listening face, suspended about ten feet above the stage. The old white face with long, outspread hair gradually emerges from the darkness. His slow and regular breathing can be heard. He is the "listener" to his own voice, a threefold voice. He expresses himself in different keys, but at the same time his voice is used as an instrument that is, as it were, short-circuited and introverted. Before he realizes what is happening, the voices that he summoned into his consciousness begin to harangue him on behalf of himself and to feed back acoustically in the resonant cavities of his head. In Beckett's novels, characters such as Watt, Molloy, and the Unnamable yearn for silence, yet are unwilling or unable to free themselves from the sound of their own obsessive voices, which never cease to randomly interrupt each other.

The head, the smallest possible acoustic space, is the location where most of Beckett's miniature dramas take place. Inside the skull, the inner ear attentively listens to the resonating words. In the head, where the voices literally come to life and the deepest stirrings of the soul are put into words, thoughts are transformed into sound material. At the moment of expression they appear to make contact with the outside world, but in fact they are merely ghosts around in the mind.

Concentration through Introversion

While speaking and listening to their own voice and their inner voices, most of Beckett's characters close their eyes. In *That Time* the Listener closes his eyes after the first line or two of the monologue. In *Company*: "By the voice a faint light is shed. Dark lightens while its sounds deepens when it ebbs.... Whence the shadowy light? What company in the dark! To close the eyes and try to imagine that." The characters close their eyes with the same intention as the Irish ballad singers do—to concentrate, shutting themselves off from the uproarious outside world, drawing the story from the depths of their hearts with heightened sensitivity, and allowing it to develop in their heads.

It is usually toward closing time that a singer in a pub feels the urge to make a statement of emotional importance. A farewell to the day begins, melancholy takes over. The pub audience, which was a noisy crowd only minutes ago, silently listens to his ironic lyrics about death and decay. The traditional Anglo-Irish ballad singers, especially those who tell "Sean Nós," the old stories, are folk poets, composing in an ancient, improvised narrative medium with an unusual idiom; the medium involves striking distortions in both content and form. Sometimes it is a woman, but in most cases it is an old man singing stilled and in a subdued mood. Especially in the case of a sad, piercing song, the singers sometimes appear to be far removed from the prosaic world, enclosed in a magic circle.

Like Beckett's characters, the singer, thinking aloud, engages in a conversation with his inner voices. In a rugged song format, sometimes divided into strophes, and a discontinuous narrative form, the narrator mentally transports himself into situations with such vividness that he appears to have seen these with his own eyes and indeed to be still in the midst of events as a participant and observer. Because he both presents the vicissitudes of various characters through dialogue and comments on these, he is also the director. Past and present and expectations about the future intermingle, as the story keeps turning in circles in a timeless self-contained no-man's-land.

QUESTION AND ANSWER

In the Irish tradition of rhetoric about waiting, the ballad singer asks himself questions about events from the past, about the "heroes" in his tale, and about the possible outcome of their deeds. He answers himself by presenting various options and offering his own opinion.

Beckett goes further: not only do his answers give arise to new questions but they also raise questions about questions and answers. The characteristically Anglo-Irish rhetorical questions can be found in various works of Beckett. He often divides them up into small question sequences and repeats them in many variations. For example, in *Words and Music* Words asks, "What?" and then "[Pause. Very rhetorical] Is love the word?" *The Unnamable* starts with a voice asking a series of questions. "Where now? Who now? When now? Unquestioning. I, say I. Unbelieving. Questions, hypotheses, call them that." Molloy poses himself questions and wonders why the answers fail to come, why he experiences words purely as sound and how he should react to this. In *Not I*, the mouth spouts propositions about questions and answers in a canonlike form and gets stuck in circular arguments while the rivulets of words move too fast for comprehension, even for attentive listeners. Finally, after an accelerando that is comparable to that in Irish songs, the stream ends on three equivalent "closing notes": "Pick it up." In *Embers*, Henry ends his story on "Not a sound"; and *Footfalls* finishes with "It all, it all, it all."

Beckett often gives the question-and-answer construction a musical form. The spoken answer is made to sound like an echo by including part of the answer in the formulation of the question. Another echo is created by repeating the question in the answer. When question and answer are simultaneously spoken by a number of characters, this produces a polyphonic contrapuntal relation between the first voice and its counterparts.

Echo effects are a favorite technique for musicalizing the text: the frequent repetition of sentences and clauses, words and syllables, sometimes with minimal variations, creates echoes reverberating throughout the text, as in *Footfalls* and *Rockaby*. In the mysterious structure of echoes in *Footfalls,* where the mother and daughter change roles of narrator and listener, it is never certain who listens to whom. Echoes sound in "the same where she [pause] The same where she began. [pause] Where it began. [pause] It all began. [pause] But this, this, when did this begin?" In *Not I*, when the woman's voice is musing on the functioning of her mouth, the echo effects give the stream of gurgling words an undulating, repetitive character similar to minimal music. The repetition of themes with variations, spoken through a number of "voices," and the apparent superposition and infraposition of melodic sentences by shifts in time or place render pieces such as *Embers* and *All That Fall* fugal. Other texts, such as *Cascando,* contain short strings of words that reappear in almost retrograde fashion, as if using one of the techniques of serial music.

Across the Bar

Another feature that is essential to some Irish songs and ballads is the division of the text into irregular strophes. This is a form that is very familiar to Beckett, as can be seen in his short, originally English prose, *Worstward Ho*, *Stirrings Still*, and *Company*. The recurrent refrain is also a means Beckett uses to add chant to a text. Usually these are theater texts like in

Ohio Impromptu, where three successive sections end on the words "then disappeared without a word." In *That Time* the recurrent refrain functions as an inventory, a brief moment of contemplation serving as a conclusion to the strophes: "when was that" results in the closing song "not a sound." The evaluative function of the "chorus" is repeated in the a capella trio in *Play*, spoken in alternating 2/4 time bars.

When a rest between words or sentences has a real value, Beckett indicates this by recording in the form of spaces or dots the number of beats that such a rest should last. In some cases, when he wishes to indicate the rhythm with greater precision, he uses bars or places the sentences below one another, like in the song of Words, "Age is when to a man" and the song in *Watt*: "We shall be here tonight."

Like an Irish singer, a Beckett stage character takes the liberty of letting the text overrule the music whenever the story demands this. He crosses bars, suddenly produces ligatures to emphasize a word, or draws out the end of a sentence. He occasionally combines words for sound effect or breaks them off prematurely. When he slows down into murmuring or muttering and raises the tension, making his breath audible by tensing his vocal chords, he must accelerate to regain this "stolen time" and rejoin the steadily continuing rhythm. Sometimes the melody crosses the bars in syncopation or, on the contrary, lags behind as the result of the speed of the hurtling words, the rattling over small details, or turning around the main theme in jumpy figure sidetracks.

The loose narrative style employed by the Irish ballad singer does not have an ordered narrative structure or a fixed meter, but it does have clear time divisions and pauses, which depend on the structure of the sentences. He usually sings a capella, with a dark and hoarse, yet melodious, speaking voice without the traditional accompaniment of violin, harp, flute, or bagpipe of other song styles. However, the ballad singer can mark his story by means of sound effects in order to announce various episodes or "voices," and he can increase tension by means of light rolls or darkly pounding beats on the Bodhrán frame drum and accentuate the storytelling rhythm by rattling bones.

Beckett achieves comparable effects of timing and atmosphere using this discontinuous narrative technique and by making his characters stamp a club on the floor, beat their thumbs on the table at certain intervals, or ticking an admonitory baton on the music stand. He uses many sound effects, often involving the feet, the sound of walking in all its forms. More important are vocal techniques such as in "minimal" music based on a long series of "fathers" and "mothers" and various types of laughter. (In *Watt*,

Beckett lists a multiplicity of laughs: "Haw! You heard that one? A beauty. Haw! Hell! Haw! So. Haw! Haw! Haw! My laugh, Mr. ——? [. . .] Of all the laughs that strictly speaking are not laughs, but modes of ululation, only three I think need detain us, I mean the bitter, the hollow and the mirthless. [. . .] The bitter laugh laughs at that which is not good, it is the ethical laugh. The hollow laugh laughs at that which is not true, it is the intellectual laugh. [. . .] But the mirthless laugh is the dianoetic laugh, "down the snout—haw!—so. It is the laugh of laughs, the *risus purus,* the laugh laughing at the laugh, the beholding, the saluting of the highest joke, in a word the laugh that laughs—silence please—at that which is unhappy."

Other effects are the murmur of the sea, street sounds, and the sound of the wind, the wind as breath. The sea splashes "all around us." The wind can pant and can fondle like a caress. Likewise in the ballads the wind blows like a hot breath down our neck and announces fate with a threatening sound or, like the breath of a deceased person, it hangs above its tombstone. In "I Never Will Marry" a girl hears herself screaming when she is standing by the sea. The wind is whispering and the water is roaring. Her beloved has left her, reason enough to drown herself. In Beckett's television play *Eh Joe*, the woman's voice accuses Joe of the suicide of his former girlfriend. She has drowned herself in the sea. Death is also one of the most recurring themes in ballads and appears in many different shapes in these macabre song forms. The words for darkness and death are richly represented in the Anglo-Irish language.

Beckett has been called a moralist more than once. Many of his characters are very close to death, although they keep postponing the actual dying. In Irish, one does not die, one "gets death" *(bas d'fhaghail).* In only one work a character sincerely wishes to die. Malone sighs at the very beginning, "I shall soon be quite dead at last in spite of all."

Beckett wrote a number of dramas with particular actors in mind, just as composers create pieces for a special soloist. The coloring and intonation of a text and the adding of the accents in a changing interpretation can differ to such a great extent that the musical meaning is totally changed. Especially in Beckett's texts that either require a fragile silence or ask for a powerful, loud approach in a scanted rhythm, the atmosphere is dependent on the performer. *Rockaby* and *Not I* were created for the melodious and rhythmically flexible voice of Billie Whitelaw. After hearing Patrick Magee read *Molloy* on BBC radio, Beckett's fascination with this grating voice prompted the writing of *Krapp's Last Tape*. He had a predilection for strong personalities, preferably with a deep voice, such as David Warrilow and Klaus Herm. During rehearsals with these actors he explored various methods in order to fully realize the movement in the language and the emotional values through intonation, dynamics, and rhythm.

Sound

Those who have seen a play by Beckett performed by actors with an Anglo-Irish accent and intonation will have been struck by the balladlike cadences of the jerky, rather bouncy rhythm, by the nasal sound, the dragging mobility of the vowels and the rolling *r*'s. The aspiration with audible breath or the lengthening of consonants, the buzzing *ng* at the end of recurring words such as "going," "being," and "seeing," the rapid staccato articulation and the quavery reverberation at the end of sentences—all are typically Irish. Beckett's own English, although he does not use dialect, has a distinct Dublin quality of the kind often called a Trinity accent. Beckett studied and later on taught at Trinity College in Dublin, but the origin of his accent lies in the middle-class Dublin Southside speech, hard to acquire unless one or one's parents grew up in the Georgian squares or the red-brick suburbs. Both Joyce and Shaw also spoke with this Trinity accent, though neither of them went to that college. Beckett was also familiar with the North County Dublin accent ("Fingal"), and the lower-class Dublin accent *(Watt* and *All That Fall).*

In his most "Irish" texts, a much exploited feature of the Anglo-Irish dialect is its distinctive pronunciation of certain common words, which are used to extend the meaning of the text. Much of the "sound sense" of the works, which requires that it be read with an "aural eyeness," is based on Anglo-Irish pronunciation. This speech preserves the eighteenth-century pronunciation of a large number of words containing the sound usually represented in standard English by the digraph *æ*. This is such a prominent feature of the dialect that the pronunciation of one such word, Jesus as Jaysus, is regarded by many as the sine qua non of Dublin speech.

The tone of voice has explicitly physical qualities because of required audibility of the breath and emotion. Stage directions such as "sad," "suppliant," "very excited," "irritated," "laughing," "explosive," "melancholy," and the individual diction for different characters indicate how much importance he attached to these matters and show how his words should be voiced. Another musical feature of Beckett's language is the associative sentence structure, which is based on the broad spectrum of sounds, repetitive assonances, and alliteration. The form of the text is calculated to show the ways in which the characters think and talk. Their tone reveals their state of mind.

The Body

Life as Beckett saw it was not a process of growth but a process of continuation of deterioration, decay, and destruction. Many miniature dramas in which his figures play their parts are set in half-dark, dusk, an omen of death. All of Beckett's stage figures, even those that appear to be nearly disembodied souls or to experience their bodies as a lifelong burden, possess a voice that is highly physical. Equally, the sounds of footsteps, which appear in many of his plays, create association with a physical, almost earthly, quality. "Not a living soul in the place only yourself and the odd attendant drowsing around in his felt shuffles not a sound to be heard only every now and then a shuffle of felt near then dying away," voice C relates in *That Time*. These soft shuffling sounds have a much more nostalgic meaning than the resolute paces, a "clearly audible rhythmic thread," the daughter makes in *Footfalls*. The daughter walks like an echo in her mother's tracks. These steps were probably inspired by the footsteps that Beckett heard as a child, when his mother wandered around the house. Another influence may be the Irish set dance, the first form of tap dance, in which the dancers tap their feet on the afterbeat and to other irregular rhythms. Beckett records these step patterns in highly detailed rhythmical and tonal descriptions, and in a number of cases the movements are even indicated in the form of choreographic drawings.

In many respects, these movements are comparable to those of the Irish step dance, which emphatically—like Beckett's choreographies—is not a proper dancing dance but involves a solo dancer walking figures, turning in steps, away from and back to his initial position. These dancinglike, turning patterns that Beckett shows in his poem "Roundelay" form small or larger magical circles in which the "dancers" are caught: "Steps sole sound / long sole sound / on all that strand / at end of day." Comparatively, the chorus of the song "Lanigan's Ball" is as follows: "I stepped out, I stepped in again / I stepped in again and I stepped out / I stepped out, I stepped in again / learning to dance for Lanigan's Ball."

In the course of Beckett's dramatic work a phased reduction of the human body can be observed. In *Waiting for Godot* two complete men walk in circles. In *Eh Joe*, the protagonist is reduced to sitting on the edge of his bed while listening to a woman's voice. By the slightest movements of his back, we get to know his emotions. In *Happy Days*, Winnie's movements are restricted to her upper body, because the lower part is locked up in a sandhill. She is left with only the ability to gesticulate. The bodily function is even further reduced in *Play*, where only the heads remain: their bodies are stowed away in urns. They merely have the command over their mimics and the ability to (literally) change their point of view.

Not I leaves us with nothing but a mouth that keeps talking until breath, the vehicle of the voice, is all that remains. A breath moves through its extremely brief life story in *Breath*. After its birth from the dark acoustics of the head, it emerges and comes to life in the light for a brief contact with the outside world, then withers away in the twilight—until the last breath is exhaled and darkness falls.

A Short Statement with Long Shadows: *Watt*'s Arsene and His Kind(s)

JOHN PILLING

*W*ATT is such a "bone-shaker" of a book that its critics can perhaps be forgiven for fragmenting it still further, confining themselves to one or other of the "precipitates" left over from six large exercise books and willingly suspending any lingering conviction that "anatomy is a whole."[1] The voice that tells Watt that "the only cure is diet"[2] recommends a kindred therapy, though too late in the day—on page 225 of the 1963 English edition—for its addressee to have much opportunity to put this remedy into practice. This said, it is arguably too stringent a diet that has conditioned commentaries on Watt's encounter with his immediate predecessor at Mr. Knott's house, Arsene, who irrupts into the novel from out of nowhere, dominates it for twenty-five pages, and then vanishes—though a footnote (p. 79) and an item in the addenda (p. 248) prolong and expand his fictional life an iota or two.

In the available monographs and essays,[3] Arsene has enjoyed, admittedly, some kind of celebrity, although almost the only passages from this episode that are recurrently evoked are (1) his excursus on the laugh culminating in his identification of the *risus purus;* (2) his ladder joke, for Beckett of distinctively Welsh origin,[4] though the ladder has sent critics off in search of Vico, Kierkegaard, Wittgenstein, Mauthner, and others; (3) his anecdote of Mr. Ash on Westminster Bridge.[5] The situation is similar to that which obtains with respect to Beckett's first published essay, "Dante...Bruno. Vico..Joyce," from which his sudden outburst on the question of form and content is invariably cited. Yet, much as with the essay, there is a great deal more to Arsene than critics have, for the most part, been prepared to allow, and perhaps properly so, given that Arsene is Beckett's first first-person narrator and, as such, something of a progenitor of the mature, middle-period figures in the French *nouvelles* and *Trilogy*. It is not just the privileged trio of items referred to ad nauseam but the whole of Arsene's so-called "short statement" that casts long shadows, and backwards as well as forwards, as of course befits the topsy-turvy world of the book that contains it.[6]

Watt's meeting with Arsene raises especially acutely the question that this novel is always, either extrinsically or intrinsically, asking: What? In one sense, irrespective of any debt Beckett may owe to Aristotle,[7] this is a question that inescapably involves considerations of a distinctively generic kind, issues indeed that oblige us to flesh it out more fully—even if "the only cure is diet"—in the form "What *kind* of . . . ?" Arsene is not the only figure in *Watt* to have asked this question or something like it; had it been otherwise, we should not have learned that Watt is "an experienced traveller" and that it is "highly probable" he has been "a university man."[8] But no one else in *Watt*, not even Watt himself, seems nearly so concerned with *kinds* as Arsene manifestly is. It is Arsene, after all, who distinguishes between "voluntary" and "solicited" information, between "superficial loitering" and "disinterested endeavour," between "the intellectual type of chap" and "the luxurious kind of fellow," and (as if anticipating the Vladimir and Estragon of *Godot*) between "big, bony, shabby seedy haggard knock-kneed men" and "little fat shabby seedy juicy or oily bandy-legged men."[9] In the same spirit, it is Arsene who seeks to inculcate in the hapless Watt[10] the sense of each of them participating in a series, along with Vincent, Walter, Erskine, Micks, and Arthur. For Arsene, if not for Watt, it is important to establish the genus "Mr Knott's servant," so that the particular species can have a background against which to figure. Indeed, it is Arsene's concern for both the genus and the species that fuels his interest in genealogies (the who-begets-whom structure that irresistibly brings biblical chroniclers to mind), and his attempts at ordering them along a line from first to last, which inevitably provokes thoughts not only of generations but of *de*-generations, as if a distinct kind were in some danger of ultimately dying out. These latter are given an effective pivot around which to operate by way of Arsene's stress on being "in his midst at last,"[11] where "his" can refer equiponderantly to a given servant or to Mr. Knott himself. It is as if Watt, who until he meets Arsene has no way of knowing that he is not the first (nor of knowing that he is very nearly the last), is being offered the opportunity of occupying the "midst" or distributed middle ground between them, albeit courtesy of Arsene's unusually systematic orientation toward kinds of things.

Arsene's emphasis on genus, species, and kinds of things generally looks at first glance highly (perhaps even nostalgically) recidivist in the face of *Watt* as a whole, where Beckett seems determined not to circumscribe his options by deciding what kind of novel he is writing. Yet the way in which Arsene's manner and his matter point in opposite directions—the one so anarchic, the other so formalized—surely makes this episode the type and measure of the novel, if such a thing is possible in the circumstances. As such, one might have expected commentators on *Watt* to concentrate less slavishly on the obviously charismatic elements of the Arsene excursus, a "short statement," an "eleventh-hour vision" or a "declaration,"[12] depending upon how you look at it and depending upon how concerned you are to designate or define a thing according to the doctrine of kinds. Arsene himself is of course overwhelmingly (and perhaps pointlessly) concerned to do exactly this, so much so that he casually neglects to indicate that his long farewell, already generically atavistic as the kind of "interpolated tale" beloved of Cervantes and the eighteenth-century English novelists[13] goes back beyond them to the kinds of material that—with the rediscovery of classical models in the Renaissance—were once considered the codifiable property of anyone speaking or writing for effect, to persuade an audience of either the *dolce* or *utile* aspects of utterance. "I speak well, do I not, for a man in my situation?" asks Arsene,[14] a question Watt is in no position (and not given the chance) to respond to, but that we as readers must unequivocally answer in the affirmative.

Apart from absolutely offending against the cardinal rhetorical rule that manner and matter must be adapted one to another, Arsene is a most accomplished rhetorician, who must (it would seem) have spent so much of his time at Knott's reading handbooks of rhetoric that he has—very unlike himself—forgotten to specify by name the "figures of speech" and "figures of thought" with which he haphazardly studs his short statement. (In my own "addenda" [see below] I supply the technical terms, or a selection from the huge available stock of them, that would once have been known to any serious orator or writer, and learned by rote as part of the extremely formalized training of Elizabethan grammar schools.) Arsene in fact uses so many "figures of speech" and "figures of thought" over the relatively short space of twenty-five pages that one suspects his creator of a quasi-Joycean attempt of exhausting his capacities, the better never to have to repeat himself. The staple of the "Eumaeus" episode in *Ulysses* is the cliché, as is well-known; the staple of the Arsene episode in *Watt* is the figure of thought or speech more or less systematically tabulated in handbooks like Puttenham's *Arte of English Poesie* (1589; reprinted 1895).

It will be clear from my addenda that the majority of the long shadows cast by Arsene's short statement point backward in time to a period when kinds of things, and all the varieties of genus and species, could be confidently assigned their names and their places in a well-defined and well-ordered hierarchy. Arsene's manner—as distinct from his matter—projects those shadows forwards, however, into an ethos where, before long, there will be nothing but "nameless images" and "imageless names."[15] In Arsene the continuum exposes the impulse to classify to a "withering," even as it threatens to "bud" in a way unprecedented in Beckett's writing career.[16] There could in fact hardly be a better illustration of Beckett's possession of a mind, like that of the narrator of *From An Abandoned Work*, "always on the alert against itself."[17] Yet in this connection Beckett's experiment with Arsene seems to retain a positive value as well as a negative one. If *Watt* generally was to make a change to the French imperative, and if in French it was "easier to write without style"[18] (an ambiguous remark that I take to mean "without rhetoric" as systematically codified), there was to be no corresponding dismantling of the structural base that had underpinned Arsene's short statement. A decade on from *Watt*, with the *Trilogy* having so decisively intervened that *Watt* could be written off as "just an exercise,"[19] the narrator of *From An Abandoned Work* dreams of "a long unbroken time without before or after, light or dark, from or towards or at" but cannot rid his mind wholly of "*kinds* of things still [. . .] life and death all nothing, that *kind* of thing."[20] And even with "the old knowledge of when and where gone, and of what"—or with only its relics partitioning the mind of *How It Is*—the speaker in the latter is obliged to admit that he has "never quite fallen from [his] species" and still finds it profitable to apply, however vainly, "all [his] great categories of being."[21] The spirit of Arsene may glimmer only fitfully thereafter, although it is even possible to detect him, or his kinds, in the dense thickets of *Worstward Ho*, which is utterly dependent upon grammatical transformations at once generative and degenerative, as if "the old knowledge . . . of what" had not atomized after all,[22] or had somehow contrived to keep itself miraculously alive in the impossible interstices of the void.

Notes

1. Cf. *Dream of Fair to Middling Women*, p. 124 ("If ever I do drop a book . . . it will be ramshackle, tumbledown, a bone-shaker"); "Enough," in *Collected Shorter Prose 1945–1980* (London; John Calder, 1984), p. 140 ("One day he halted and fumbling for his words explained to me that anatomy is a whole"). For a pioneering analysis of the *Watt* manuscripts, see: J. M. Coetzee, "The manuscript revisions of Beckett's *Watt*," *Journal of Modern Literature* 2 (1972); and, for a more extensive treatment, see Ann Beer, "*Watt*, Knott and Beckett's Bilingualism," *Journal of Beckett Studies* 10 (1985).

2. The source of this dictum is unusually recondite even for Beckett. It translates *sola diaeta curari* from the *Tardes passiones* of the fifth-century physician Caelius Aurelianus, book 2, chapter 12. See Lewis and Short's Latin dictionary under the entry for *diaeta*. Beer, *"Watt,* Knott," p. 72, interprets the remark as a critique of Watt's regressive proclivities, but it is perhaps best seen in the context of Beckett's pervasive concern with food. Cf P. J. Murphy, "The Art of Hunger," in: *Reconstructing Beckett: Language for Being in Samuel Beckett's Fiction* (Toronto: University of Toronto Press, 1990).

3. High-quality individual essays on *Watt* are particularly numerous, no doubt partly as a consequence of the novel's disunified fabric. To those already mentioned in these notes could be added: Heath Lees, *"Watt*: Music, Tuning and Tonality," *Journal of Beckett Studies* 9 (1984); John J. Mood, "The Personal System; Samuel Beckett's *Watt,*" *PMLA* 86 (1971); Thomas J. Cousineau, *"Watt*: Language as Interdiction and Consolation," *Journal of Beckett Studies* 4 (1979).

4. Beer, *"Watt,* Knott," p. 41 n. 17.

5. For a quasi-Kantian reading of this incident, see my "From a (W)horoscope to *Murphy,*" in John Pilling and Mary Bryden, eds., *The Ideal Core of the Onion: Reading Beckett Archives* (Reading, U.K.: Beckett International Foundation, 1992), p. 16.

6. The Arsene material was originally independent of the story of Quin from which *Watt* was quarried. See Beer, *"Watt,* Knott," p. 56.

7. Beckett appears to have begun *Watt* by way of Aristotle's famous "Categories." Cf. Aristotle, *Categories and De Interpretatione,* trans. and ed. J. L. Ackrill (Oxford : Oxford University Press), 1963, and my discussion in *Samuel Beckett* (London: Routledge and Kegan Paul), 1976, p. 125.

8. *Watt* (London: John Calder, 1963), pp. 18, 21.

9. Ibid., pp. 44, 39, 48, 58.

10. More than usually hapless when it comes out (ibid., p. 77) that he has not been listening, the "rational" explanation of why the tenth item in the "Addenda"—"Note that Arsene's declaration gradually came back to Watt" (p. 248)—could never be incorporated into the book proper, the evidence of the manuscript notwithstanding.

11. Ibid., p. 39.

12. Ibid., pp. 37, 79, 248.

13. A prefiguration of sorts, therefore, for Arthur's tale of Mr. Louit, Mr. Nackybal, and "The Mathematical Intuitions of the Visicelts" in part 3 of *Watt*. But it is also a species apart insofar as it contains a brief interpolated tale of Mr. Ash within it.

14. *Watt*, p. 57. Cf. *Murphy* (London : John Calder, 1963), p. 15: "Scratch an old man, and find a Quintilian."

15. *Molloy, Malone Dies, The Unnamable* (London: John Calder, 1959), p. 411.

16. *Watt*, p. 57. On the continuum and other aspects of continuity, see my essay "Beckett: 'That's Not Moving, That's *Moving,*'" *Europe* 770–71 (1993): 21–28.

17. *Collected Shorter Prose*, p. 131.

18. Beckett, as reported by Niklaus Gessner in *Die Unzulänglichkeit der Sprache: Eine Untersuchung über Formzerfall und Beziehungslosigkeit bei Samuel Beckett* (Zurich: Juris, 1957).

19. Personal communication to Ruby Cohn.

20. *Collected Shorter Prose*, p. 136; my italics.

21. *How It Is* (London: John Calder, 1964), pp. 138, 15.

22. Arsene's back-formation "foremore" (*Watt*, p. 55) is perhaps the first instance in Beckett of what will dominate *Worstward Ho*.

Addenda

To illustrate the pervasiveness of figures of thought and figures of speech in Arsene's short statement, I have applied a selection of the categories itemized by Brian Vickers, *In Defence of Rhetoric* (Oxford: Clarendon Press, 1988), and Lee A. Sonnino, *A Handbook to Sixteenth-Century Rhetoric* (London: Routledge and Kegan Paul, 1968), with illustrations taken sequentially from the novel. When a choice in terminology between Latin and Greek offers itself I have generally favored the more familiar word.

p. 37 (*Watt* [London: John Calder, 1963])
The dawn! The sun! The light! Haw!
(*ecphonesis*, Vickers, *In Defence,* p. 493)

p. 38 there are no roads, no streets any more [. . .] the little sounds that demand nothing, ordain nothing, explain nothing, propound nothing . . .
(*asyndeton*, ibid., p. 493; also *epistrophe* and *ellipsis*)
the birds never the same darting into hiding. And all the sounds, meaning nothing.
(*homoioteleuton*, ibid., p. 495)

p. 39 And he knows this. No. Let us remain calm. He feels it.
(*epanorthosis* or *metanoia*; ibid., p. 494)

p. 40 I was sitting on the step, in the yard, looking at the light, on the wall. I was in the sun, and the wall was in the sun. I was the sun, need I add, and the wall, and the step, and the yard . . . (*epanodos*; ibid., p. 494).

p. 41 for my—how shall I say?—personal system . . .
(*adynaton*; ibid., p. 491)
But let us not linger on my breast. Look at it now—bugger these buttons!—as flat and—ow!—as hollow as a tambourine.
(*aposiopesis*, with *apostrophe*; ibid., p. 492; a possible parody of the end of *King Lear*; Arsene's prose is certainly "unbuttoned")
Hymeneal still it lay . . .
(*hysteron proton*, also *hypallage*; ibid., p. 495)
these moments together have changed us [. . .]—ticktick! ticktick!
(*onomatopoeia*; ibid., p. 496)

p. 42 What was changed, and how? What was changed [. . .]. What was changed [. . .].
(*anaphora*, also *anthypophora*; ibid., pp. 491–92)

p. 43 To hunger, thirst, lust . . .
(*brachylogia*; ibid., p. 493)
For do not imagine me to suggest that what has happened to me, what is happening to me, will ever happen to you . . .
(*paralipsis*; ibid., p. 496)

	But that and the rest, haw!, the rest, you will decide for yourself, when your time comes . . .
	(*epitropis/concessio*; Sonnino, *Handbook,* p. 50; with a possible *antanaclasis* on "rest"; Vickers, *In Defence,* p. 491)
p. 44	It was blowing heavily. It was also snowing heavily. I nodded, heavily.
	(*ploche*, with *homoioteleuton* and a possible *antanaclasis* on "heavily"; Vickers, *In Defence,* p. 497)
p. 45	and the long summer days and the new-mown hay [. . .] and the wasps in the jam and the smell of the gorse and the look of the gorse . . .
	(*isocolon*; ibid., p. 496)
p. 46	*We shall be here all night,*
	Be here all night shall we, etc.
	(*antimetabole*, with *hyperbaton*; ibid., pp. 492, 495)
	the passage from the one to the other is the passage from the lesser to the greater, from the lower to the higher, from the outer to the inner, from the gross to the fine, from the matter to the form.
	(*auxesis*; ibid., p. 493)
	They correspond to successive, how shall I say successive . . . excoriations of the understanding.
	(*aporia/dubitatio*; Sonnino, *Handbook,* p. 82)
p. 47	Personally of course I regret all. All, all, all.
	(*anadiplosis*, with *epizeuxis*; Vickers, *In Defence,* pp. 491, 494)
	And the laugh that once was bitter. Eyewater, Mr. Watt, eyewater.
	(*meiosis*; ibid., p. 496)
	without however pausing in my career
	(*syllepsis*; ibid., p. 498; Arsene is using "career" to apply both to his curriculum vitae and to the velocity of his delivery)
p. 49	Let [. . .] Let [. . .] Let (also p. 51).
	(*dialysis* or *divisio*; Sonnino, *Handbook,* p. 81)
p. 50	Erotic cravings? Recollections of childhood? Menopausal discomfort? etc.
	(*interrogatio*; ibid., p. 117)
p. 51	Let him, Jane
	(*solecismos*; ibid., p. 211)
p. 53	Now when speaking of Mary's mouth I make use of the expression full to overflowing, I do not merely mean to say that it was so full, nine-tenths of the time, that it threatened to overflow, but in my thought I go further and I assert, without fear of contradiction, that it was so full, nine-tenths of the time, that it did overflow. . . .
	(*periphrasis*; Vickers, *In Defence,* p. 497)
p. 54	And the former, on its way down to be filled, meets the latter on its way up to be emptied, at a point equidistant from their points of departure, or arrival.
	(*parison*, with *antithesis*; ibid., pp. 497, 492)

| p. 55 | But another evening shall come and the light die away out of the sky and the colour from the earth and the door open on the wind or the rain or the street . . .
(*polysyndeton*; ibid., p. 497)
and the reason for that is this
(*etiologia*; Sonnino, *Handbook,* p. 145) |
| p. 56 | . . . (for I am not illegitimate) . . .
(for they always spoke freely before me)
(*parenthesis*; ibid., p. 115) |
| p. 58 | But that he has never had any . . . seems certain
(*oxymoron*; Vickers, *In Defence,* p. 498) |

As Sterne would say: "Shall I go on?—No." But any interested party could extend this list indefinitely by way of *adinventio, adjudicatio, admonitio, acclamatio,* or *circumductio, commutatio, consolatio,* to use only Molloy's favorite letters *A* and *C*.

Beckett's Trilogy and the Limits of Autobiography

FRANK MATTON

ONE of the persistent themes in Beckett's work is the problem of identity. In its exploration of identity, Beckett's trilogy seems to conduct an ongoing dialogue with the practice of autobiographical writing, which has traditionally tried to contain and express identity.[1] But rather than elucidate the question of identity, it turns out that the trilogy's dialogue with autobiography has some far-reaching aesthetic implications.

By the time Beckett starts writing the trilogy, his work has undergone a movement of interiorization of which the use of first-person narrators is perhaps the most visible sign. The result of this movement is a decreasing distance between the Beckettian narrator and his narrative. The narrator is no longer telling just any story, but his own "story": "I have only to open my mouth for it to testify to the old story, my old story."[2] Being as isolated from the world as he is with only very few memories, it seems as if the Beckettian narrator has nothing but his own autobiography to work with: "I simply believe I can say nothing that is not true, I mean that has not happened" (p. 216). Similarly, the narrator of *The Unnamable* wants to "set about saying what [he] was, and where, during all this long lost time" (p. 304). Malone, too, has arrived at a moment when he believes he can "close off" his life: "All my life long I have dreamt of the moment when, edified at last, in so far as one can be before all is lost, I might draw the line and make the tot. This moment is now at hand" (p. 167). The representation of that "total" does not imply exhaustiveness, as Molloy knows: "you cannot mention everything in its proper place, you must choose between the things not worth mentioning and those even less so. For if you set out to mention everything you would never be done" (p. 39). Molloy follows the example of one of the first works of the genre, Saint Augustine's *Confessions;* it only provides us with a limited number of events, which are then supposed to be "representative." So, concerning all the little details of his life Moran says: "I shall not record them. Let us be content with paradigms" (p. 159). The combination of those paradigmatic events produces a metaphor for the life of the autobiographer. This is at least the view of James Olney and Jean Starobinski, two important theorists of autobiography.

For both Olney and Starobinski, the order that autobiography imposes on life should be seen as a metaphor. Metaphor enables the individual to fit his or her previously opaque and confused experiences into a meaningful metaphorical pattern.[3] Both theorists also believe that the self thoroughly controls the resulting metaphoric representation of its life.[4] Take the case of Moran. He sits down to communicate something about himself while writing a report for his alleged employer, Youdi. Moran writes: "He asked for a report he'll get his report" (pp. 110–11). "But I shall conduct it in my own way, up to a point" (p. 121). The self, then, can accommodate itself adequately—"up to a point"—in the language and mode that govern its representation. Many theorists of autobiography believe that the autobiographer can thus make a virtue out of a structural necessity.

Following the line of enquiry above, we could start to conceive of the trilogy as an autobiography by regarding its four narrators as autobiographers and autobiography as a simple "narrative device."[5] But there is a different way of conceiving of Beckett's trilogy as an autobiography. And this way not only impugns genre distinctions or contests the traditional artistic power structure (and thereby the commanding role of the self in the autobiographical triad of *autos*, *bios*, and *graphē*), but it also questions the very structure of representation on which both language and autobiography depend.

For one thing, a *considerable* number of elements from Beckett's biography can be found in the trilogy, from Beckett's kindergarten teachers, the Elsner sisters in *Molloy*, to Malone's exercise book, which curiously resembles the one Samuel Beckett himself was writing in at that time, as John Fletcher has pointed out.[6] This might lead us to look upon Beckett's trilogy as an autobiography in a "perverse" negation of the laws of genre. The trouble surfaces, however, when one starts realizing that those two ways of considering the trilogy bear a close relation to each other.

Many critics have already pointed to the autobiographical aspects of Beckett's writings, but they have always been very careful not to threaten the traditional genre distinctions. For example, they point out how everything that smells of autobiography in Beckett is "thoroughly fictionalized"[7] or they even invent an in-between category such as "autography" to fit Beckett's work, a category "that moves him out of fiction altogether."[8] The thing to avoid at all costs seems to be a conflation of the two that would make autobiography a form of fiction and fiction a form of autobiography. Yet, this is exactly what the trilogy seems to suggest.

For example, if we were asked "Who is the creator of *Murphy* and *Molloy*?" we could complacently answer "Samuel Beckett," a historical person (1906–89). Yet a fictional character also claims the authorship of *Murphy* and *Molloy:* viz., Malone. Legal author and fictional narrator have become interchangeable here, just as the legal author Samuel Beckett and the narrator's (i.e., Malone's) fictional creation Saposcat (whose physical description matches Samuel Beckett's) become interchangeable. Questioned by John Fletcher about this, Beckett only answered: "He got a bit out of hand."[9] Characters get out of hand when they suddenly become identified with authors, just as authors get out of hand when they turn into characters.

However, in order to observe this interplay between fiction and reality or between the demands of story and autobiography in Beckett's trilogy, it is not necessary to make Beckett's biography the focus of our attention, since the "lawful" reading of the trilogy is already concerned with the possibility and impossibility of its "perverse" reading. The narrators of the trilogy themselves give us different versions of a struggle with the same problem. For example, as a storyteller, Malone decides to insert explicit autobiographical sections so he can control them and prevent them from contaminating his stories. So when he gives us a description of Sapo, he also refers to himself, but only in order to emphasize the difference between himself and Sapo all the better:

> Nothing is less like me than this patient reasonable child. [. . .] My concern is not with me but with another, far beneath me and whom I try to envy, of whose crass adventures I can now tell at last, I don't know how. Of myself I could never tell, any more than live or tell of others. How could I have who never tried ? (Pp. 178–80)

The anticipation of certain autobiographical entries in his exercise book was even explicitly stated: "I have also decided to remind myself briefly of my present state before embarking on my stories. I think this is a mistake. It is a weakness. But I shall indulge in it" (p. 167). However, this weakness or indulgence is not something that could just as easily have been avoided:

> I must simply be on my guard, reflecting on what I have said before I go on and stopping, each time disaster threatens, to look at myself as I am. This is just what I wanted to avoid. But there seems to be no other solution. (P. 174)

Malone's commitment to look at himself in order to avoid doing so puts him in very tight corner. Paradoxically, in order to keep his fiction pure he has to rely on autobiography. The line that separates autobiography from fiction has two sides: by marking one side one also seems to mark the other. We pointed to Malone's ambition to tell himself stories (p. 165). Stories differ from autobiography in that they have no referential or objectivity requirement. But then again, Malone knows that his inventions need a little "life" to make a nice illusion, for the lives he will create must appear to be "true lives" (p. 181)—in order to succeed as illusion: "They will not be the same kind of stories as hitherto [. . .] they will be calm, there will be no ugliness or beauty or fever in them anymore, they will be almost lifeless like the teller" (p. 165). But here's the catch: by being almost lifeless the stories become like their author, who is almost lifeless.

Malone's stories thus become a displaced kind of autobiography, in spite of his explicit intentions. When Malone describes the green cabs in the town where he "finds" his character Sapo, he writes: "I must have seen them myself, and even driven in them, I would not put it past me" (p. 209). Later he wonders: "How many have I killed, hitting them on the head or setting fire to them ?" (p. 217). At the end of the novel we will see a fictional character, Lemuel, doing the same thing (cf. pp. 262–64). His stories are contaminated by elements from his autobiography to such an extent that, at the very start of his stories he already had to ask himself: "I wonder if I'm not talking yet again about myself. Shall I be incapable, to the end, of lying on any other subject?" (p. 174). Especially after Sapo becomes Macmann does the character's situation come to resemble the narrator's more and more: the room, the pot and dish routine, the possession of useless little objects, and so on. From the very beginning his intention to play and tell stories was threatened by autobiography. Since it was not impossible that he would find himself "without anything to play with," he resolved: "Then I shall play with myself" (p. 166). Thus the self became subject to the play that Malone reserved for his fictional stories.

By virtue of their common border, what goes for Malone the storyteller goes for Malone the autobiographer as well. Just as much as Malone's stories turn out to be displaced autobiographical sketches, so the account of his actual situation turns out to be imbued with fictional elements. For example, Malone describes how Macmann receives a visit from a bizarre character called Lemuel (cf. pp. 244–45). Only two pages later Malone himself suddenly receives a visit from an unnamed character who closely resembles Lemuel. The fictional situation seems to have shifted planes and transposed itself to Malone's own situation. But not all is lost, for in spite of this cross-pollination of fiction and autobiography, Malone the autobiographer still believes that he can use the conflation of the two realms to his own advantage by using the stories to enhance his autobiography.

For example, at the same time that Malone is denying the similarity between himself and the other, the lure of showing himself through the other lurks: "To show myself now, on the point of vanishing, at the same time as the stranger, and by the same grace, that would be no ordinary last straw" (p. 180). Similarly, the narrator of *The Unnamable* wants to show himself through others—whom he calls "vice-existers" (p. 289). Through Basil, Mahood, and Worm, the narrator of *The Unnamable* hopes to show himself by stripping them of their own characteristics: "mutilate, mutilate, and perhaps some day, fifteen generations hence, you'll succeed in beginning to look like yourself, among the passers-by" (p. 289).[10] Note that the idea of escaping into a fiction to illuminate the self still has the same didactic purpose as traditional autobiographies: "I slip into him, I suppose in the hope of learning something" (p. 208). The narrator of *The Unnamable* gives his autobiographical project a similar didactic function: "I suppose the wisest thing now is to live it over again, meditate upon it and be edified. It is thus that man distinguishes himself from the ape and rises, from discovery to discovery, ever higher, towards the light" (p. 233).

This kind of complicity between fiction and autobiography cannot remain uninvolved and perfunctory, for it not only collapses the distinction between narrator (Malone) and character (Sapo/Macmann), but it likewise challenges the distinction between the narrator (Malone) and the author (Samuel Beckett). If Sapo(scat)/Macmann is just a persona for Malone, then by the same token what is personal for Malone could turn out to be a persona for the author, Samuel Beckett. Thus the line between fiction and autobiography is crossed not only by Malone but also by Samuel Beckett.[11]

The implications of all this are not so much psychological (as Deirdre Bair's biography of Beckett seems to suggest) but aesthetic. Beckett appears to be very much concerned with the dislocation of the traditional artistic power structure at this time.[12] We can find a plethora of examples in the trilogy that would illustrate how both author and narrator renounce the power traditionally invested in their function. For example, when Sapo throws the master's cane out of the closed window, Sapo's creator, Malone, expresses surprise that Sapo wasn't thrown out of school and declares: "I must try and discover, when I have time to think about it quietly, why Sapo was not expelled when he so richly deserved to be" (pp. 174–75).[13] The lines drawn between author, narrator, and character give way and one role becomes entangled with the other, "the other who passes for me" (p. 284). The author not only writes but he is also written; he becomes both "the teller and the told" (p. 284): "What if we were one and the same after all [. . .]?" (p. 289).

This possibility to be both author and protagonist pivots on an intrinsic division of the self: "Everything divides into itself, I suppose" (p. 168). And this may account for the trilogy's flirtation with autobiography, for this self-division is structurally inherent in autobiography. The autobiographical self necessarily divides itself into author, narrator, and protagonist. In autobiography the autobiographical subject has to become the object of its own enquiry, whereby the self has to split itself into subject and object. This disintegrated nature of the self is most visibly borne out in autobiography by the central function of memory, which both contrasts and connects the past with the present self. It is because of this disjunction—an interval or caesura in identity, so to speak—that a genre like autobiography becomes possible at all.

Time and again we can observe how the trilogy's narrators try to bring this split in the autobiographical self to the readers' attention. Molloy, for example, makes a contrast between his present existence and the story of his past actions: "Thus from time to time I shall recall my present existence compared to which this is a nursery tale. But only from time to time, so that it may be said, if necessary, Is it possible that thing is still alive ? Or again, Oh, it's only a diary" (pp. 57–58). The narrator of *The Unnamable* assumes different masks in an attempt to speak about himself alone and to make subject and object coincide. One of those masks is the guise of a worm. But the narrator also recognizes that talking about himself, even if it is in the guise of someone or something else, inevitably means turning himself into an object for his subjective understanding. He recognizes that "that is the way to speak of him, *as if* he were alive, *as if* he could understand, *as if* he could desire, even if it serves no purpose" (p. 329; italics mine).

Paul de Man writes: "The autobiographical moment happens as an alignment between two subjects involved in the process of reading in which they determine each other by mutual reflexive substitution."[14] This "specular structure" implies differentiation as well as similarity.[15] So if autobiography draws a line across the self, it also crosses out this line. For autobiography can only exist by positing a relation of identity between author, narrator, and protagonist.[16] Whereas traditional autobiography will try to emphasize the fundamental unity of the self, Beckett's trilogy, in its exploration of the limits of fiction and autobiography, constantly hints at how this relation of identity between author, narrator, and protagonist could easily be undermined. Malone, for example, promises: "I shall not watch myself die, that would spoil everything" (p. 165). To watch himself die would mean that he is not the one dying, that the real narrator does not coincide with Malone; it would confirm his split identity, which he wanted to cover up by talking about Sapo/Macmann. These discrepancies between Malone and the narrator frequently surface, as when Malone loses his pencil: "I fear I must have fallen asleep again. In vain I grope, I cannot find my exercise book. But I still have the pencil in my hand" (p. 191). But where is Malone writing the above, if not in the exercise book? He realizes his mistake and adds: "I have just written, I fear I must have fallen, etc. I hope this is not too great a distortion of the truth" (p. 191).

We suggested that the disintegrated nature of the self is best borne out in autobiography by the central function of memory, which both contrasts and connects the past with the present self. But if autobiography depends on memory, then memory structurally depends on language, as Augustine already realized:

> Can it be that the memory is not present to itself in its own right but only by means of an image of itself? When we describe the past correctly, it is not past facts which are drawn out of our memories but only words based on our memory-pictures of those facts. [. . .][17]

Memory is constituted by images; it works on the principle of representation or language. Autobiography partakes of the fundamental structure of language as representation through its insertion of a distance in time and space between the representation and what is represented. Language signs (just like autobiography itself) can only present themselves in a temporal sequence. This is carried to an extreme in *Molloy,* where Molloy tells us about his own new language to get money from his mother. Molloy gives his mother four knocks on the skull and at the same time puts a banknote under her nose so that, in time, she will come to associate the four knocks with money. But by the time the signifier or the four knocks have realized themselves, Molloy's mother has forgotten the first blows already; we have an incomplete signifier that is not understood: "It was too far for her, yes, the distance was too great, from one to four. By the time she came to the fourth knock she imagined she was only at the second" (p. 19).

The central role of memory in autobiography (which reminds us that the "narrator" is separated from the "protagonist" in and through time) suggests that we could conceive of this split, this caesura in identity, as a function of time. In 1930 Beckett already wrote that, through time, the individual has to be conceived as "a succession of individuals."[18] Yet, to the extent that autobiography can only exist by positing a relation of identity between author, narrator, and protagonist, it will aspire to undo this distance in time. In the following example from *Molloy* this happens through an unwarranted confusion of grammatical tenses: "I *stopped* to think. It *is* difficult to think riding for me. [. . .] I speak in the present tense, it is so easy to speak in the present tense, when speaking of the past. It is the mythological present" (p. 26; italics mine).

It is because the individual is constituted in and through time that it always contains a moment of difference or absence from itself:[19] "No object prolonged in this temporal dimension tolerates possession, meaning by possession total possession, only to be achieved by the complete identification of subject and object."[20] Time perpetuates the split between subject and object because time introduces a fundamental difference or absence that undermines the relationship and communication between subject and object.[21]

This is worrying because autobiography, as Elizabeth Bruss has analyzed it, could be regarded as a speech act.[22] And, as such, autobiography presupposes an origin of that speech act, i.e., the speaker's presence to his own utterance and hence an intentional continuity between speaker and utterance. Yet exactly this relation is denied in the trilogy, which constantly reminds us of the discontinuity between a speaker and his words. "What I mean is *possibly* this" (p. 190; italics mine), Malone says, and "I shall say nothing that is not false, I mean nothing that is not calculated to leave me in doubt as to my real intentions" (p. 190). For Molloy "not to be able to say what you want to say, not to be able to say what you think you want to say, and never to stop saying, or hardly ever, that is the thing to keep in mind, even in the heat of composition" (p. 27). As the narrator of *The Unnamable* writes: "I speak [. . .] but I do not listen" (p. 281).

The same precarious language signs that can only present themselves in a temporal sequence are also relied upon to re-present the self in an autobiographical narrative. When autobiography comes to stand for a person, for someone who says "I," then "I" is no longer a referent but a sign. From the moment something is said about a referent, it is no longer a referent, but a sign, something that stands for something else. Strictly speaking, this also means that a person can only be the referent of autobiography when autobiography says nothing *about* that person.[23] For as soon as something is said about a person, that person becomes a sign, subject to temporality, self-division, and death. The narrator of *The Unnamable* appropriately refers to "the *fatal* leaning towards expressiveness" (p. 359; italics mine). "I hope this preamble will soon come to an end and the statement begin that will dispose of me" (p. 277). As Molloy's "communication" with his mother via the knocks on the skull already made clear, language, and by implication autobiography, only comes to exercise its real function in the absence (or the death) of the referent.[24] That is why Paul de

Man called the proper figure for autobiography *parousia*. For Moran, "a simple prophetic presence, on the model of those employed by Youdi" (p. 100) is the only possible presence of a person in autobiography, because it is not a presence but an absence. A "prophetic presence" in "the mythological present." The presence is "prophetic" partly because is not marked by the referent but only by *reference to* the referent, which has to remain unpredicated if it wants to remain a referent. Only by being another, i.e., not oneself (or dead), can one live in autobiography. As Malone writes: "And on the threshold of being no more I succeed in being another. Very pretty. [. . .] To show myself now, on the point of vanishing, at the same time as the stranger, and by the same grace, that would be no ordinary last straw" (pp. 178, 180). It is this extraordinary unveiling of oneself that the trilogy aims at. We recall that this conflation was strictly resisted at the beginning, whereas now it seems to be the only way out for the narrator.

Together with this strict division between fiction and autobiography, the notion of autobiography as a metaphor will also have to be abandoned. The distance and delay inherent in the structure of representation puts autobiography in an allegorical rather than a symbolical or metaphorical relation to the life it purports to represent, at least in Paul de Man's understanding of these terms. De Man believes that the symbol relies on "an intimate unity between the image that rises up before the senses and the supersensory totality that the image suggests."[25] We have seen how in Olney's and Starobinski's descriptions of autobiography as metaphor, metaphor is based on a close unity between the image and what it suggests.[26] According to de Man this intimate unity between sign and meaning is displaced in an allegorical relationship, for allegory "suggests a disjunction between the way in which the world appears in reality and the way it appears in language."[27]

The trilogy constantly evokes that disjunction, viz., the discontinuity between sign and meaning. Witness Molloy's description of his experience with the sounds of language and visual images:

> sounds unencumbered with precise meaning were registered perhaps better by me than by most. [. . .] Yes, the words I heard, and heard distinctly, having quite a sensitive ear, were heard a first time, then a second, and often a third, as pure sounds, free of all meaning, and this is probably one of the reasons why conversation was unspeakably painful to me. [. . .] And my eye too, the seeing one, must have been ill-connected with the spider, for I found it hard to name what was mirrored there, often quite distinctly. (P. 47)

To be sure, Molloy hints that "all things hang together, by the operation of the Holy Ghost, as the saying is" (p. 39). But the addition of the last phrase only emphasizes the rhetoricity of the unity and puts its factuality in doubt. When Moran thinks about Molloy he recognizes that there are different Molloys, which he opposes to "the real one as the saying is" (p. 106). Even the real one is recognized as a figure.

The trilogy seems to insinuate that the formalizing and controlling power of metaphor is not so much "of our own making" but that we are the product of a process of metaphorization.[28] In Molloy's version:

> Saying is inventing. Wrong, very rightly wrong. You invent nothing. [. . .] And every time I say, I said this, or I said that, [. . .] or find myself compelled to attribute to others intelligible words, or hear my own voice uttering to others more or less articulate sounds, I am merely complying with the convention that demands you either lie or hold your peace. (Pp. 31, 81)

This would suggest that language rather than the self controls the autobiographical project. We recall here that it was language that was ultimately responsible for the confusion of fiction and autobiography, as their confusion depended largely on the fact that both were constructed in exactly the same medium: "I write about myself with the same pencil and in the same exercise-book as about him" (p. 191). The narrator of *The Unnamable* is surprised by this same possibility: "Me, utter me, in the same foul breath as my creatures?" (p. 275). Language not only promotes the confusion of fiction and reality, but it is also responsible for the self-division of the autobiographical subject, as we have seen.

The trilogy repeatedly illustrates that language rather than the self controls the autobiographical project. When Molloy is describing Ruth or Edith, he writes: "She had a somewhat hairy face, or am I imagining it in the interests of the narrative?" (p. 53). The interests of the narrative appear to determine the narrator's past: "But perhaps I was stunned with a blow, on the head, in a forest perhaps, yes, now that I speak of a forest I vaguely remember a forest" (p. 169). The interests of the narrative are a far cry from the revealing metaphoric pattern that is shaped and controlled by the narrator. But however botched the tool might be, it is the only one available to the narrators of the trilogy, as the very last words of *The Unnamable* confirm:

> you must say words, as long as there are any, until they find me, until they say me, strange pain, strange sin, you must go on, perhaps it's done already, perhaps they have said me already, perhaps they have carried me to the threshold of my story, before the door that opens on my own story, that would surprise me, if it opens, it will be I, it will be the silence, where I am, I don't

know, I'll never know, in the silence you don't know, you must go on, I can't go on, I'll go on. (P. 382)

He uses language to find the self, to let them say "I," while at the same time language can only take him to the threshold of a selfhood that is wrapped in silence. While language necessarily distorts, divides, and hides the self, without this language the silence in which the true self manifests itself could not even be approached. The final decision of whether the narrator has been able to reach the threshold of selfhood in language is left up to the reader. The narrator himself keeps it at a "perhaps." And because of this perhaps, he can't be sure and he has to go on, even though it's impossible, even though it will only aggravate his plight and carry him further away from the silence he desires. Significantly, Beckett once called the key word of his work "perhaps."[29] In the words of the narrator of *The Unnamable*: "The essential is never to arrive anywhere, never to be anywhere. [. . .]" (p. 311).

At the beginning we saw how Malone arrived at a moment in his life when he believed he could "close off" his life (cf. p. 167). In light of the above, this seems very improbable. Because of the fundamental absence that time and language introduce, closure is not possible in autobiography. The inevitable "delay" in the structure of representation seems to annihilate the possibility of self-possession. In the trilogy, however, there is no shortage of attempts to turn back on oneself and possess oneself. Molloy starts his account by mentioning that he has taken his mother's room, and thereby he tries to link up the beginning of his own text with the place of the beginning of his own life: in the same place where she gave birth to him, he will give birth to himself in language in an attempt to become his own mother, as it were. Indeed, conceive himself, for he describes himself with "my prick in my rectum" (p. 20). At the end of his narrative Moran refers back to the opening sentences of his report: "Then I went back into the house and wrote, It is midnight. The rain is beating on the windows. It was not midnight. It was not raining" (p. 162). With this Moran puts the referential value of his account under erasure and invites us to read the affirmations of his report as negations and the negations as affirmations, including the last sentence, which will invite yet another reading, and so on, ad infinitum. Moran's self-reference does not result in any form of self-possession or self-containment but reveals the essential open-endedness of his narrative. Malone, too, tries to possess his own writing; he mentions how he found the exercise book he is writing in: "I drew a line no, I did not even draw a line, and I wrote, Soon I shall be quite dead at last, and so on" (p. 192). But he also realizes the difficulties of making his life coincide with his narrative: "My story ended I'll be living yet. Promising lag" (p. 260).[30]

Time introduces a moment of difference that prevents closure. It is difficult for Malone to accept this fact, however, and his autobiographical project therefore goes one step further than ordinary autobiographies in that Malone wants to keep on writing until the very moment he dies in order to include the dying itself. It becomes important to fail here, for successfully recording his own death would expose his autobiographical project as a fraud. But his attempt also draws the attention to the paradox of self-possession of any autobiography. For there always remains a time lag between living and writing, however small, so that "to live it over again, meditate upon it and be edified" can never be a pure living over because of the "distance" that has intervened.[31] If turning back on oneself constitutes the moment of autobiography, then this turning back cannot comprehend the very movement of turning back itself. Since autobiography is not constructed in one single moment, autobiography itself is caught up in the temporality it describes. And if one wants to include the moment of writing the autobiography in the autobiography, then there is still the moment left of writing about the writing of the autobiography, and so on. As Molloy writes: "It is in the tranquillity of decomposition that I remember the long confused emotion which was my life, and that I judge it. [. . .] To decompose is to live too, I know, don't torment me, but one sometimes forget" (p. 25). Later he remarks: "My life, my life, now I speak of it as something over, now as of a joke which still goes on, and it is neither, for at the same time it is over and it goes on [. . .]" (p. 35). Beckett's texts proceed with this kind of double movement that prevents closure and that prevents the text and representation as such from taking itself for granted.

Rather than elucidate the question of identity, it turns out that the trilogy's dialogue with autobiography has provided a tacit critique of the traditional conception of autobiography (and thereby of the crucial role of the self in the autobiographical triad). By engaging in a displaced autobiographical project, Beckett has been able to resist its temptations and expose the fundamental discontinuity between the narrator and "his" texts (and, indeed, "his" life) while rendering identity and the traditional artistic power structure even more problematical than before, questioning the very structure of representation on which both language and autobiography depend.

Notes

1. The tradition Beckett evokes includes confession, memoir, diary, and, to a certain extent, even apology and autobibliography.

2. Samuel Beckett, *The Beckett Trilogy: Molloy, Malone Dies, The Unnamable* (London: Picador, 1979), p. 216. All page references in the text refer to this edition.

3. Olney writes: "The self expresses itself by the metaphors it creates and projects, and we know it by those metaphors" (James Olney, *Metaphors of Self: The Meaning of Autobiography* [Princeton: Princeton University Press, 1972], p. 34). For Starobinski, metaphor is "that by which the lonely subjective consciousness gives order [. . .] to itself" (Jean Starobinski, "The Style of Autobiography" in James Olney, ed., *Autobiography: Essays Theoretical and Critical* [Princeton: Princeton University Press, 1980], p. 76).

4. Metaphor, according to Starobinski, is "something known and of our own making, or at least of our own choosing, that we put to stand for, and so to help us understand, something unknown and not of our making" (Jean Starobinski, "The Style of Autobiography," p. 76).

5. Porter Abbott, *The Fiction of Samuel Beckett: Form and Effect* (Berkeley: University of California Press, 1973), p. 96.

6. John Fletcher, "Malone 'Given Birth into Death,'" in J. D. O'Hara, ed., *Twentieth-Century Interpretations of Molloy, Malone Dies, The Unnamable: A Collection of Critical Essays* (Englewood Cliffs, N.J., Prentice-Hall, 1970), p. 61.

7. Andrew Kennedy, *Samuel Beckett* (Cambridge: Cambridge University Press, 1989), p. 121.

8. Porter Abbott, "Narratricide: Samuel Beckett as Autographer," *Romance Studies* 11 (Winter 1987): 43.

9. John Fletcher, *The Novels of Samuel Beckett* (London: Chatto & Windus, 1964), p. 175.

10. Although the technique may be the same, the intention is different. While Malone wants to avoid talking about himself, it seems as if he can never avoid doing so. And while the narrator of *The Unnamable* wants to talk about himself, it seems as if he can never succeed in doing so: "I've told another little story, about me. [. . .] But once again the fable must be of another" (p. 366).

11. According to Deirdre Bair's biography of Beckett, "*Malone meurt* is the most autobiographical of all Beckett's fiction" (*Samuel Beckett* [London: Jonathan Cape, 1978], p. 376). She points to "Beckett's relentless pursuit of himself through Malone" (p. 377).

12. Cf. the 1956 interview with Israel Shenker in the *New York Times* in which Beckett opposes an aesthetics of powerlessness and impotence to Joyce's aesthetics of power and omniscience. At that time Beckett had just finished translating *Malone meurt* into English and was about to embark on the English translation of *L'Innommable*.

13. We can also find counterexamples in which the narrator does avail himself of his authorial power. But this is always done with a "show" of force that exposes this power; for example, the change of names from Sapo to Macmann (p. 210), or Malone's sudden decision to kill Moll (p. 242). Similarly, the narrator of *The Unnamable* sometimes talks about his "puppets" (p. 267).

14. Paul de Man, *The Rhetoric of Romanticism* (New York: Columbia University Press, 1984), p. 70.

15. Ibid., p. 70.

16. This *common* identity seems to be guaranteed by the *proper* name of the title page, which reassembles author, narrator, and protagonist and renders them interchangeable as if they unproblematically formed one indissoluble subject.

17. Augustine, *Confessions* (London: Penguin, 1961), pp. 222, 267.
18. Samuel Beckett, *Proust and Three Dialogues with Georges Duthuit* (London: John Calder, 1987), p. 19.
19. Beckett's assertion that "the only true Paradise is the Paradise that has been lost" (*Proust*, p. 26) is an early denial of the possibility of an ultimate presence.
20. Ibid., p. 57.
21. Cf. ibid., p. 17.
22. Elizabeth Bruss, *Autobiographical Acts: The Changing Situation of a Literary Genre* (Baltimore: Johns Hopkins University Press, 1976).
23. Cf. Barbara Johnson, *The Critical Difference: Essays in the Contemporary Rhetoric of Reading* (Baltimore: Johns Hopkins University Press, 1980), p. 64.
24. Sticking a banknote under his mother's nose is only an element of the learning process. The "proper" use of the four knocks on the skull gains its intended effect in the absence of money. The same goes for autobiography.
25. Paul de Man, *Blindness and Insight: Essays in the Rhetoric of Contemporary Criticism* (London: Methuen, 1983), p. 189. The symbol should be conceived as "an expression of unity between the representative and the semantic function of language. [. . .]" (ibid., p. 189).
26. Olney talks about "the metaphoric bridge [. . .] from subjective self-consciousness to objective reality" (James Olney, *Metaphors of Self*, p. 36). "It is only metaphor that thus mediates between the internal and the external" (p. 53). In metaphor, then, there is no fundamental disjunction between the way in which the world appears in reality and the way it appears in language.
27. De Man, *Blindness and Insight*, p. 207. "Whereas the symbol postulates the possibility of an identity or identification, allegory designates primarily a distance in relation to its own origin, and, renouncing the nostalgia and the desire to coincide, it establishes its language in the void of this temporal difference. In so doing it prevents the self from an illusory identification with the non-self. [. . .]" (p. 207).
28. Both Olney and Starobinski believe that the metaphor is also is fully controlled, if not shaped, by the self. But even in *Proust* Beckett already wrote that "no amount of voluntary manipulation can reconstitute in its integrity an impression" (*Proust*, p. 72). "The most successful evocative experiment can only project the echo of a past sensation, because, being an act of intellection, it is conditioned by the prejudices of the intelligence which abstracts from any given sensation [. . .] whatever word or gesture, sound or perfume, cannot be fitted into the puzzle of a concept. But the essence of any new experience is contained precisely in this mysterious element. [. . .]" (pp. 71–72).
29. In the 1961 interview with Tom Driver in the *Columbia University Forum* (Lawrence Graver, *Samuel Beckett: The Critical Heritage* [London: Routledge and Kegan Paul, 1979], p. 218).
30. Augustine, for example, lived for thirty-two more years after his *Confessions* were finished.
31. This distance is an essential ingredient of autobiography, as Malone realizes: "Yes, the event is past, but it's too soon to use it, hence the delay, that's what I tell myself" (p. 216).

Mourning, Schopenhauer, and Beckett's Art of Shadows

ANGELA MOORJANI

> Je ne sais plus quand je suis mort.
> I don't know when I died.
> —*Le Calmant/The Calmative*

IN the French fiction of the forties, Beckett situates the writer writing within a ghostly site, the domain of the unborn and the dead, where "Death is dead because Time is dead" (Beckett, *Proust,* p. 56). The *Innommable/Unnamable* speaks of "the time of the ancient dead and the dead yet unborn" that "buries you grain by grain neither dead nor alive" (p. 389). Writing about the *Innommable*, Maurice Blanchot points to the work's "imaginary" space, inhabited by phantoms, in which the writer in order to write must fall into timelessness to die a death without end ("Où maintenant" pp. 685–86). In Blanchot's own experimental fictions one finds a similar spectral temporality and a "neuter" narrative voice "qui dit l'oeuvre à partir de ce lieu sans lieu où l'oeuvre se tait" [giving utterance to the work from the placeless place where the work falls silent] (*L'Entretien infini,* p. 565; my translation).

Sharing Beckett's and Blanchot's intimations of a timeless entombment, numerous writers and artists of the first half of the century have linked this inner crypt to the artistic imaginary. For Marcel Proust, there is "une région de toi-même où les barrières de la chair et du temps n'existent plus, où il n'y a pas de mort, parce qu'il n'y a pas de temps, ni de corps, et où on vit doucement dans la société immortelle de ce qu'on aime" [a region within yourself where the barriers of flesh and time no longer exist, where there is no death because there is no time, nor body, and where one lives serenely in the immortal company of what one loves] (p. 208; my translation). Similarly, Paul Klee's 1920 artistic credo and later epitaph place the artist among the dead and the unborn in a far-off proximity to genesis (p. 427). Rilke, on the other hand, associates the inner domain of the unborn with the Egyptian cult of the dead (pp. 896–99), or with the underworld of Osiris, Orpheus, and Persephone.

In this paper I examine the poemagogic notion that conceives of generativity as the activity of an anonymous (or neuter) other within an entombment in the psyche. First, I trace the parallels of such creative self-estrangement in mystic and philosophic thought, especially that of Schopenhauer, whose influence on Proust, Beckett, and psychoanalytic and aesthetic theory has been amply documented.[1] Secondly, I suggest that psychoanalytic theories of refused mourning help to explain the linkage between cryptic exile and generativity shared by mystics, philosophers, and artists. Finally, I use these poemagogic conceptions to work toward an understanding of the phantom time, space, and ungendered shadows in several of Beckett's late works.

Mystic and Philosophical Precedents

Beckett's and other artists' reiterated experience of an inner tomb as a creative womb has its parallels in mystic evocations of divine creativity. Gnostic and kabbalist creation stories speak of a space of inner exile in which a divided divinity's female element—the gnostic Sophia, the kabbalist Shechinah—creates the world out of nothing. The act of creation fractures a previous harmony and introduces darkness, death, and sinfulness into the world. This story, with its simultaneous emphasis on maternal creativity and destructiveness, was influenced no doubt by Mother Goddess lore, with its underworld cycles of death and regeneration bound up with the Great Mother/muse and her dead and reborn child. The trajectory of the gnostic-kabbalist conception of a divided creator creating from an inner entombment can be traced from the teachings of the Protestant mystic Jakob Böhme (1575–1624) to the nineteenth-century idealist philosophies of Schelling and Schopenhauer (Henry, *Proust romancier,* pp. 38–42). It would appear most likely that it is from them, and from Schopenhauer in particular, that artists and writers of the twentieth century took their conception of a spectral artistic subject.[2]

In *The World as Will and Representation*, Schopenhauer separates the ego [Ich] into an inner and outer subject. The inner ego, the will, linked to generativity (Eros) or the life impulse, exists outside of time and space, endlessly, eternally unborn and undying. For in contrast to the notions of birth, death, and afterlife, the will's timelessness is akin to the eternal now of transmigrating dead and unborn souls. The outer ego or the intellect, on the other hand, pits its awareness of birth and death and time's passing against the will's intimations of timelessness and immortality. Clashing with the will, the intellect bound to space-time can know the timeless will within itself only piecemeal and as something other and foreign to itself. The will "falls" into consciousness as a figment or an apparition; in itself the will eludes representation (Schopenhauer, *Die Welt,* 2:590–651; chap. 41). Specifically, in wanting to grasp our inner self, we can get hold of nothing but a fleeting ghost "indem wir so uns selbst ergreifen wollen, erhaschen wir mit Schaudern nichts als ein bestandloses Gespenst" (1:384 n. 1; § 54).

For Schopenhauer, it is the will to live that gives impetus to the will's ghostly materializations whether in art or otherwise, whereas the negation of the will leads to the nirvana of oblivion (2:779–81; chap. 48). Since the world is knowable only as a representation, art's partial objectifications are representations of representations or repetitions of what is already a repetition in the manner of a play within a play. Owing to this contemplative distantiation or *mise en abyme,* art stills temporarily the suffering and terror of existence (1:371–72; § 52). Ultimately, though, finding no justification for the world's pain, let alone the tragedy of birth, Schopenhauer agrees with asceticism's negation of the will to live and its dissolution of the world into nothingness (1:514–40; § 68; 1:554–58; § 71).

A post-Freudian reader of Schopenhauer cannot help but notice the affinity between Freud's Eros and Thanatos and Schopenhauer's affirmation and negation of the will. Freud did, of course, tie Thanatos to the Nirvana principle via Schopenhauer (Laplanche). "We have unwittingly steered our course into the harbour of Schopenhauer's philosophy. For him death is the 'true result and to that extent the purpose of life,' while the sexual instinct is the embodiment of the will to live," Freud was to write in *Beyond the Pleasure Principle* (pp. 49–50). It is of little surprise that Beckett would quote both the philosopher's and the psychoanalyst's versions of Nirvana-Thanatos. Schopenhauer's divided subject and the inner subject's unbornness and deadness suggest further parallels with the timelessness of the Freudian unconscious and the splitting of the ego in refused mourning.

Psychoanalytic Theories of Abandoned Mourning

An imaginary exile in the ego, outside of time, has intrigued not only mystics, poets, and philosophers but also a number of psychoanalytic theorists of mourning. For Freud, the usual path of mourning involves progressive detachment from the lost one. Rejecting detachment, however, the mourner, who refuses to mourn, incorporates a lost object into an enclave in the ego where it is kept simultaneously dead and alive. This cryptic host, then, which has been encapsulated within the ego, is identified with the ego's otherness or strangeness, which becomes the target of the affection and aggressiveness felt for the unmourned object. Unmourned loss produces a festering wound within the ego ("Mourning," pp. 243–58).

Extending the views of Freud on mourning, Melanie Klein emphasizes that grief is first and foremost related to the fantasized loss of the mother as the first other. Whereas in describing the splitting of the ego in refused mourning, Freud spoke of real losses, Klein's early childhood mourning often results from imaginary losses that build on the anxiety of separating from the mother. If the child's losses, whether real or fantasized, are not adequately mourned, the maternal object, in the manner of Freudian unfinished mourning or melancholy, will be incorporated as a split-off self within the self. And this incorporated phantasm may take the shape of a phallic mother or a combined mother-father. Each later experience of mourning will reactivate the earlier griefs and lead to projections outward of the maternal phantasm or of the foreign fragments within the self. Klein, in particular, linked mourning to the reparative work of art (pp. 210–18, 262–89, 344-69).

Following similarly on the Freudian concept of a division within the ego during failed mourning, Nicolas Abraham and Maria Torok describe a permanent incorporation of a lost one into a cryptic space, an unconscious entombment, a place of exile within the interiority of the ego. Held permanently within this inner crypt, the incorporated lost one is neither dead nor alive, but the living dead. Abraham and Torok insist on the difficulty of deciphering the cryptonymic signs concealing the lost ones from whose traces there is no release.

Abraham and Torok's "cryptonymy" would seem to owe its popularity partly to Derrida's introductory essay to *The Wolf Man's Magic Word*, which interrogates the metaphysical life-death opposition, and partly to its explanatory power for the artistic imaginary. Their theories are beginning to rival the currency of Schopenhauer's a hundred years ago. Could the preoccupations then and now with the death of time and the death of death have anything to do with an end-of-the-century and an end-of-the-millennium concern with time's passing?[3]

Spectral Scenarios

In returning to the artists and writers who, under the influence of Schopenhauer, bonded their art to the realm of the dead and unborn, the parallels between Schopenhauer's divided, unknowable, and ghostly subject and the exiled and encrypted shadows of refused mourning become apparent. In Kleinian terms, the earliest experiences of loss, if unmourned, result in a split within the self, constituting a wounded otherness concealed in the artistic imaginary. Writing, then (and painting, too, if we follow Klee, is a form of writing), retraces the shadowy exteriority within a self constituted by endless mourning.

But how is one to represent encrypted shadows or the spirits of the dead and the unborn? What is their gender? Or is there gender without a body? If the inner subject, akin to the spirits of the dead and the unborn, is ultimately unrepresentable, then cryptic phantasmagoria and the figurations of dreams and fictions are examples of what the series of Beckett narrators have condemned as "vice-existers" or "avatars" or "caricatures" or "surrogates" (*Unnamable,* pp. 315, 392). Accordingly, Beckett and Blanchot not only conceive of an anonymous or "neuter" subject speaking from an inner exile, but by means of aporias and self-contradictions dramatize the impossibility of representing the phantom state in fiction or theater. In Blanchot's *Thomas l'obscur*, Thomas at one point is described as follows: "Il était réellement mort et en même temps repoussé de la réalité de la mort. Il était, dans la mort même, privé de la mort, homme affreusement anéanti, arrêté dans le néant par sa propre image" [He was really dead and at the same time banished from death's reality. He was, in death itself, deprived of death, a man horribly annihilated, detained in nothingness by his own image] (p. 40; my translation). The *Innommable/Unnamable*'s anonymous and disembodied subject similarly vociferates that in being made to speak it is humanized by the very language that fails to represent its unborn deadness. Thus Blanchot's and Beckett's cryptic subjects neither dead nor alive are exiled from death as they are from life. As Molloy suggests, it is by filling in the holes that words have pierced into blankness, that the spectral subject might best undo the humanness inflicted upon it by language (Beckett, *Molloy*, p. 13). This unwording in the *Innommable/Unnamable* is partly carried out by the unsaying of the pronouns needed to assign reference to the participants in discourse, leaving only a ghostly figment or a "not I."

Throughout the trilogy of the forties, Beckett probes the predicament of representing the unrepresentable by having his autodiegetic (teller-told) narrators speak from within the buried timelessness within the psyche. Thus Molloy, writing in his mother's room or tomb, uses the "mythological present," the spectral now of the unborn dead (*Molloy*, p. 26). The narrated subject, to the contrary, would appear to journey in space and time. Yet, the nonlinear and labyrinthine structure and eventual annulment of this diegetic temporality contradict expectations of a chronological story-time. As it were, it is all only a game the timeless teller plays with a pseudoself in pseudotime. On the other hand, hermeneutical temporality, or reading as process, clashes with the narrating-narrated atemporality. And as this temporal process of reading or reader's time, unlike story time, cannot be annulled, its duration points to the inevitable passage of time. Similarly, in the process of reading in sequence more than one version of the same text, such as the two parts of *Molloy*, the reader experiences repetition as the text differing from itself in time. This discourse time, which, along with reader's time, encodes the inevitable progression of time towards death, conflicts with the narrative's spectral timelessness. In being invited to anchor simultaneously in these clashing temporalities, readers experience the disorienting contradiction between the inner subject's timelessness and the conscious awareness of mortality. The difficulty of the Beckettian texts has more than a little to do with such postmodernist imbrication of conflicting temporalities resulting in a text fluctuating between otherworld reference (spectral temporality), world-reference (hermeneutical time), and fictional self-reference (the annulled story time).[4]

Gender and genderlessness similarly clash in the trilogy and later texts. A firm gender identity is no more certifiable than a fixed temporality. Since the narrating subject is outside of space-time, this specter is without body and gender. On the other hand, the two narrated personages of *Molloy* are gendered as male. Or are they? Within the diegesis femaleness lurks within maleness and maleness within femaleness, blurring gender distinctions. Finally, in its parodic disdain and ultimate obliteration of matric and phallic creativity myths, *Molloy* moves toward the ungendering of artistic activity. With the pre-Socratics, the gnostics, and the German romantics, to all of whom he makes frequent intertextual allusions, Beckett from *Molloy* onward attempts to conceptualize creative process in dehumanized, nongendered, anonymous terms.[5]

At the end of the twentieth century, the Beckettian attempts at ungendering, at de-metaphorization, at staging the unrepresentable as unrepresentable, at writing the unnamable as unnamable, appear postmodern even as they hearken back to a heretical tradition. For the postmodern reader or viewer, the shift outside of gender brings to mind the radical feminist call for an end to the gender divide, the enclosing categories lined up for maleness and femaleness within a male dominant culture. For whatever Beckett's aim may have been, by preventing readers or viewers from anchoring their identities to stable gender representations, he brings into question the either/or of gender dichotomy.[6]

Loss and the Art of Shadows

The short pieces Beckett composed in the last fifteen years of his life are increasingly works of mourning featuring shades dressed in black or gray, voices heard faintly, images barely glimpsed. As hypothesized by the theories of unfinished mourning, Beckett's late works suggest that it is the wound of loss that is the wellspring of art. And given that the spectral otherness can be glimpsed only through language and figuration, be they under erasure, Beckett alternately imagines seemingly male or seemingly female "moribunds" (*Unnamable,* p. 308) whose gendered humanness, however, is tentative or eventually merged with a genderless ghostliness. As Schopenhauer had warned, the intellect can apprehend the inner subject only as a ghostly apparition.

Like the French trilogy of the forties, *Ohio Impromptu* (1981) situates the grieving artist at work, self divided from self, within an inner entombment, reading from the book of memory or a script inscribed within. The inner crypt, inhabited by the spirits of the dead, among whom artists labor, is projected before the eyes onto the stage. With their streaming white hair, partially hidden faces, and enveloping black coats, the play's twin apparitions appear to come from another world. They bring to mind the *pleurants* of funeral monuments, grieving figures of uncertain age and gender, or shades returned from the dead.

In an example of the paradoxical *mise en abyme* Beckett favors, and of the play-within-a-play structure Schopenhauer praised for its aesthetic distanciation, *Ohio Impromptu*'s onstage Reader would seem to be reading about an offstage reader reading the tale the Reader is reading. The telling and the told both concern the solace brought by repeated storytelling, the comfort received by hearing always the same story or stories within stories in the face of death. In the tale told, the quest for relief from the loss of a loved one begins with a flight to an unfamiliar place, a room on the far bank, and steps retraced on the Isle of Swans.[7] The failure of the flight from grief and the return of the terror of night move the absent shade to send a reader to read night after night the same tale to comfort the bereaved. At story's end, reader and listener, or the artist listening to himself, descend into the region within, where, as Proust wrote in the letter of consolation to his friend quoted earlier, "one lives serenely in the company of what one loves" (p. 208). Mourned and mourner are reunited in the realm of the dead and the unborn from which issues the art of solace.

In the play's story, the return of the "old terror of night," which "[a]fter so long a lapse that as if never been," recalls the scenes in Beckett's earlier short fiction in which a child is calmed by storytelling (p. 286). "Le Calmant/ The Calmative" and the first of the *Textes pour rien/Texts for Nothing* tell of the narrator's father reading always the same tale to soothe the child he was then in face of the terrors of night. In the first work, the narrator insists that the story had to be read, not told: "He might have simply told me the story, he knew it by heart, so did I, but that wouldn't have calmed me, he had to read it to me, evening after evening, or pretend to read it to me, turning the pages . . ." ("The Calmative," p. 28). For the narrator of *Texts for Nothing I*, the purpose of telling himself stories is "to lull me and keep me company" (p. 74). By dividing himself into teller and hearer he experiences again the solace felt while listening as a child to his father's story:

> Yes, I was my father and I was my son, . . . I had it told to me evening after evening, the same old story. . . . And this evening again . . . I'm in my arms, I'm holding myself in my arms. . . . Sleep now, as under that ancient lamp, all twined together, tired out with so much talking, so much listening, so much toil and play. (P. 75)

In the same vein, Beckett told the actor David Warrilow to treat the Reader's tale in *Ohio Impromptu* as a soothing bedtime story (Brater, *Beyond Minimalism,* p. 125). As is well known, and we don't need Proust's bedtime saga to remind us, children cannot do without night lights, stories, or lullabies, if they are haunted by the terror of night associated with separation and death. And more often than not the stories themselves tell of terrors overcome, as in the father's story of Joe Breem or Breen or the onstage Reader's tale. The telling of stories for comfort, for company, in the face of loss, responds repeatedly to traumas of real and imaginary grief and is very much what writing is about for Proust and Beckett, Freud and Klein.

The familiar teller-told dualities, too, recur in *Ohio Impromptu*, as the ghostly state of Reader and Listener is contradicted by their offstage doubles' movement in time, space, and gendered identity. Both the tale's calming reader and grieving listener are given male gender, whereas anonymity enshrouds the person whose loss is being mourned. At the end of the play, however, motion and identity are suspended, as the embedded reader and listener turn into stone and in a progressive descent are buried in thought—then buried still deeper, all sight, hearing, and thought stilled, "[b]uried in who knows what profounds of mind" and finally, entombed in "profounds . . . [o]f mindlessness" (p. 288). Merging with their spectral doubles, they enter the psychic crypt from which the artistic subject, divided from itself, tells its comforting tales of loss and mourning.

The mortuary monument motif, within and without the tale, gives visual force to the fusion of story time with cryptic time and of figure with stone.[8] This calm intermingling of the animate with the inanimate, beyond sound, sight, and thought, is surely a knowing wink in the direction of the pleasure principle hypothesized by Freud in *Beyond the Pleasure Principle*. Aware of its affinity with Schopenhauer's philosophy, Freud identifies the pleasure principle with the wish to mute inner and outer sensations and return to an inanimate state before life (pp. 36–38). A child's desire to hear always the same story, too, along with other instances of repeating, falls in with the pleasure principle's aim (pp. 35–36). No wonder Beckett in *Molloy* referred to it as "the fatal pleasure principle" (p. 99), because of its bondage to death.

Along with *The World as Will and Representation*, *Beyond the Pleasure Principle* is surely one of the most important intertexts of Beckett's works. Beyond the direct and indirect allusions to the pleasure principle they contain, many of Beckett's works can be read as repeating *fort/da* games.[9] Further, the following quote from Gottfried Büttner's book on *Watt* leaves no doubt about Beckett's sympathy for Freud's book:

> Beckett's relationship to stones, which he called "almost a love relationship," was associated by Beckett himself with death (conversation of September 9, 1967). As a child he frequently picked up stones from the beach and carried them home, where he built nests for them and put them in trees to protect them from the waves and other dangers. On the same occasion, Beckett mentioned Sigmund Freud, who had once written that man [sic] carried with him a kind of congenital yearning for the mineral kingdom. (P. 163 n. 200)

Just prior to and overlapping with the writing of *Beyond the Pleasure Principle*, Freud made an incursion into aesthetics with his 1919 essay "Das Unheimliche" (The uncanny). One of Freud's most quoted essays, owing to its own uncanniness and tie-in with cryptonymic concealment, "Das Unheimliche," too, haunts Beckett's play. Doubles stalked by doubles, the terror of night, the return of ghosts, and uncertainty about aliveness and deadness are among the uncanny effects Freud investigates. For Freud, the "Unheimliche," literally "away from home," is something familiar that through repression has become unfamiliar and frightening. Instead of recurring, such disquieting strangeness should have remained concealed and forgotten. The manifestations of the uncanny, such as the compulsion to repeat and the double as a messenger of both immortality and death, are traced back to a number of anxieties, of which the earliest is the terror of night.

It would seem that the foregrounding of the search for unfamiliarity in *Ohio Impromptu*—"Relief he had hoped would flow from unfamiliarity. Unfamiliar room. Unfamiliar scene" (p. 285)—which at the tale's end is doubled by the inner strangeness of "profounds . . . of mindlessness," echoes Freud's essay on the uncanny's secret "familiarity/unfamiliarity," the very words used throughout Strachey's English translation. Finally, the uncanny is an effect of endless mourning, which in *Ohio Impromptu* gives voice to the repeated telling of stories in the face of the terror of night.

The clash of the atemporality of ghosts (and stone?) and the temporality of mortals in *Ohio Impromptu* is an example of the uncanny oscillation between imaginary time and represented story time. To these must be added the spectator's time linked to the performance, as it moves from opening to closing, and to the performance within the performance proceeding from "little is left to tell" at play's beginning to "nothing is left to tell" at play's end. The contradiction between timelessness and time is thereby exacerbated as spectators simultaneously experience time's passing, with its implications of mortality, and see disorienting intimations of timelessness. Concurrently, listening to the story about art's consolation and soothed by the rhythmic tempo of the reading, spectators experience the calming pleasure of art.[10]

The "nothing is left to tell," however, recalls Schopenhauer's distinction between the temporary solace of art and the ultimately desired nirvana of extinction. The telling of the tale has brought momentary comfort, but the fugitive consolation of art leaves nothingness still unattained. Written for a symposium of scholars of his work, *Ohio Impromptu* has moments of comic relief, for which Beckett is renowned, along with the solace of the tale of mourning. For the relief of his audience, he embedded inexhaustible intertextual winks, many of them humorous, and one of his most poetic statements of his art's genesis, purpose, and ultimate failure.[11]

The play's motif of the twin as the other of the artist is replaced in many of the late works of mourning by the phantom of the (m)other. This I take to be the maternal phantasm, the image harbored, loved, and hated from childhood onward that Klein suggests. According to the psychoanalytic theories of impossible mourning I have summarized, this phantasm—not the real mother—is incorporated into the cryptic unconscious, endlessly mourned, identified with, hated and loved; it is a living dead, from whom there is no escape. At the same time she is the figure of the self's cryptic otherness.

Emphasizing the maternal phantasm because it is likely to be the child's first, Klein nevertheless counts paternal and mother-father incorporations as important effects of unfinished mourning (pp. 344–69). Her insight is borne out by Beckett's and other artists' masking of their shadow otherness by a double or a twin, by maternal/paternal figments, or, even more likely, a mother-father phantom. With these specters artists share the exile in the inner tomb that doubles as creative womb.

From the forties to the seventies, a blocked birth from the imaginary womb was one of Beckett's preferred images of artistic failure or of the unrepresentable. The artist, pregnant with his twin or, having incorporated the mother-father, pregnant with himself, are variations on the theme.[12] In the later works of mourning, though, ghostly figments, more often than not, shift the focus from womb to tomb and from the unborn who cannot be born to phantoms not fully faded into the night.

The concern in much of my work has been to trace the categories related to the powerful maternal phantasm and its undoing in Beckett's work. Somewhat in the manner of H. D., who in her 1944 *Tribute to the Angels* teasingly calls up Great Mother iconography only to deny its resemblance to her unnamable vision, Beckett in *Molloy* and more than thirty years later in *Mal vu mal dit/Ill Seen Ill Said* multiplies mythic and religious allusions to a phantom muse. Among the most apparent are hints of the Great Mothers Ishtar, Cybele, Astarte-Aphrodite, Demeter, and the Christian Mother of God, each associated with a dead and reborn child. Of special significance, too, are the lunar goddess Hecate and the gnostic Sophia, the Creator in female form. These Great Mothers embodying the creative cycles of birth, death, and rebirth are figurations of the encrypted phantom both dead and not dead, loathed and loved, whose creative power the writer envies and emulates, and from whom he would wrench writing free. The ubiquitous temptation of "gynesis," the female gendering of creativity's unknowable otherness, which we find in myth, religion, philosophy, and art, is much in evidence in Beckett's, as well as Blanchot's, works, in both of which it is ultimately replaced by indifferentiated shadows.[13]

In what follows, I will only briefly highlight the process of the dimming of female figures into ghostliness in three late works of mourning. In *Molloy* the writer angrily sought to erase all trace of the powerful rival/muse haunting him; in *Ill Seen Ill Said* the wish to obliterate the figure is more wistfully expressed: "If only she could be pure figment. Unalloyed. This old so dying woman. So dead. In the madhouse of the skull and nowhere else" (p. 20). The weariness incurred in "[s]laving away forever in the same place" (p. 58) comes to expression in the 1981 prose piece, along with the ultimate powerlessness of seeing and saying or unseeing and unsaying once and for all the cryptic (m)other/other self.

A tomb, a dolmen, stones obliterating pastures, a bereaved figure in black and white petrified into stone, and the pall of winter and night relate the prose piece to *Ohio Impromptu*'s statues and to the pleasure principle's imaginary entombment. The Great Mother/muse turned to stone goes counter to two millennia of Pygmalions appropriating matric generativity by fantasies of male parturition or animating Venus statues. In this late fiction, the will to animate stones gives way to the "pleasure" of merging with their lifelessness.

Finally, in *Ill Seen Ill Said*, the maternal shade haunting the artist in the timeless domain of the dead and unborn is once again unsaid, or as the narrator puts it: "The already ill seen bedimmed and ill seen again annulled" (p. 48). The obliteration is staged more ferociously in the piece's final words, which in reversing early oral fantasies of devourment would have the skull's "carrion," the living dead phantom of (m)other and self, reduced to crumbs, devoured, consumed (p. 59).[14]

Each time the unsaying or fade-out of the shadowy muse is a repetition only, as on the stage, where the lights come on again, and the same words—or variants—repeat another round of dim grapplings with indelible traces within. In *Footfalls* we find a ghostly apparition listening to and telling stories while endlessly going over the same space in the timeless sepulcher within. This 1976 play, perhaps more than any other, brings to mind that for Beckett writing had to do with listening for a lost self that "never got born" or with "groping in the dark for a shadow" (Harvey, *Samuel Beckett,* p. 247). As May paces rhythmically to and fro, she pauses to listen to the voice of the maternal phantom (V), a ghost within a ghost, tell the simulacrum of the story she is acting out by her shadowy actions.[15] Mother and daughter, like the ghostly apparitions of *Ohio Impromptu*, are dreamlike variants of each other (and of the artist), and the action told (doubly) is the action performed, with the listener-teller retelling the story telling her. As we have seen, this collapse of inside and outside is a paradox much favored by Beckett and other artists staging the cryptic self outside the self. Such aporetic duplications result in a drastic disorientation of readers and spectators who cannot situate themselves in relation to these ungraspable shadows in illusive spaces.[16]

The three abysmal stories of *Footfalls*—May and V, V's story of May, May's of Amy—are variations on the same unbornness and undeadness. They are examples of the "vicissitude of hardly there and wholly gone" (*Ill Seen,* pp. 37–38). The spectral muse/other self, divided into a listener and teller of tales, is evoked in *Footfalls*, and again in the later *Rockaby*, but drastically dehumanized by ghostly rhythms and the gradual shading into impenetrable darkness and stillness.

How the progressive dimness of the late nocturnal plays leads to a simultaneous ungendering is described by Peter Gidal in *Understanding Beckett:* "The woman becomes more and more of a skeleton, less sexed, as the light dims. A bisexual/unsexual image is produced by the annihilation of light," he writes about *Rockaby* (p. 140). There is a clash, he finds, between the perception of the figure as a woman, who dressed in her finery would appear to be an icon of femininity, and the progressive ungendering, occasioning the unraveling of the audience's hold on gender and human identity. One might also add that the very excess of the feminine costume in *Rockaby* points to a possible transvestism, the exaggerated (and outmoded) finery suggesting a bisexual fantasy of a male figure dressed as a woman. Here, one gender masquerades as another, with both screening the ultimate genderlessness.

Within the cryptic domain of enlessly mourned shadows, outside of time, outside of language, outside of gender, male and female representations are only the play with simulacra that come and go and fade away. As "[t]he 'rockaby' of the title becomes a child's song of sleep and an old woman's song of death" (Ben-Zvi, *Women in Beckett,* 179), the play's maternal specter, mother and daughter fused into a ghostly rocker, fades into the anonymous shadows of the artist in the realm of the unborn and the dead.[17] From this "placeless place" in between life and death sound art's consoling elegies in the face of the ultimate lessness.

Notes

1. On the importance of Schopenhauer for Proust's *A la recherche du temps perdu,* see Beckett, *Proust*; Descombes, *Proust,* p. 35 and Henry, *Proust romancier,* p. 41. Henry maintains that the intellectual movements of the second half of the twentieth century, whether structural, Marxist, or psychoanalytic, are basically the products of German romantic philosophy (p. 31). She emphasizes particularly the influence of Schelling's early aesthetic theories on Schopenhauer, whose spectacular popularity during the second half of the nineteenth century led to the adoption of a "mysticisme laïque" [secular mysticism] (p. 40) by many writers of the nineteenth and twentieth centuries.

Several critics have pointed out the more-or-less explicit references to Schopenhauer in Beckett's early work and his affection for the pessimistic philosopher. For a sampling, see Harvey, *Samuel Beckett,* pp. 73–78; Hesla, *Shape of Chaos,* pp. 51–55; Pilling, *Samuel Beckett,* pp. 126–27. Paul Davies's essay, "*Stirrings Still*: The Disembodiment of Western Tradition," on the other hand, draws attention to the mystical traditions of Hinduism, Buddhism, Taoism, Sufism, esoteric Christianity, Rosicrucianism, etc., and to previous gnosiological readings of Beckett to elucidate the narrator's wish for the "one true end to time and grief and self." Whereas Davies only mentions Schopenhauer as the source of Beckett's knowledge of Buddhism (p. 148), I argue below that the desire for the dissolution into nothingness and the coupling of an "end to time" with an end to "grief and self" smacks of Schopenhauer as the mediator of a long lineage. It is also important to note that the dissolution into nothingness or nirvana is not the same as fusing an entombed and enwombed subjectlessness with artistic generativity.

2. For the gnostic and kabbalist sources, see Pagels, *Gnostic Gospels,* pp. 57–70 and Scholem, *Major Trends,* pp. 260–78. I relate Sophia to a number of Great Goddess figures in my "The *Magna Mater* Myth in Beckett's Fiction." Beckett's own familiarity with this material—including the Shechinah and Böhme—is evident as early as *Dream* (written in 1932), which abounds in explicit ironic references to mystical and philosophical intertexts and which repeatedly refers to an inner "wombtomb."

3. In "Beckett's Devious Deictics," a paper presented at the 1986 Beckett Conference in Stirling, Scotland, I first turned to Klein's and Abraham and Torok's theories of unfinished mourning in order to interrogate the puzzling use Beckett makes of expressions of time, place, and person. The interrelation between mourning and the postromantic imaginary is further illustrated in my book *The Aesthetics of Loss and Lessness,* in which may be found a more complete presentation of the theoretical framework of the present article. See also Hill, who relates encrypting to the larger theme of incorporation, particularly of the father.

4. The importance of hermeneutical temporality and of the processing of textual contradictions in Beckett's later works is emphasized by Gidal and Locatelli. My discussion of reader's time and discourse time is indebted to them. Gidal, for example, writes: "[T]here are texts which produce, throughout their duration, both a contradiction between what is said and how it is said *and* a contradiction between what is referred to and what for the viewer is the actual reference, i.e. the material of speech and gesture" (p. 66). For an incisive discussion of hermeneutic temporality, see Locatelli's chapters entitled "Repetition Against the False Movement of the Text" (pp. 120–25) and "The Problem of Temporality" (pp. 134–46).

5. On Beckett's demystifying and degendering maneuvers, see my *Abysmal Games,* pp. 96–120, 147–51; "The *Magna Mater* Myth"; and *The Aesthetics of Loss,* pp. 175–95. It is also clear that when it comes to gender, Beckett parts company with Schopenhauer, for whom the will (inner self) derives from the "superior" paternal principle, whereas the intellect is of maternal origin (*Die Welt,* 2:660–78; chap. 43).

6. For a brilliantly sustained discussion of the ways in which Beckett's late drama blocks identification with or through figures of determinable gender, see Gidal, *Understanding Beckett.*

7. The Allée des Cygnes, an artifical island where Beckett used to walk with Joyce (Brater, *Beyond Minimalism,* p. 126), is located downstream from the Eiffel Tower between the Pont Bir-Hakeim and the Pont de Grenelle.

8. For an excellent discussion of the play's statue motif in relation to *The Winter's Tale,* see Foster, "Beckett's Winter's Tale."

9. On the implication of the *fort/da* in Beckett's fiction, see my *Abysmal Games,* p. 33.

10. See Ermarth, *Sequel to History,* who finds that rhythmic time, which she compares to musical rhythm, is the preferred temporality of postmodernism. In "Time as Rhythm," she writes: "Postmodern narrative encourages new rhythms of attention by pluralizing voice and by sustaining contradiction. . . ." (p. 68). The rhythmic temporality of Beckett's late plays and prose fictions is, of course, part of the overall pleasure and complexity of these texts. For Schopenhauer, music, unlike the other arts, is not a representation of a representation but gives voice directly to the inner self (the will) (*Die Welt,* 1:356–67; § 52).

11. See Brater, *Beyond Minimalism,* for a description of the first performance of *Ohio Impromptu* on 9 May 1981, at the Ohio State University International Beckett Symposium, for which occasion Beckett wrote the play, and for Beckett's humorous allusions to the situation (pp. 125–38). Brater recounts that Beckett warned Alan Schneider, the play's director, that the audience of Beckett scholars would laugh when the curtain opened on *Ohio Impromptu.* Brater writes: "He was right. Taken by the austerity of the situation, two lookalike 'philosophes' bent over an ancient tome at a table where a soigné Latin quarter hat lies abandoned, the audience in Ohio could appreciate the irony of the stage event" (p. 126). As I joined in the laughter that day, I remember being struck more by the self-parody of the mirror image on stage. Ironic figures of the audience, or parodic shadows of the artist, or both, the play's twinlike apparitions are examples of Beckett's inexhaustible stage images, which in their dreamlike condensation *(Verdichtung)* add to the power of the plays to stir.

12. In agreement with the Kleinian incorporation of the mother-father, Ehrenzweig chronicles the artist's fantasy of self-generation from an imaginary womb: "Ultimately the divine child himself absorbs the creative powers of both parents. He incorporates the mother's womb. He bears, expels and buries himself in a single act" (*Hidden Order,* p. 187). In Beckett's trilogy, writing is indeed conceived as an endlessly varied birth-into-death (Moorjani, *Abysmal Games,* pp. 119–30). In "The Difficult Birth: An Image of Utterance in Beckett," Lawley aptly relates the recurring themes of blocked passage, male pregnancy, and male birth fantasies in Beckett's theater to the writer's preoccupations with "imperfect being, utterance and the process of creation" (p. 10). On the same themes in Beckett's short fiction, see Lawley's "*First Love*: Passage and Play." In addition to Lawley, two psychoanalysts, Anzieu and Simon, have been particularly intrigued with Beckett's phantasm of a twin's obstructed birth. Both Anzieu and Simon believe that W. R. Bion's article, "The Imaginary Twin," is based on Beckett's analysis with him in the thirties. Beckett did indeed tell a number of people that the fantasy of an unborn twin/dead other self is related to his own situation as a writer (Harvey, *Samuel Beckett,* 247; Juliet, "Un Vivant," p. 16).

13. It is interesting to note to what extent the intertextual resonances with goddess lore mystify many readers who, unlike Beckett's generation, lack familiarity with Frazer's *Golden Bough.* For more extensive discussion of these allusions in *Molloy* and *Ill Seen Ill Said*, see Tagliaferri, *Beckett,* pp. 47–70 and the works listed in note 5. On "gynesis," see Jardine.

14. For a comparison between *Ill Seen Ill Said*'s final passage and Beckett's 1935 poem "The Vulture" and their relation to the pleasure principle, see my *Abysmal Games,* pp. 81–82, 150–51. Murphy discusses more extensively the relation between the two texts (*Reconstructing Beckett,* pp. 161–63). See also Graver for a reading of the end in terms of a "heartily satisfied appetite" ("Homage," p. 147). Locatelli has analyzed the inscriptions of duration in the text, such as the repeated "on" (*Unwording,* pp. 208–12). These inscriptions, however, I would add, must be read against the text's "mythological present," which in *Molloy* already most closely approximated timelessness: "All this in the present as had she the misfortune to be still of this world" (*Ill Seen,* p. 8). The conflation of time and timelessness is beautifully expressed in *Ill Seen Ill Said*'s "Death again of deathless day" (p. 40).

15. See Worth for a reading of the play as a ghost story ("Beckett's Ghosts," pp. 69–72).

16. In his study of *mise en abyme,* Dällenbach defines "aporetic duplication" as "a sequence that is supposed to enclose the work that encloses it" (*Mirror,* p. 35). I agree with Jardine that Derrida's corresponding term, "invagination," is a problematical instance of "gynesis" (pp. 34–35).

17. For a far-reaching discussion of disembodiment in *Rockaby*, see Oppenheim, "Female Subjectivity," pp. 222–26. Cohn reads the end of the play as a birth-into-death or a "fatal birth" ("Femme Fatale," p. 171).

Given the importance of figure fusing with rock and stone in *Ohio Impromptu* and *Mal vu mal dit*, both of which along with *Rockaby* date from 1981, I cannot help but be struck by the word *rock* in *rocker*. It is another instance of cryptonymic *Verdichtung*.

Works Cited

Abraham, Nicolas, and Maria Torok. *The Wolf Man's Magic Word: A Cryptonymy*. Translated by Nicholas Rand. Minneapolis: University of Minnesota Press, 1986. Originally published as *Cryptonymie: le verbier de l'Homme aux Loups* (Paris: Aubier-Flammarion, 1976).

Anzieu, Didier. "Beckett and Bion." *International Review of Psycho-Analysis* 16 (1989): 163-69. Originally published as "Beckett et Bion," *Revue de Psychothérapie Psychanalytique de Groupe* 5-6 (1986).

Beckett, Samuel. "The Calmative." In *Stories. No's Knife: Collected Shorter Prose 1945-1966*. London: Calder and Boyars, 1967. Originally published as *Nouvelles et Textes pour rien* (Paris: Minuit, 1955).

———. *Dream of Fair to Middling Women*. New York: Arcade, 1993.

———. *Footfalls*. 1976. In *Collected Shorter Plays*. New York: Grove, 1984.

———. *Ill Seen Ill Said*. New York: Grove, 1981. Originally published as *Mal vu mal dit* (Paris: Minuit, 1981).

———. *Molloy*. 1955. *Three Novels*. New York: Grove-Black Cat, 1965. Originally published in French as *Molloy* (Paris: Minuit, 1951).

———. *Ohio Impromptu*. 1981. In *Collected Shorter Plays*. New York: Grove, 1984.

———. *Proust*. 1931. New York: Grove, 1957.

——— *Rockaby*. 1981. In *Collected Shorter Plays*. New York: Grove, 1984.

———. *Texts for Nothing I*. In *No's Knife:* In *Collected Shorter Prose, 1945–1966*. London: Calder and Boyars, 1967. Originally published as *Textes pour rien I: Nouvelles et Textes pour rien* (Paris: Minuit, 1955).

———. *The Unnamable*. 1958. In *Three Novels*. New York: Grove, 1965. Originally published as *L'Innommable* (Paris: Minuit, 1953).

Ben-Zvi, Linda, ed. *Samuel Beckett*. Boston: Twayne, 1986.

———. *Women in Beckett: Performance and Critical Perspectives*. Urbana and Chicago: University of Illinois Press, 1990.

Bion, W. R. "The Imaginary Twin." 1950. In *Second Thoughts*. New York: Jason Aronson, 1974.

Blanchot, Maurice. *L'Entretien infini*. Paris: Gallimard, 1969.

———. "Où maintenant? Qui maintenant?" *Nouvelle Revue Française* 1 (1953): 678–86.

———. *Thomas l'obscur*. 1941. New ed. Paris: Gallimard, 1950.

Brater, Enoch. *Beyond Minimalism: Beckett's Late Style in the Theater*. New York: Oxford University Press, 1987.

Büttner, Gottfried. *Samuel Beckett's Novel "Watt."* Philadelphia: University of Pennsylvania Press, 1984. Originally published as *Samuel Becketts Roman "Watt": Eine Untersuchung des gnoseologischen Grundzuges* (Heidelberg: Carl Winter Universitätsverlag, 1981).

Cohn, Ruby. "The Femme Fatale on Beckett's Stage." In Ben-Zvi, ed., *Women in Beckett*, pp. 162–71.

Dällenbach, Lucien. *The Mirror in the Text.* Chicago: University of Chicago Press, 1989. Originally published as *Le Récit spéculaire: essai sur la mise en abyme* (Paris: Seuil, 1977).

Davies, Paul. "*Stirrings Still*: The Disembodiment of Western Tradition." In *The Ideal Core of the Onion: Reading Beckett Archives,* edited by John Pilling and Mary Bryden, pp. 136–51. Reading, U.K.: Beckett International Foundation, 1992.

Derrida, Jacques. "*Fors*: The Anglish Words of Nicolas Abraham and Maria Torok." Translated by Barbara Johnson. In Abraham and Torok, *Wolf Man's Magic Word.*, pp. xi–xlviii. Originally published as "*Fors*: les mots anglés de Nicolas Abraham et Maria Torok," in Nicolas Abraham and Maria Torok, ed. *Cryptonomie: le verbier de l'Homme aux Loups* (Paris: Aubier-Flammarion, 1976), pp. 7–73.

Descombes, Vincent. *Proust: philosophie du roman.* Paris: Minuit, 1987.

Ehrenzweig, Anton. *The Hidden Order of Art: A Study in the Psychology of Artistic Imagination.* 1967. Berkeley: University of California Press, 1971.

Ermarth, Elizabeth Deeds. *Sequel to History: Postmodernism and the Crisis of Representational Time.* Princeton: Princeton University Press, 1992.

Foster, Verna. "Beckett's Winter's Tale: Tragicomic Transformation in *Ohio Impromptu.*" *Journal of Beckett Studies* 1 (1992): 67–75.

Frazer, Sir James G. *The Golden Bough: A Study in Magic and Religion.* 1890. 3d ed. 13 vols. New York: Macmillan, 1955.

Freud, Sigmund. *Beyond the Pleasure Principle.* 1920. In vol. 18 of *Standard Edition.*

———. "Mourning and Melancholia." 1917. In vol. 14 of *Standard Edition.*

———. *The Standard Edition of the Complete Psychological Works.* Ed. and trans. James Strachey. 24 vols. London: Hogarth, 1953–74.

———. "The Uncanny" *(Das Unheimliche).* 1919. In vol. 17 of *Standard Edition.*

Gidal, Peter. *Understanding Beckett: A Study of Monologue and Gesture in the Works of Samuel Beckett.* Language, Discourse, Society. London: Macmillan; New York: St. Martin's, 1986.

Graver, Lawrence. "Homage to the Dark Lady: *Ill Seen Ill Said.*" In Ben-Zvi, *Women in Beckett* 142–49.

Harvey, Lawrence E. *Samuel Beckett: Poet and Critic.* Princeton: Princeton University Press, 1970.

H. D. *Tribute to the Angels.* 1945. In *Collected Poems 1912–1944*, edited by Louis L. Martz, pp. 545–74. New York: New Directions, 1986.

Henry, Anne. *Proust romancier: le tombeau égyptien.* Paris: Flammarion, 1983.

Hesla, David H. *The Shape of Chaos: An Interpretation of the Art of Samuel Beckett.* Minneapolis: University of Minnesota Press, 1971.

Hill, Leslie. *Beckett's Fiction: In Different Words.* Cambridge and New York: Cambridge University Press, 1990.

———. "Late Texts: Writing the Work of Mourning." *Samuel Beckett Today/Aujourdhui* 1 (1992): 10–25.

Jardine, Alice A. *Gynesis: Configurations of Woman and Modernity*. Ithaca: Cornell University Press, 1985.

Juliet, Charles. "Un Vivant." *Magazine Littéraire* 231 (1986): 16–17.

Klee, Paul. *Tagebücher 1898-1918*. Edited by Felix Klee. Cologne: DuMont, 1979.

Klein, Melanie. *Love, Guilt, and Reparation and Other Works, 1921–1945*. London: Hogarth, 1975.

Laplanche, Jean, and J.-B. Pontalis. "Principe de Nirvana." In *Vocabulaire de la psychanalyse*. Paris: Presses Universitaires de France, 1973.

Lawley, Paul. "The Difficult Birth: An Image of Utterance in Beckett." In *"Make Sense Who May": Essays on Samuel Beckett's Later Works*, edited by Robin J. Davis and Lance St. J. Butler, pp. 1–10. Totowa, N.J.: Barnes & Noble, 1989.

———. "*First Love*: Passage and Play." *Samuel Beckett Today/Aujourd'hui* 2 (1994): 189–95.

Locatelli, Carla. *Unwording the World: Samuel Beckett's Prose Works After the Nobel Prize*. Philadelphia: University of Pennsylvania Press, 1990.

Moorjani, Angela. *Abysmal Games in the Novels of Samuel Beckett*. North Carolina Studies in the Romance Languages and Literatures. Chapel Hill: University of North Carolina Press, 1982.

———. *The Aesthetics of Loss and Lessness: Language, Discourse, Society*. London: Macmillan; New York: St. Martin's, 1992.

———. "Beckett's Devious Deictics." In *Rethinking Beckett: A Collection of Critical Essays*, edited by Lance St. John Butler and Robin J. Davis, pp. 20–30. London: Macmillan, 1990.

———. "The *Magna Mater* Myth in Beckett's Fiction: Subtext and Subversion." In *Beckett Translating/Translating Beckett*, edited by Alan Warren Friedman et al. University Park: Pennsylvania State University Press, 1987. Rpt. in Ben-Zvi, *Women in Beckett*, pp. 134–41.

Murphy, Peter J. *Reconstructing Beckett: Language for Being in Samuel Beckett's Fiction*. Toronto: University of Toronto Press, 1990.

Oppenheim, Lois. "Female Subjectivity in *Not I* and *Rockaby*." In Ben-Zvi, *Women in Beckett*, pp. 217–27.

Pagels, Elaine. *The Gnostic Gospels*. New York: Random-Vintage, 1981.

Pilling, John. *Samuel Beckett*. London and Boston: Routledge and Kegan Paul, 1976.

Proust, Marcel. "To Robert Dreyfus." 10 Nov. 1910. Letter 98 in *Correspondance*, edited by Philip Kolb, 10:207–8. Paris: Plon, 1983.

Rilke, Rainer Maria. "To Witold Hulewicz." [13 Nov.?] 1925. Letter 410 in *Briefe*, edited by Ruth Sieber-Rilke and Karl Altheim, 3:894–901. Frankfurt: Insel-Taschenbuch, 1987.

Scholem, Gershom G. *Major Trends in Jewish Mysticism*. Rev. ed. New York: Schocken, 1946.

Schopenhauer, Arthur. *Die Welt als Wille und Vorstellung*. 1819–44. Vols. 1 and 2 of *Sämtliche Werke*, 5 vols., edited by Wolfgang Frhr. von Löhneysen. Stuttgart and Frankfurt: Cotta-Insel, 1987.

Simon, Bennett. "The Imaginary Twins: The Case of Beckett and Bion." *International Revue of Psycho-Analysis* 15 (1988): 331–52.

Tagliaferri, Aldo. *Beckett et la surdétermination littéraire.* Paris: Payot, 1977. Originally published as *Beckett e l'iperdeterminazione letteraria* (Milan: Giangiacomo Feltrinelli, 1967).

Worth, Katharine. "Beckett's Ghosts." In *Beckett in Dublin,* edited by S. E. Wilmer, pp. 62–74. Dublin: Lilliput, 1992.

Re-Mythologizing Beckett: The Metaphors of Metafiction in *How It Is*

WANDA BALZANO

How It Is, upsetting the taxonomic certainties of genre classification, does not obey any order and cannot be put into any category; its numerous possible readings challenge and transgress the very notion of genre. The text seems to question "how it is" and, as in the course of writing this enigma is not solved, the presumed rhetorical question changes into a play of tracks that refers to a metonymical sense, to a *mise en abyme* of the text itself or, better still, to a self-questioning of writing about its formal im/possibility. The scansion, in middle-length verses and sometimes even one-line verses that are gathered together and divided among themselves by one simple blank space, is a very effective stylistic device that suggests that this is a story told by a voice among the various rest-breaths: "when the panting stops."[1]

Such a stylistic and formal divertissement is made more evident by the lack of punctuation marks and, often, of conjunctions, articles, and main verbs. Syntax is abolished; language is both degrammaticized and subverted. Anarchy is the driving force. The black of writing seems to blend with the white of page into a gray, muddy, entropic form of writing, in which there is neither order nor hierarchy. On the one hand, the phonic expression has the same value as the graphic one; on the other hand, the concepts of repetition and authenticity, traditionally contrasted, here become equivalent. And, with their recurrence, both these joint relationships (speech-writing, repetition-origin) give form to the structural frame of the story—symptom of a metafictional will.

Repetition and Difference: Variations on a Theme

The secret power of *How It Is* consists of repetition. In the fictional reign of tautology, the voice "says" *how it is* in the process of writing, while the writing, in its turn, reflects this oral effort. Voice and writing (or, let me say, Echo and Narcissus), which correspond to the forms of narration, here appear redundant. Each is the reflection of the other, endlessly repeating it and re-calling it (*petere* = to recall, to claim, to desire). Palinodying the myth of Echo and Narcissus, *How It Is* can be read as an amorous *surenchère* of forms; as the nymph Echo, bound by a passion for Narcissus, throws the words onto the wind ("this voice these voices as if borne on all the winds but not a breath another antiquity," p. 14), so the oral dimension of this text repeats, "loves" the written dimension, with a continuous exchange between them.

As a silent reverie, the purest among the jeux d'esprit, *How It Is* is the result of a clear contradiction. Though it is the next step made by Beckett, after *The Unnamable*, in his search for expressive forms that are increasingly skeletal, it is based on recursive structures that, turning in a circle, do nothing but strengthen—instead of destroying—its ontological guarantee. In all three sections of the book, *repetition* is a central dimension for language, structure, and plot, whereas *originality* is openly rejected by the narrating voice, which, since the beginning, affirms that it is only quoting: "I say it as I hear it" (p. 7). In this way the voice, puppet of a diachronic ventriloquist, confesses that it is repeating the discourse of someone (presumably the author) of whom it is ignorant. That voice, described as "the quiver of the lower face" (p. 48), belongs to a traveling narrator who gropes his way forward in a slime. Provided with a sack containing tins and an opener, he murmurs the same meaningless sentences in an attempt to reproduce sounds, odors, and colors that can keep him company during his journey. The need to go on talking, to repeat the word already said, reflects the wish to deafen silence in order to fill the void of an increasingly pressing solitude.

Hence, the speaker's need to create a character to interact with, to create a second self who can strengthen the ontological barrier against his vanishing self. Bom's approach to his duplicate, whose name is Pim, is a violent one. In the second part of the book, Bom torments Pim with punches, scratches and engravings made with his own nails and the opener he has, under pretense of leaving a trace of communication. In the third part, then, Bom is brutalized in the same way by other torturers, who alternate repeatedly on his back. In the next fourteen sections, the roles switch and switch back, but the extorted words, quotations of a life "ill-said ill-heard ill-recaptured ill-murmured in the mud" (p. 7), are always the same. As we go on reading, the sensation of being before a palimpsest-like work that continuously, because ineffectually, rewrites, rereads and rehears itself at a frantic and jerky rhythm becomes more palpable.

Inevitably, the idea of *repetition* matches the existence of an *original* that, in the metaphysics of presence, goes back to Being as a rudiment and to the thought of purity and centrality as authentic values. Nevertheless, in an ontologically "weak" world,[2] in which the metaphysical notions of subject and object, of reality and truth, lose weight, repetition must not be considered as subordinate to the original; instead it must be considered as being mutually interdependent. Origin and repetition must be seen as moments of an unceasing process of reciprocal definition and redefinition, according to the logic of the modern fractals, that is, bright iridescent images infinitely repeating extraordinary combinations of colors. Similarly, *How It Is* takes on the shape of a monochromatic fractal, whose shining effects change from white to black according to a spectrum of shades. As a self-defining fractal follows an inner principle of repetition determined by casuality, so the Beckettian writing flows unceasingly by deriving ever-new geometries from its architecture. Moving on the axis of "different repetition" (Deleuze, *Différence et répétition*), Samuel Beckett suggests a new idea of seriality that frees the thought of difference from the execrated metaphysics of presence; in *repetition* it is possible never to be the same twice, and in *difference* the Same is retaken, but with a variation on retaking. If repetition differs, difference repeats.

It is chiefly the action that is eternally scanned by an equal and different alternation, at the speed of a frantic carousel; he who tortures is in turn tortured. So, in the scene of the violent representation, Pim and Bom alternate, exchanging the role of subject and object, sadist and masochist:

> so eternally now Bom now Pim something wrong there according as left or right north or south tormentor or victim these words too strong tormentor always of the same and victim always of the same. [. . .] (P. 124)

The prose of *How It Is*, like a grotesque rigmarole, produces a hypnotizing verbal melody: echoes, returnings, and altered repetitions flash to the rhythm of a stroboscope effect.

Once it is established that both canvas and plot (literary process and *factum*) unceasingly endure, the first part has necessarily to repeat itself in the third one, the second part in the fourth one and in the sixth one, and so on. From a condition of solitude in the first part, the narrator finds a sort of company in the second one, and then goes back again to the initial condition in the third part. But, from the first part to the third one, something has changed: during the process, a variation has taken place: "part three there's another difference" (p. 27). The two solitudes that frame the section "with Pim" show a variation in mood: the first solitude is the solitude of a person journeying toward another, while the second solitude is that of the same person who is abandoned by the other one. Such *variations on a theme* are typical of the sonata form, with the characteristic ternary scheme (exposition, development, repeat of the two contrasting themes, and conclusion) upon which the first movement of the sonata articulates (Webb, *Samuel Beckett,* pp. 151–69).

Even more suggestive is the proposal of studying *How It Is* as a serial work. Because it is based on the repetition of sentences or phrases, varied on one subject, its compositional technique is, indeed, construed by following the serial organization of contemporary music; there are neither sudden bounces nor abrupt changes, but everything turns into an imperceptible difference, during the suspended interval between stopping and restarting:

> In the postmodern period however, we have a music whose changing sequence of events may depend upon no such rhythmic drive, goals, or points of culmination. In the most extreme cases it is simply there, between stopping and starting. (Butler, *After the Wake,* p. 70)

It is there, in that "Other" place where the Same is refracted. It is in that elliptical uncanny space, in the mirror's refractive surface, in the voice's repercussive place—in that paraxial place of resonance and refraction—that *How It Is*, greedily, re-turns.

The Re-flection of Forms

In *How It Is*, metafiction represents another form of very complex and problematical repetition. Writing itself, the voice that speaks and "says" *how it is* is that of the author who, surviving the announcement of his own death (in a Barthesian way), mingles with the narrated topic. So, there is not a real narrator who imposes his point of view; therefore, it is unclear who writes or what is written. Like a game of Chinese boxes or Borgesian mirrors, an infinite series of returnings and rebounds is produced. Consequently, to inquire about "what" the work means has no importance; on the contrary, the question shifts to "how" it means. The ghost of cyclical repetition comes back: content returns to form and form to content. The words that Beckett employed to take up the cudgels for Joyce's writing well fit his own writing, which "is not *about* something: *it is that something itself*" (*Disjecta*, p. 27). What is told is the telling itself, flexing and re-flecting forms that are devoid of content. Beckett himself, in a letter to Hugh Kenner, designated the narrative character of *How It Is* as "narrator/narrated." The secret charm of the text reveals itself in this contradiction in terms; the voice that quotes (not specifying from who or what) is, in its turn, narrated—and written. Voice is mirrored in its own writing and writing reechoes through the voice, Echo and Narcissus-like. Each attempt toward originality is of no use.

The story, a voice's writing, has neither beginning nor end, neither content nor frame. Such a structure deprives the text of any beginning or decidable border, reproducing the Russian babushka's structure. Frame without content and content without frame.[3] The nontheme of *How It Is* is a questioning and reflecting on the story's possibility or impossibility—both written and spoken. Bom, engraving—i.e., writing—some capital letters on Pim's bleeding back, tries to cause exhaustive verbal answers, to know how life is, how death and the telling itself are; but the extorted words are senseless, useless, inconclusive. In this way, the questioning of the book about itself frustrates any possible expectation. It will never reveal what it is. On the contrary, it will return to the initial "how." To Narcissus's question, Echo answers in a palimpsest-like talking that unrelentingly builds itself and falls to ruin, calling and recalling to itself on all sides.

The narrative of *How It Is* reproduces a self-begetting form (Kellman, *Self-begetting Novel*) that loves itself. Narcissus falls in love with the image he has produced. The narcissistic nature of a narrative whose compositive process is visible and autogamous nestles in this sort of paradox. The novel has nourished an obsessive love and hate for itself, as it looks at itself in the mirror and then, just as Narcissus did, enters its own death, to survive in different forms (cf. Narcissus's transformation into a flower). Here myth has become play and repetition.

If the paper of the page is the spring and the text reflects its own narcissistic image in it, that verbal process which is disappearing little by little among the lines of *How It Is* is incarnated in Echo, whose essence, however, becomes increasingly insubstantial. A text claiming its autonomy because it can produce itself still cannot avoid the interaction of at least two connected agents of narration; the text exists as a re-flexing screen between author and reader. While the author is writing, under his pen, under the text he is composing, the reader's reflection inevitably takes form. Thus, s/he becomes the author's reversed duplicate, becomes s/he who writes the text with the author, but on the other side of the mirror. Therefore, writing becomes a transparent operation that implies the existence of a reader who "writes." At this point, then, to establish whether the author is the reader's reflection or vice versa has no more importance, because both are figures that are born of the mirror of desire, that is, the desire of creation.

Beckett's writing presents itself as an integration of history and speech. The "I," present in *How It Is* as an instance of the narrative discourse, not only glides toward the "he" of the *histoire* ("if they see I am a monster of the solitudes he sees man for the first time," p. 14) but reifies itself in fiction, which coincides with the narrated matter.[4] As the echo fades, the silent written word, subject/object of desire, makes its own way through the text. The "scripteur," longing for his own writing, sinks in the text's most secret recesses, being perpetuated in a process of "infinitation." More than an optical illusion, it is a *mise en abyme:* "an image inside an infinitely sinking well, with progressive lessenings as one goes down to the abyss" (Barilli, *Tra presenza e assenza,* p. 286, translation is mine).[5]

That's how the macrocosm, then, mirrors itself in the microcosm. As in Las Meninas by Velázquez, the sight is captured in infinite resightings:

it's the sack Pim left me without his sack he left his sack with me I left my sack with Bem I'll leave my sack with Bom I left Bem without my sack to go towards Pim it's the sack. (P. 120)

A) it's the sack = beginning (and end)
B) Pim left me without his sack _____ (denies and asserts)
   he left his sack with me

C) I left my sack with Bem _____ (asserts and denies)
   I left Bem without my sack
D) it's the sack = end (and beginning)
   I'll leave my sack with Bom _____ opens the fault in
   to go towards Pim   the discourse; the future tense
                              guarantees continuity, making
                              returning all into circulation.

Microcosm into microcosm, the chiasmus:

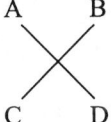

How It Is exhibits its forms at the same time as it reflects them, thereby impregnating them with itself. On the basis of the Lacanian distinction between Imaginary and Symbolic Order, here presided over by Echo and Narcissus, in *How It Is* it is possible to establish an amorous relationship between these two forms. While Echo, voice's incarnation, is being recorded in an imaginary reign of pure sonorous signifiers and is explicating her functions in the auditive field, she tries to enter the order of the signified in order to become image herself ("an image too of this voice," p. 138) and to again join the writing. But Narcissus, writing's personification, rejects this love because he is in his turn attracted by his own reflected image; and yet, involuntarily, the passionate words that he addresses to her bounce back because of Echo. Narcissus's drives, therefore, tend to be recorded in an imaginary world, whereas Echo, for her part, yearns for inclusion in the Symbolic (the voice aims at the order of the written code).

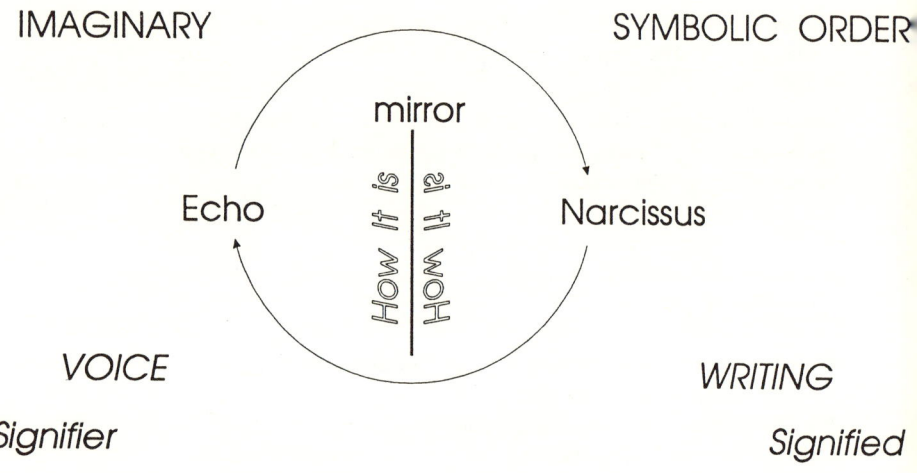

Thus, Echo and Narcissus, in subverting the orders of which they are part, both defer their own passions; none of the pairs in the myth succeeds in joining the object of desire, and love remains unsatisfied: Echo's passion is not satisfied, Narcissus—longing for Eros—has married Thanatos . . .

In the maze of the bend something is lost, a difference has occurred: between voice and writing a fissure has opened. A mirror has penetrated. On the wave of continuous refraction, Echo pursues Narcissus and Narcissus returns in Echo; but, magically, beyond myth and history, beyond reality and fiction, the two halves join. Secretly, silently, contravening the laws of necessity and the principle of reality, their encounter becomes true on the mirror's surface. Abandoned to the pleasure principle, words merge with images and satisfy an age-old desire: between pantings and allurements, between enticements and reluctances, *How It Is* dreams of love on a looking glass.

Notes

1. Quotations of *How It Is* that follow will refer to the John Calder edition (1977).
2. The adjective is here borrowed from the so-called "weak thought," a contemporary Italian philosophical movement. In a world whose reality is "lightened," the "weakers" propose philosophical strategies in contrast with the logocentric metaphysics' "strong" ideology (Vattimo, *La fine,* 1985).
3. It is also the case of an interesting small book by Maurice Blanchot that represents the structural duplicate of *How It Is*: *La folie du jour* (1980).
4. As indicated by Patricia Waugh (*Metafiction,* p. 135), it is a particular level of subjectivity that provides the author's presence only in the terms of his real absence. The cipher of this attentive analysis is borrowed by Barthes, whose book *Roland Barthes par Roland Barthes* turns out to be a clear example of authorial reification. In it we read: "I myself am my symbol, the story that happens to me" (p. 71).
5. Elsewhere, in Barilli's book, the *mise en abyme* is defined as that "infinitation effect which can be obtained, for example, by putting two photographic objectives or two mirrors facing each other" (*Tra presenza e assenza,* p. 243; my translation).

Works Cited

Barilli, Renato. *L'azione e l' estasi.* Milano: Feltrinelli, 1967.
———. *Tra presenza e assenza. Due ipotesi per l' eta' postmoderna.* Milano: Bompiani, 1981.
Barth, John. "La letteratura dell' esaurimento." In *Postmoderno e Letteratura,* edited by Carravetta and Spedicato, 49–60. Milano: Bompiani, 1984.
Barthes, Roland. *Roland Barthes par Roland Barthes.* Paris: Editions du Seuil, 1970.
———. *S/Z.* Paris: Editions du Seuil, 1970.
Beckett, Samuel. *Comment C'est.* Paris: Les Editions de Minuit, 1975.
———. *Disjecta: Miscellaneous Writing and a Dramatic Fragment.* Edited by Ruby Cohn. London: John Calder, 1983.
———. *How It Is.* London: John Calder, 1970.
Blanchot, Maurice. *La folie du jour.* Montpellier: Fata Morgana, 1980.
———*L'Entretien infini.* Paris: Gallimard, 1969.
Borges, Jorge Luis. "Borges y yo." In *Obras Completas,* 3:50–51. Buenos Aires: Emecé Editores, 1967.

———. "El jardín de senderos que se bifurcan." In *Obras Completas,* 2:97–111. Buenos Aires: Emecé Editores, 1967.

Butler, Christopher. *After the Wake: An Essay on the Contemporary Avant-Garde.* Oxford: Clarendon Press, 1980.

Connor, Steven. *Samuel Beckett: Repetition, Theory, and Text.* Oxford and New York: Basil Blackwell, 1980.

Deleuze, Gilles. *Différence et répétition.* Paris: Presses Universitaires de France, 1968.

Derrida, Jacques. *L'Ecriture et la différence.* Paris: Editions du Seuil, 1967.

Foucault, Michel. *Les Mots et les choses.* Paris: Gallimard, 1966.

Kellman, Steven G. *The Self-begetting Novel.* London: Macmillan, 1980.

McHale, Brian. *Postmodernist Fiction.* London: Methuen, 1987.

Vattimo, Gianni. *La fine della modernitá: Nihilismo ed ermeneutica nella cultura postmoderna.* Milano: Garzanti, 1985.

Waugh, Patricia. *Metafiction: The Theory and Practice of Self-Conscious Fiction.* London and New York: Methuen, 1984.

Webb, Eugene. *Samuel Beckett: A Study of His Novels.* London: Peter Owen, 1970.

Entering Beckett's Postmodern Space

ELIZABETH KLAVER

Dream of a silence, a dream silence, full of murmurs." And so *The Unnamable*, Beckett's last novel of his 1950s trilogy, ends in the thwarted desire for silence, a silence permeated with sound, "words [. . .] all words," even as it is thought (p. 414). Through out the narrative, the unnamable has been trying to reach or at least consider the possibility of existence and subjectivity in a realm devoid of semiosis, but cannot find a way to proceed that does not lead him back to repetition (Connor, *Samuel Beckett*, p. 73) and to the impossibility of getting rid of language (Locatelli, *Unwording*, p. 51). He does not even find a silence between texts, because rather than being awakened from silence the unnamable has been generated out of the interstices of previous Beckettian narratives and has already been returned by Beckett before the trilogy ends into the murmur of *Waiting for Godot*. Before *The Unnamable* can be switched off, Beckett has already inscribed the semiotic problematic of the "unword" onto a series of dramatic texts, which begins to generate a postmodernist rise in his theater.

It is this series of texts that begins with an oblique step from the prose onto the stage that I want to examine in the light of Beckett's postmodernist aesthetic. To be sure, there is a certain arbitrariness to citing works such as *The Unnamable* and *Godot* as making apparent the rise of Beckett's post-modernism, given the fact that there is little agreement among critics as to precisely when Beckett became postmodernist. Allen Thiher, for instance, seems to locate it at the beginning at *Murphy* (*Words in Reflection,* p. 106), while Nicholas Zurbrugg sees it at *Watt* ("Seven Types," p. 34/42). However, I think Carla Locatelli is accurate in pointing out an alteration that occurs in Beckett's project during the trilogy, a project that begins with a certain way of writing reality and ends with an attempt to get rid of words altogether (*Unwording*, p. 55). This change broadly describes the turn from a modernist skepticism about and refusal of the validity of linguistic referentiality to the postmodernist doubt of linguistic forms themselves. By the ending of *The Unnamable*, Beckett has discovered the impossibility of getting outside of words in a universe that is linguistic and textual. Because I will be focusing on Beckett's attempts to display, work out, or go beyond this semiotic problematic, I place the onset of his postmodernist project during the writing of the latter part of the trilogy (a time that includes the writing of *Godot*), particularly building during *The Unnamable* when his text begins to display a thorough entanglement in a linguistic universe.

Of course, the debate over the onset of Beckett's postmodernism is really part of a larger question about whether Beckett should be charted as postmodernist at all. H. Porter Abbott, for instance, recognizes features throughout Beckett's work that coincide with the late modernist spirit of opposition and uses some of the same texts *(Watt, Godot)* Zurbrugg invokes in his taxonomy of postmodernist trends. This debate will most likely remain unresolved, not simply because of the critical desire to categorize but because Beckett, as a writer who spans most of the twentieth century, is apt to demonstrate both modernist and postmodernist trends in his work. If literary and cultural movements are difficult to periodize at the best of times, Beckett makes it virtually impossible to identify in his work a radical, chronological rupture between modernism and postmodernism.

Moreover, one way of looking at postmodernism demands the articulation of two competing ideas: postmodernism as a development and as a rejection of modernism. Postmodernism continues the project of rejection begun by modernism in the destabilization of various entrenched master narratives—the classical transparency of the sign, the unified self, the myth of Victorian progress described by Abbott—but rejects the aesthetic groundings modernism installed in their place. In other words, while it continues to expose many of the same Western axioms as modernism did, postmodernism involves a more complex configuration of semiotics, structure, and subjectivity that interrogates related modernist sensibilities. I believe the nontrivial act of thinking these competing ideas at once is partly responsible for both the appearance and the interpretation of modernist and postmodernist features in Beckett's mid-to-late century work. Ironically, though, this contrary project adds more weight to the case for a turn by Beckett to postmodernism, because such competing propositions parallel the sort of convoluted postmodernist space found in his work.

I would also argue that the project of assessing Beckett's postmodernism does not spring from the desire to appropriate a late modernist, but from the wish to understand his position in the literary and cultural era associated with the mid-to-late twentieth century. There can be no doubt that Beckett critically examines similar philosophical questions of language and being as Sartre and Derrida, and that he has had a tremendous impact on later writers like Len Jenkins, Adrienne Kennedy, J. M. Coetzee, and, of course, John Barth. By viewing Beckett as one of the first writers to recognize and reflect a literary and cultural rezoning, the absurdist label of the 1960s can disintegrate, allowing Beckett's plays to be seen as in step with the ways postmodernists structure the universe.

And yet, the critical effort to align the structures of postmodernism with Beckett's work also raises the twin problematics of definition and totalization. It is more accurate today to speak of postmodernism(s), since the term has spread out to name the consumer culture, the media culture, a nonessentialist feminism, and hyperreality, as well as the crisis of representation. All of these postmodernisms structure the world differently. Furthermore, the title of a session, "Beckett and Postmodernist Aesthetics," at the Beckett Symposium (The Hague, 1992) invoked the issue as well, for the term "aesthetic" suggests an umbrella, a process of definition that cannot "fit" a postmodernist paralogia. Indeed, a similar discordance is apparent in the debate between Jean-François Lyotard and Jurgen Habermas over the consensus community, a totalizing effort on the part of Habermas that does not come to terms with the postmodern condition of discontinuity and heterogeneity.[1] In fact, the work of defining, cataloguing, or totalizing postmodernism into an aesthetic has much in common with the work of unifying Beckett's plays into an acceptable academic project, acts that inevitably involve the delimiting of indefinite, heterogeneous space into narrow, logical lines of reasoning. Despite the fact that subject matter may be working against totalization, there is always a demand on the part of critical discourse to synthesize and refine, a practice that can, ironically, generate self-deconstruction.

A case in point is Ihab Hassan's schematizing of modernism and postmodernism (a practice that could go under the labels "form," "purpose," and "design" in his "Modernism" column), which he produces in the form of a table. While useful for a general range of the possible differences between these movements, one immediately realizes that much of the "Postmodernism" column ("antiform," "chance," "anarchy") simply cannot be itemized ("Culture of Postmodernism," p. 312). Because of the incompatibility of postmodernism and the "consensus community" of critical discourse, I want to invoke Wittgenstein's notion of the "indistinct" concept as more "exactly what we need" (*Philosophical Investigations,* p. 34e), and map my discussion not as a glovelike fit between a definition of postmodernism and Beckett's mid-to-late work, but rather as the uncovering of a postmodernist trajectory, in the form of a semiotic problematic, that travels through the much wider scope of Beckett's plays and of postmodernism(s) in general.

Interestingly, the effort to write critically on Beckett itself raises the topic of semiosis, because any discussion of his work makes a representation of his work and, therefore, opens all sorts of questions about referentiality and the relation of one set of signs to another. Beckett's plays are thoroughly concerned with the issue of how semiosis functions in all the sign systems of the stage and its relation to meaning and the actualization of existence, subjectivity, and the void. Very simply put, the plays continually pose a dilemma: If a universe is constructed of signs, is it possible to be anywhere but in signs?

Is it possible to discover meaning, a sense of existence or subjectivity without being mediated through language? Is it possible to render a purely empty void? Is it possible to be in silence without murmurs? And when a serious attempt is made to work out this problematic, the shape of space begins to change, distorting the usual illusory play world into graphic manifestations of semiotic functioning.

Beckett's hard look at semiosis is part of what Fredric Jameson and others term the "crisis of representation" (*Postmodernism,* p. viii), a postmodernist phase of linguistic and semiotic theory that actually began early in the twentieth century with the end of the classical economy of the sign as the articulation of function and structure, the coherence of referent and sign (Baudrillard, *Selected Writings,* p. 125). Saussure's notion of the autonomy and arbitrariness of language radically altered the representational equation of language with the referent, shifting the emphasis to a relational network of difference among signs. But, as Allen Thiher points out, the most radical attack on the classical sign has come since midcentury from Jacques Derrida (*Words in Reflection,* p. 92), who problematized the availability of meaning itself within the sign by deconstructing the privilege of content over form, the intelligible over the sensible (*Writing and Difference,* p. 281).

The early history of semiotic theory, then, coincides with the modernist abandonment of the enlightenment narrative of referential transparency in favor of a centering within language and literature on the grounds of meaning, depth, latent structure, and truth, all available within a vehicular and expressive form. This expressive model posits a transcendence within semiosis by reducing the exteriority of the sign and by privileging its content (Derrida, *Positions,* p. 22). Lately, however, the postmodernist concentration precisely on the exteriority of the sign suggests that the depth model of modernism has given way to the surface play of chains of signifiers, the transcendence of meaning and latent truth to the economy of *différance*. As Beckett recognizes by the end of *The Unnamable*, semiosis, having already abandoned classical referentiality, is now refusing its vehicular function and has become the thing itself.

It should not be surprising, then, that *Godot*, in appearing out of the interstices of the trilogy, is entangled in similar semiotic complexities. This dramatic piece is self-consciously generated out of various kinds of play—ludic, theatrical, linguistic. Didi and Gogo play at being the tree and at being Pozzo and Lucky; Pozzo and Lucky recite; Lucky and Didi dance; Didi and Gogo play word games. Ostensibly, the point of all this play is to fill up time while waiting for the arrival of Godot. But another way of looking at the play suggests that all this activity is an attempt to stand in for Godot, to fill the lack generated by his nonpresence, to fill the space produced by what is implied is the "real" purpose of the play—waiting for Godot.

If signs are indeed inhabited by Derrida's notion of the deferral of full presence and are generated out of this lack within them, then it should not seem absurd that the play is demonstrating both a lack (of Godot) and an excess of semiotic play. The play is giving a performance of the very functioning of semiosis *and* producing itself by trying to fill the lack always opening in its sign structures.

In *Godot*, we are given a look at the semiotic problematic represented as an endless waiting in a universe of signs for the only "meaningful" activity in the play; but since the arrival of this meaning is impossible in the economy of *différance*, the semiotic functions begin to spatialize into endless chains or loops. This sort of effect occurs because Beckett focuses on the exteriority of the sign rather than on a modernist depth model of semantic connotation. For instance, it is pointless to search for hidden meanings beneath Lucky's speech when the words not only permute themselves into more words but return to themselves in loops as if they were skidding across a surface:

> *tennis* football running cycling swimming flying floating riding gliding conating camogie skating *tennis* of all kinds dying flying sports of all sorts autumn summer winter winter *tennis* of all kinds.... (P. 29; my emphasis)

While words may produce more words, the general effect of *Godot* is one of flattened spatiality, for regularly the words do not produce a teleology of meaning but curl horizontally back to virtually the same place from whence they started:

> Didi: Say, I am happy.
> Gogo: I am happy.
> Didi: So am I.
> Gogo: So am I.
> Didi: We are happy.
> Gogo: We are happy.
>
> (P. 39)

Even the phrase—"waiting for Godot"—performs a semiotic loop, for its appearance always reminds us of an earlier reinvocation, not to mention the title of the play.

Nevertheless, it is Beckett's parallel concentration on the other languages of the stage that makes his step into theater more significant than simply incidental to the Unnamable's entanglement in words. Of course, theater is the perfect place to examine a semiotic problematic, because it offers an abundance of semiotic systems in an architectural site in which signs, including the linguistic, are already relatively tactile. As Steven Connor points out, a number of critics have seen Beckett's turn to the theater during the writing of *The Unnamable* as relief from its epistemological disintegrations (*Samuel Beckett,* p. 115); yet, what he found there was a hard exteriority traversing the languages of the stage and a space where sign systems may evolve into strange, postmodernist constructs. Beckett's swerve from the trilogy into *Godot* rather than providing relief displaces the conundrums he was uncovering in the prose into the spatiality of theater.

By scoring the stage properties, the gestures, and the actors' bodies and expressions with the semiotic problematic, *Godot* begins to open a three-dimensional space that can be itself realized as postmodernist. Like the spoken dialogue, a great number of the nonlinguistic sign functions, such as the continual trying on of the boots, are also spatializing themselves into endless chains or loops. Perhaps the best example is the hat trick, which demonstrates in the circular exchange of hats how stage properties as nonverbal signs enact the same loop of semiotic play. Because there are three hats and two heads, an infinite loop is very simply produced out of the impossible task of trying to keep a lack filled, and the episode can only end, as it does, in frustration rather than resolution.

In fact, Beckett's generation of postmodernist space in *Godot* is similar to Jameson's notion of space in the Westin Bonaventure Hotel in Los Angeles. Interestingly, Jameson's analysis of the Bonaventure reflects the literary origins of the concept of postmodernism in the architectural community, a concept that recognizes built structures as narrative, buildings as sign systems, and internal space as semioticized (Klotz, *History,* pp. 128–30). Of the Bonaventure, Jameson describes an inner space that does not correspond to the language of volume or perception, a suppression of depth that goes against the fundamental property of architecture (*Postmodernism,* p. 43).

One negotiates the flattened space of the lobby either by riding on elevators that have become "reflexive signs and emblems of movement" (p. 42) or by walking through a topology of color-coded signs (p. 43). When one visits the Bonaventure, it becomes apparent immediately that space has turned not only into a semiotic universe but has also inscribed a problematic similar to *Godot*'s: in the desire to find an exit, entrance, or the registration desk, one can wander the lobby for hours.

And, of course, Didi and Gogo wander the space of *Godot* for hours as well, carving out convoluted, semiotic loops as they (don't) go. While their (lack of) movement suggests the same type of nontotalizing space found in the Bonaventure, the most obvious clue that the stage languages are forming the play into a postmodernist space is the dog song Didi sings at the beginning of act 2. As this song suggests, the actions that follow in act 2 will evolve into a virtual re-presentation of act 1, so that the various signifying functions, in basically repeating themselves, make up the play's universe as a series of spatialized, semiotic loops or cycles. Because this universe is being depicted as a relentless spiraling through the signifying processes of verbal and nonverbal signs, it actually makes sense that Godot would never arrive and that various substitutes—Pozzo, Lucky, and the boy—would appear and reappear in this space instead.

Beckett creates a similar universe in *Endgame* by ending the play with virtually the same tableau that began it, Hamm in his wheelchair, face covered with an old, bloodstained handkerchief, implying that the play is about to repeat itself. As in *Godot*, Hamm and Clov have been playing various kinds of word, narrative, and theatrical games in an effort to stand in for the equivalent of Godot's nonarrival—Hamm's death. In fact, the play with the toy dog Hamm and Clov engage in throughout *Endgame* can be seen as a transformation of Didi's dog song into a nonverbal semiotic loop, one semiotic system into another. The toy dog is semiotically opaque, "not even a real dog," as Hamm complains (p. 69); it is always "unfinished," because it "lacks a leg," a sex, and a ribbon (pp. 39–40). Near the beginning of the play Clov retrieves it from the place to which Hamm threw it at the ending, so that like the dog song in *Godot* the toy dog suggests a nonfinishing cycle. In other words, both of these early plays can be seen as opening Beckett's work to a sort of flattened spatiality generated by the deliberate foregrounding of the exteriority rather than the content of the various stage sign systems, a move that entraps activity, behavior, speech, and props in the permutations of postmodernist space.

Such endlessly looping space in these plays seems to reject the sort of universe perceived and depicted by the modernists. The universe created by Virginia Woolf in *Mrs. Dalloway*, for instance, shows the experience of space as deeply subterranean, an architecture of volume. Woolf uses her "tunnelling" process to "dig out beautiful caves behind [her] characters" where something like "humanity, humor, depth" becomes available (p. 59). On the contrary, Didi and Gogo, Hamm and Clov as subjects play within a system more akin to the loop mode of computer processing, in which a command in the program tells the computer to start over, than to the Bergsonian or Jamesian model. Beckett's plays seem horizontal: they make no pretence to the availability of deep structure, whether of space, the universe, memory, or psychology. There are no Freudian slips here.

Curiously, though, it is just the sort of subjectivity that Beckett allows his figures that ends up differing from Jameson's notion of the guests who wander the Bonaventure, for Jameson argues that human subjectivity, still formulated as the high modernism of Woolf, does not have the perceptual ability to be at home in a postmodernist space (*Postmodernism,* pp. 38–39). And yet, Beckett's figures, no matter how hopelessly entangled in language, are always at home in their universe, because they are an inseparable aspect of the functioning of semiosis. For instance, in *Godot* the figures engage in various activities that give them, as Gogo says, "the impression we exist" (44). The existentialist ground of authentic selfhood or Camus's self-present certainty of existence is simply not available to Didi and Gogo. Rather, they are busy making signs to themselves in order to achieve an impression, like an image pressed into wax, of existence. The enmeshing of existence and subjectivity with the semiotic in *Godot* can be seen as an abandonment of the high modernist aesthetic of authenticity still operational in existentialism (*Postmodernism,* p. 12), which itself has already abandoned the illusion of an essentialist coherent and unified self. In Beckett's hands, Sartre's famous question—Does existence precede essence?—becomes the question, Does existence precede signs? If Didi and Gogo cannot be outside mediation, if language structures their subjective "reality," then every game they play simply deflects the experience of existence into any one of the semiotic loops circulating throughout the play.

Furthermore, because Didi and Gogo are not present to themselves—cannot get through the impression—they go on to counter the modernist idea that language, while autonomous from the outside world, still ought to be transparent to some state of the inner mind, to some form of Bergsonian immediate experience. Despite the fact that playwrights like Eugene O'Neill and Susan Glaspell have complicated and ambiguous approaches to the way language refers to reality and to the subject, they nevertheless attempt to "tunnel," in O'Neill to a Freudian latency *(Desire Under the Elms)* and in Glaspell to a Saussurian separation of thought from words *(The Verge)*. Glaspell's artistic heroine, Claire, for instance, continually attempts to break out of form, a project that suggests the ability to isolate a pure signified. While Glaspell recognizes the complexity of such an endeavor, Claire seems to achieve her transcendent goal at the play's ending. *The Verge* portrays the artist as a modernist imaginer capable of creating an autonomous work of art that can reach ultimate meaning without having to participate in a network of traces within form.

On the other hand, Didi and Gogo specifically deconstruct the binary opposition of form and content by being discovered as both the producers and the products of semiosis. Beckett undercuts the very ideas a modernist like Glaspell wants to legitimate in the place of a master narrative of referentiality—namely, that language can be submitted to thought, that meaning can arrive without form, and that a center or a centered being can exist. In Beckett's play, Godot never arrives, indicating that Didi's and Gogo's purpose in life, unlike Claire's, cannot be legitimated; more importantly, though, the transparency of meaning as a ground cannot be legitimated either. Jeffrey Nealon sees this lack of legitimation as proof that Didi and Gogo, because they believe nostalgically in the master narrative of Godot, have a modernist worldview in a postmodern universe ("Samuel Beckett," pp. 521, 526). Accepting this claim means that, once again, Didi and Gogo would have to be seen as absurd. Rather, I would propose that the postmodern invades Didi and Gogo as well, for their games, repetitions, and lack of accessibility to unmediated subjectivity and existence are part of the semiotic problematic functioning in the play's universe. Once we recognize that the entire universe of *Godot* and *Endgame*, including the figures in it, is dictated by the functioning of semiotic processing, that the lack of Godot is generated out of the same mediated status as the lack forming in the figures, Didi and Gogo, Hamm and Clov, no longer appear absurd or out of harmony. Their entanglements are consistent with postmodernists inhabiting a postmodernist space.

Many of Beckett's subsequent plays are on this postmodernist trajectory in which the semiotic problematic is scored across the figures as well as their universes, making it impossible for them to uncover an essentialist or existentialist moment of transcendent subjectivity. Plays such as *Embers, Cascando, Happy Days,* and *Krapp's Last Tape* depict figures who are inseparable from their semiotic functions, their storytelling, their writing, their prattling, their tapes. *Krapp's Last Tape* is an interesting example. At first glance this play may appear to present the sort of modernist character Abbott finds in Beckett's work, a character with integrity of being over time and whose discontinuities resolve in performance ("Late Modernism," pp. 85–87). But Beckett quickly entangles Krapp in semiotic structures similar to those of *Godot* and *Endgame*. Krapp's life is full of narratives, contained in the spools of tape he holds up, peers at, knocks on the floor, and croons to: "Spool five. Spool. Spooooool" (p. 56). Krapp experiences his memory, his subjectivity, his existence, and ultimately the play's universe as a fabric of semiotic loops, a "box of spools" represented physically as these props. In fact, the spools are not only tropes for the play's universe but actually provide its structure when Krapp plays, rewinds, and replays Spool Five, causing the verbal signs imprinted on the tape to return the play to the same passage over and over, circling back to virtually the same point, much as *Godot* circled back with its repetitions. Each time Krapp rewinds the spool (runs it backwards), the "spool" becomes "loops."

As the play goes on, Krapp becomes less interested in and less capable of sustaining the illusion of modernist expression. He becomes less tolerant of the Glaspellian conception of the artist, the visionary who believes in the availability of meaning and truth—himself at age thirty-nine. Rejecting the epiphany contained in the tape, Krapp tries to locate the memory of his beloved, but the memory is accessible to him only as an imprint on the tape. In other words, the play is depicting Krapp's memory not as transparent thought but as writing mediated through a semiotic processing machine. Krapp's mind has become both the composer and the composed, an act that scores subjectivity with inescapable language and generates Krapp as a Lacanian incoherent and mediated subject.

In a way that is similar to Didi's and Gogo's game playing, the tape playing, then, performs the operation of constructing Krapp's "impression" of existence and (him)self as semiotic, and opens the play to a formulation of his characterization as postmodernist rather than modernist. It seems that Abbott's analysis of Beckett's characters as modernist assumes that the physicality of theater and the phenomenology of performance are equivalent to character and that the dis-integration of the subject in the prose text is somehow solved in the presence of theater space ("Late Modernism," p. 86). I would posit that Krapp is always discontinuous in performance, precisely because he undergoes a dis-integration of subjectivity across time and space, appearing not simply as the onstage Krapp but also as the younger taped voice and its reference to an even younger Krapp. Furthermore, keeping in mind Beckett's stage direction, "A late evening in the future" (p. 55), an offstage Krapp seems to be occupying the locus of "real" time. Krapp is performed, then, not as one character, but as four subject positions dispersed across the four points of a "reel," a dance realized in time as remote past, past, present, and future.[2] (Beckett seems to have considered calling the play "Krapp's Last Reel" (Gontarski, *Intent of Undoing,* p. 58). In this way, Krapp participates in what Connor calls "a shadowy dance of repetitions" (*Samuel Beckett,* p. 76), a subjectivity constituted out of the traces he repeats as a reel over time. Yeats's query to the modernists in "Among School Children," "How can we know the dancer from the dance?" becomes in *Krapp's Last Tape,* How can we know an essential subject from the trace?

Discovering that a trace structure inhabits Krapp's seeming integrity of character means that the semiotic problematic has altered the theater, as Connor puts it, "from a place of being to a place of writing" (*Samuel Beckett,* p. 131). Rather than playing out his life as a character in the usual illusory play world, Krapp appears as a trace in a graphic manifestation of semiosis. But at the play's ending, does not Krapp finally hear in the hiss of blank tape the premonition of his own death, the silence of his grave, a space without words? After the play is over, cannot Krapp look forward to achieving a Beckettian void?

Not if one considers that Beckett's attempts to render a void, particularly in the presumably empty site of the grave, are always language-driven. In *Worstward Ho,* for instance, the void is not only generated out of language by being "said" into existence but also contains other voids: "say a grot in that void. A gulf" (p. 17). This void is permuting internally. Rather than consciousness and language coming into the world as a hole of being, language appears before being to say being, in the form of a void, into existence. Krapp may be listening to a void at the end of the play, but it is not the void of postsemiotic existence.

Neither is it Kawin's ineffable, a transcendent silence that lies outside language ("On Not Having," pp. 196–201). Nor is it L. A. C. Dobrez's Irreducible, a nothingness viewed as a sort of numinous presence, an existential being-nothing that is nevertheless there (*The Existential,* p. 63). Krapp is listening to the sort of nonempty grave-site Beckett will write into *Play* and *What Where,* a space in which semiosis, rather than being submitted to the transcendence of the void, fully inhabits the void. That is to say, Beckett's voids are not really voids at all: they are the result of critically playing out the logic of semiosis; they are a graphic manifestation of the lack in language being said, a lack that permutes the act of saying (the functioning of semiosis) into more saying.

As Jameson describes the Bonaventure, this sort of postmodernist space gives the feeling of an "emptiness" that is absolutely packed (*Postmodernism,* p. 43). And, indeed, the figures of *Play* and *What Where* are trapped in a site where the void as part of the process of semiosis takes up ever more space, convolutes itself into more semiotic material, grows to indefinite proportions if not arbitrarily "switched off." The silence of the grave will always elude these figures, because there is no escape to a nothingness outside semiosis; they must experience silence as murmurs, postlife "existence" as narratives and phrases that continually repeat, that loop back onto themselves like recorded messages and permute out to infinity.[3] In these plays, where there is no sense of perceptual, psychological, or epistemological depth, the semiotic problematic spatializes into spirals and loops that etch themselves in pain across the surface of the urns and, in the later television play, across the flattened screen of the TV set.

The void as represented in *Krapp's Last Tape*, *Play,* and *What Where*, then, does not invoke an entity like Sartre's hole of being, but rather like the prompter's hole of theater, Derrida's "hidden but indispensable center of representative structure—which ensures the movement of representation" (*Writing and Difference,* pp. 235–36). Ironically, focusing on the exteriority of semiosis ultimately means focusing on this hole, the site in which semiosis marks itself and refers to itself. It is here in this hole that the semiotic problematic becomes most graphically startling. A hole absolutely packed with continually expanding semiotic functions cannot allow the possibility of being anywhere but in semiosis. And such a hole constitutes the universe as a bounded infinity, a nontotalizing site that alters the very shape of space itself.

Beckett's plays, then, are constantly involved in the sort of semiotic problematic that has been recognized as a major feature of the postmodern era. Language systems and their role in representation have been critical issues for many writers, literary and theoretical, throughout the twentieth century, but at no time have they been more significant than during the mid-to-late decades. In Beckett's case, a postmodernist rise means pushing further the modernist abandonment of classical referentiality while going on to scrutinize, doubt, and abandon the modernist ground of vehicular transparency. In universes structured as semiotic there can be no escape to ultimate meaning or to a core of existence for Didi and Gogo, to the expressive imagination or subjectivity for Krapp, to the emptiness of a void for the figures of *Play* and *What Where*. What has been seen in these plays as an angst experienced in the face of an existential confrontation with the finality of death can now be seen as a dread that death might not be final, that death itself might be inhabited by semiotic functioning.

And, of course, theater as a site that is tactile and architectural is a prime venue for displaying the semiotic problematic, because it shows in all the stage languages an experience of space, whether of the grave or of a country road, as graphically manifesting the loops, spirals, and cycles of semiotic functioning, a project the prose works can only represent tropologically. In Beckett's theater, we do not look into the sort of volume expected of a modernist play, an illusory farmhouse or greenhouse. Rather, we look into a universe that is flattening horizontally like the permutations of a computer program in loop mode, a universe in which words, hats, dogs, and memories return to repeat themselves. In his plays, Beckett structures the universe as the sort of infinite spatiality that, like postmodernism in general, ends up defying totalization, delimitation, cataloguing. Certainly, as I approach the teleology of my own essay, I am mindful of the way Beckett's work has not only impacted on literary writers of the late twentieth century but has also reverberated onto critical writers and the assumptions of representation made in our projects. It seems that his work calls on us to suspect the "fit," the design, the vehicular transparency of our own discourse, and to recognize the semiotic as the unavoidable thing.

Notes

1. The debate between Lyotard and Habermas can be followed in Lyotard's *Postmodern Condition: A Report on Knowledge*, especially pp. 71–82, and Habermas's "Modernity versus Postmodernity."
2. I am grateful to my student, James Thiele, for pointing out that Krapp's back-and-forth movements throughout the play describe reel dances.
3. Renée Riese Hubert in "Beckett's *Play* Between Poetry and Performance" points out similarities between *Play* and Sartre's *No Exit* (p. 339). However, it seems to me that Beckett challenges Sartre's play by rejecting the fourth-wall style of representation. Whereas Sartre concentrates on depth of character and motive and reveals the afterlife as the consequence of action, Beckett strips down the figures to the output of a semiotic machinery, to the production of narrative as reflex.

Works Cited

Abbott, H. Porter. "Late Modernism: Samuel Beckett and the Art of the Oeuvre." In *Around the Absurd: Essays on Modern and Postmodern Drama,* edited by Enoch Brater and Ruby Cohn. Ann Arbor: University of Michigan Press, 1990.

Baudrillard, Jean. *Selected Writings.* Edited by Mark Poster. Stanford, Calif.: Stanford University Press, 1988.

Beckett, Samuel. *Endgame.* New York: Grove Press, 1958.

———. *Krapp's Last Tape. Play. What Where.* In *Collected Shorter Plays.* New York: Grove Press, 1984.

———. *The Unnamable.* New York: Grove Press, 1970.

———. *Waiting for Godot.* New York: Grove Press, 1954.

———. *Worstward Ho.* New York: Grove Press, 1983.

Connor, Steven. *Samuel Beckett: Repetition, Theory, Text.* Oxford: Basil Blackwell, 1988.

Derrida, Jacques. *Positions.* Translated by Alan Bass. Chicago: University of Chicago Press, 1981.

———. *Writing and Difference.* Translated by Alan Bass. Chicago: University of Chicago Press, 1978.

Dobrez, L. A. C. *The Existential and its Exits: Literary and Philosophical Perspectives on the Works of Beckett, Ionesco, Genet, and Pinter.* London: Athlone Press, 1986.

Glaspell, Susan. *The Verge.* In *Plays by Susan Glaspell.* Cambridge: Cambridge University Press, 1988.

Gontarski, S. E. *The Intent of Undoing in Samuel Beckett's Dramatic Texts.* Bloomington: Indiana University Press, 1985.

Habermas, Jurgen. "Modernity versus Postmodernity." *New German Critique* 22 (1981): 3–14.

Hassan, Ihab. "The Culture of Postmodernism." In *Modernism: Challenges and Perspectives,* edited by Monique Chefdor, Ricardo Quinones, and Albert Wachtel. Urbana and Chicago: University of Illinois Press, 1986.

Hubert, Renée Riese. "Beckett's *Play:* Between Poetry and Performance." *Modern Drama* 9 (1966): 339–46.

Jameson, Fredric. Foreword to *The Postmodern Condition: A Report on Knowledge.* Minneapolis: Univerisity of Minnesota Press, 1984.

———. *Postmodernism; or, The Cultural Logic of Late Capitalism.* Durham, N.C.: Duke University Press, 1991.

Kawin, Bruce. "On Not Having the Last Word: Beckett, Wittgenstein, and the Limits of Language." In *Ineffability: Naming the Unnamable from Dante to Beckett,* edited by Peter S. Hawkins and Anne Howland Schotter. New York: AMS Press, 1984.

Klotz, Heinrich. *The History of Postmodern Architecture.* Translated by Radka Donnell. Cambridge: MIT Press, 1988.

Locatelli, Carla. *Unwording the World: Samuel Beckett's Prose Works After the Nobel Prize.* Philadelphia: University of Pennsylvania Press, 1990.

Lyotard, Jean-François. *The Postmodern Condition: A Report on Knowledge.* Translated by Geoff Bennington and Brian Massumi. Minneapolis: University of Minnesota Press, 1984.

Nealon, Jeffrey. "Samuel Beckett and the Postmodern: Language Games, Play and *Waiting for Godot.*" *Modern Drama* 31 (1988): 520–28.

Thiher, Allen. *Words in Reflection: Modern Language Theory and Postmodern Fiction.* Chicago: University of Chicago Press, 1984.

Wittgenstein, Ludwig. *Philosophical Investigations.* 3d ed. Translated by G. E. M. Anscombe. New York: Macmillan, 1958.

Woolf, Virginia. *A Writer's Diary.* New York: Harcourt, 1954.

Zurbrugg, Nicholas. "Seven Types of Postmodernity: Several Types of Samuel Beckett." In *The World of Samuel Beckett,* edited by Joseph H. Smith. Baltimore: Johns Hopkins University Press, 1991.

Part 2
Textuality and Theatricality

"My Life Natural Order More or Less in the Present More or Less": Textual Immanence as the Textual Impossible in Beckett's Works

CARLA LOCATELLI

INTRODUCTION

THE purpose of this paper is to show that Beckett's evolving conception of a literary text has anticipated critical issues later developed by theorists who imply the idea of the "open work" as the very condition of late-modernist textuality. Therefore, the theoretical focus of this paper aims at demonstrating that in Beckett textual immanence has progressively been connoted as a textual impossible. This epistemological assessment will be made evident through a diachronic reading of his works.

Beckett critics agree as to the fact that the issue of language is central to his endeavor, but not everyone would agree that it is so in ways that are by no means formalistic but are instead referential. Specifically, I want to show that, since his early works, Beckett's conception of literature implies a rejection of the notion of literary works as self-contained artifacts and that even his less realistic novels prescribe an irreducible relation of reality and textuality, of ontology and figurality.

By examining a number of Beckettian texts, produced between the 1950s and the 1980s, I propose to highlight ways in which textual immanence, implied by some contemporary critics as the distinctive feature of late-modernist and postmodernist writing, is regarded by Beckett as a semiotic impossibility. Rather than focusing on one specific text, which could not be representative of an evolving epistemology, I will take into consideration a number of examples, showing how differently Beckett's epistemic implications surface in his texts, probing into issues of existential relevance, the nature of symbolic practices of material consequence, and cultural interlocutions.

If one looks at the Beckett corpus trying to define its semiotic avant-garde quality, an important revelation is bound to take place: what makes it cogently avant-garde is precisely the pervasive implication described above, i. e., that perfect self-reflection is a textual impossible.[1] In fact, not only do Beckett's works challenge the rhetorical prescription on which realism has traditionally rested—i.e., narrating according to an *ordo naturalis* ("my life's natural order more or less")—but they demand a constant recognition of the temporal discrepancy between narrating and narration, between the "act" of telling and the "tale" told (therefore always "in the present more or less").

As a matter of fact, Beckett makes it imperative to inscribe such a discrepancy in his works, so as to give it full visibility, especially in his "Second Trilogy." In other words, even if he challenges traditional realism through discursive self-reflection, his texts ultimately exceed the discursive limits. Self-reflection in Beckett is a stylistic feature of discourse but not a semiotics of textuality.

Because of this, the discrepancies intrinsic to narration should not be overlooked, since they are both components of and conditions for the existence of these literary texts. Beckett's works confer visibility to what I would define as the ineliminable "diachronic genesis" of textuality, a term that obviously grows out of my personal uneasiness with the current hermeneutical opposition that dichotomizes (more or less overtly) "structural" and "phenomenological" interpretive options. Nowadays, we find a sort of "cleavage" in critical theory, placing on one side the contributions based on a "textual-genetic" approach (structuralist hermeneutics) and on the other the contributions based on a "pragmatic" approach (mainly known as "reception theory" and "reader response criticism").[2]

However, textual meanings do not exist only as the outcome of reading, nor as mere linguistic structure; any structure needs be interpreted in order to become a stabilizing factor of textual constitution. The simple fact that, whenever we try to describe a Beckettian text we feel the need to use quotation marks, whatever the chosen approach may be, signals the shortcomings of contemporary theory in successfully defining texts in ways that can account for the complexity of their articulation. Long before current "ethics of reading," and while formalism, structuralism, and semiotics (more or less in turn) seemed to be the best methods to avoid interpretive aberrations, Beckett's texts confronted the reader with the disquieting evidence of their open-endedness, even in the presence of textual self-reflection. They never warranted a reading implying that literary works are mere artifacts;

rather, they showed that textuality, even in the case of self-reflective texts, is never coextensive with the letter of the text.

Whether the interpretive endeavor is inspired by late developments of Russian and American Formalism, by recent "variants" of French (post)structuralism, by Italian semiotics, or by any critical tendency emphasizing the specific "construction" of a text against an idealistic interpretive tradition, Beckett's works reveal a deep concern for the problematic limits of textuality, and they do so (without ever being idealistic) by connoting the implied reader as an undefinable and yet undeniable condition of textuality, and by emphasizing the diachrony of form. For example, by insisting on the use of "on" as a sign and mark of time passing, Beckett's later works move away from the residual transcendency of the "always already," still treasured by some deconstructionists, and emphasize the life of form, the life of meaning, the life of texts. Both the opening of *The Unnamable* (1958) and of *Worstward Ho* (1983) indicate the importance of the procedural present, against the danger of conceptualization:

> I, say I. Unbelieving. Questions, hypotheses, call them that. Keep going, going on, call that going, call that on. (P. 291)

> On. Say on. Be said on. Somehow on. Till nohow on. Said nohow on. (P. 7)

Beckett's works offer an extremely suggestive paradigm of semiotic features that call for new, updated definitions of verbal texts, definitions that take into account the complexity of these texts, and the originality of their semiotic features. I believe that the problems raised by Beckett's innovative structural combinations, and by the changes in epistemic horizons that are reflected in his texts, offer stimulating insights for the transformation of our traditional definitions of texts. Obviously, it is not within the scope of this essay to provide a new, broader definition of textuality, but I will highlight aspects of the Beckettian texts that call for such a redefinition, since old ones have proven too limited.

The most obvious points raised by Beckett's works regard: (1) the text's self-contextualization as the ultimate opening of literary texts; (2) the role of the interpretants in the constitution of reference; (3) the dialogism of textual implications. It seems to me that all of these points, which will be discussed in this essay, require a transformation of *formal* typologies of texts into *communicative* ones; they call for a dialogical hermeneutics, investigating the link, rather than the opposition, of structuralist approaches with reader-oriented hermeneutical options.

How is the "Open Work" Open?

Between the extremes of the idealistic absolutes and the absolutist skepticism that have characterized the critical scene in our century, very few voices could be heard. Beckett, however, moved through, and beyond, both that linguistic apotheosis and that mistrust, which became pervasive in the humanities in the late 1960s (Locatelli, *La disdetta*). He did so even before such an unraveling work got to be described as a "hermeneutics of suspicion" (Gadamer, Ricoeur). As I said, I believe we are indebted to Beckett for the visibility of what now (a posteriori) can be defined as another mythology of demystification: the belief that texts exist as closed textualities (i.e., as self-contained artifacts, of no referential value), and the subsequent implication of objective interpretation.

The ending of *Malone Dies* provides an obvious example of an impossible textual closure, since the literary artifact breaks down, underscoring the limits of the mimetic convention:

> he will not hit anyone, he will not hit anyone any more, he will not touch anyone any more, either with it or with it or with it or with or
>
> or with it or with his hammer or with his stick or with his fist or in though in dream I mean never he will never
>
> or with his pencil or with his stick or
>
> or light light I mean
> never there he will never
>
> never anything
>
> there
>
> any more.
>
> (P. 288)

In spite of a generalized silence on the *actual* limits of texts, particularly before the development of theories of reading, Beckett's works showed that an "unnamable" depth could be found in/through a text, even when such a text was thematically and ideologically questioning the human power to communicate and to express "humanity."[3] Maurice Blanchot was very sensitive to this Beckettian implication when he defined *The Unnamable* as a text "producing *an utterance without proper beginning or end*, yet greedy, exacting, a language that will never stop, for then would come the moment of the terrible discovery: *when the talking stops there is still talking.*" Significantly, Blanchot contends that *The Unnamable* is more than a book"; it is a text "condemned to exhausting the infinite" ("Nouvelle Revue Française," 116, 120; italics mine).

The opening page of *How It Is* confirms this cogent movement, typical of Beckett's subsequent texts: a communicative movement that demands an implied reader willing to appreciate "open-endedness" as a "pleasure of the co(n)text":[4]

> in me that were without when the panting stops scraps of an ancient voice in me not mine / my life last state last version ill-said ill-heard ill-recaptured ill-murmured. (P. 7)

The radical quality of Beckett's prose was, especially at the time, truly provocative and compelling: critical tenets, of whatever persuasion, had to be broadened, lest reading itself would be threatened. As a matter of fact, this quotation does not "safely" close the text on a narration theme, illustrating the end of narration and its "ills"; on the contrary, it discloses the depth of a basic hermeneutics of experience, where textual movements begin "without proper beginning" ("an ancient voice in me not mine"). Thus, the idea of text implied here regards no less than the actual condition of textuality, conceived as being determined by the human "making sense" of the world, but alluded to in terms that allow no optimistic conclusions about the personal power of human knowledge.

Indeed, in order to produce the awareness of our basic hermeneutics of experience, a text has to move beyond itself, without closing on thematization, nor on a circumscribing metanarrativity; it has to include its own reading as the repetition of the "original" making sense of experience, which is to say, it has to use reference without innocence, with the awareness of the role of interpretants. In other words, the interpretant of reference has to show itself, as actualized by reading (an important point to which I will return in a later section).

The fact that when narration stops a "voice in me not mine" is still coming should come as no surprise, so that we can ask with Blanchot: "What is this void that becomes the voice of the man disappearing into it?" ("Nouvelle Revue Française," p. 117). What is this disappearing that manifests the radical human need of making sense? With its revelatory indication of "an ancient voice in me not mine" this text is actually implying that textual "excess" is the very condition of textuality, which is to say, that texts exist as their own supplement.

The thematic level of this narrative states that there is a textual supplement, not only by pointing to a "voice in me not mine" but by indicating the inevitable (but mostly hidden) occurrence of this message as part of the text itself. This indication of the performative quality of the message is stated very clearly in *Worstward Ho:* "Never since first said never unsaid never worse said never not gnawing to be gone" (p. 42).

The Text Self-Co(n)textualization

Beckett's texts point to the actualization of literary communication, not by encircling the text into its formal conventionality but by connoting the self-reflective artifact as a means of actual occurrence. If we subscribe to his assertion that art is "rhetorical question less the rhetoric," we can infer that a text is the meaning we get when the text is gone, but also that it can go only and precisely because it was there, that is, always as the result of a dynamic movement that connotes it as "text-made-context."

I think that literary textuality should be conceived as *a mobile* by which a text (conceived as a conventional referential structure), at any one moment, creates its context, a context that is not "just there," outside the text, once and for all. I am suggesting that texts exist as contexts and self-contexts, and that it is precisely this intestine meaning that provides the condition for understanding them at different historical moments (the genetic moment not being radically different from any subsequent one). A text creates a context and does not only refer to a preexisting one: thus any textual meaning is the product of this co(n)textual reference.

For example, the problematics of subjectivity developed in *Company* (1980) could not have developed without co(n)textualizing the pronominal predication as reference, and thus implying a metalinguistic description as an ontological figuration:

> Use of the second person marks the voice. That of the third that cankerous other. Could he speak to and of whom the voice speaks there would be a first. But he cannot. He shall not. You cannot. You shall not. (P. 8)

In a text like this, where the text clearly becomes its own context, it subsumes its signs as referents, not because the text is established as a self-reflective artifact but because it mirrors the ontological role of figures. In other words, metalanguage *interprets* reference rather than merely describes its linguistic structure.

As well as implying a critique of naturalism, the concluding words of the passage quoted above ("my life last state last version ill-said ill-heard ill-recaptured ill-murmured") constitute a precise indication of the life of texts, since they point to textualization as the process by which a text exists by creating, as well as reflecting, its context: "(ill)-said > heard > recaptured > murmured." As (soon as) the text is formed, the preoccupation of connecting statement to reality requires the awareness of the temporal discrepancy intrinsic to any linguistic moment, an awareness reduplicated in the act of any subsequent reading. A text cannot survive as a fetish but only by "supplementing" itself. Here "saying" is represented as the condition for inevitable hearing, and hearing as the condition for recapturing, recapturing what can only be murmured (i.e., what is not restated as statement).

Many contemporary theorists overlook the fact that a text can develop by meaning itself to itself, i. e., by textualizing itself as a context, as its own context. It goes without saying that such a co(n)textualization of the text occurs at the same level of implication as any other extratextual context.

Furthermore, it is owing to the semiotic mobilization of the text that we see the discourse of writing become the script of reading; right at the moment of writing, writing becomes one with (its) reading, in a "single series of imaginative transactions" (*Disjecta,* p. 90), i. e., through a movement that we call "text."

At times, the presence of a *doubly* addressed implied reader (I), or even the seeming textual anaphora summing up reference to a character (II), reinforces the uncertainty of textual boundaries and shows their lack of fixity and their ongoing movement. See these two examples from *Molloy*:

> I. No not *one person* in a hundred knows how to be silent and listen, no, nor even to conceive what such a thing means. Yet only then can *you* detect, beyond the fatuous clamour, the silence of which the universe is made. (P. 121; italics mine)

> II. The fact was there were three, no, four Molloys. He that inhabited me, my caricature of same, Gaber's and the man of flesh and blood somewhere awaiting me. To these I would add Youdi's were it not for Garber's corpse fidelity to the letter of his messages. Bad reasoning. For could it seriously be supposed that Youdi had confided to Gaber all he knew, or thought he knew (all one to Youdi) about his protegé? Assuredly not. He had only revealed what he deemed of relevance for the prompt and proper execution of his orders. I will therefore add a fifth Molloy, that of Youdi. But would not this fifth Molloy necessarily coincide with the fourth, the real one as the saying is, him dogged by his shadow? (P. 115)

Fidelity to the letter is qualified here as a "corpse fidelity," as a dead endeavor, and yet the "real" is a matter of saying ("the real one as the saying is"), which is like saying that the letter has to be respected. Beckett is suggesting that unlimited semiosis is not a matter of free choice, but the result of the fact that, in Molloy's words: "All language was an excess of language" (116), and thus that any text can only exceed itself as soon as it forms.

The critics' delight in finding innumerable Beckettian "deconstructed" or "self-deconstructing" oppositions, such as "mimetic/diegetic," "performative/descriptive," and "dramatic/ narrative," seems to deal with metonymical aspects of the problem rather than with its global complexity. I suggest that the late Beckett moved beyond most of the dichotomies on which phallogocentrism articulates its mythologies, and produced a textuality whose differential economy we are only now beginning to perceive. I believe that Beckett's texts "work" and "are made" precisely by mobilizing the above-mentioned oppositions, and thus that they connote the text as a "live object," i.e., as an *event* produced by the actual surpassing of the text as *object*. An example from *Worstward Ho* illustrates the text's excess, so that saying becomes visible beyond representation: "The void. How try say? How try fail? No try no fail. *Say only"* (p. 17; italics mine).

I think that the numerous critical contributions that describe the Beckettian texts as "extreme forms" of textuality prevent critical consideration of the fact that it is precisely the *mobilization* of conceptual and discursive dichotomies that establishes the Beckettian condition of textuality. The description of the pervasiveness of Beckett's oxymoronic rhetoric does not explain the strategic role of oxymorons as the very discursive figure that negates textual immanence and its corollary of incontrovertible linear coherence. Here is a cogent example from *Worstward Ho:*

> First the body. No. First the place. No. First both. Now either. Now the other. Sick of either try the other. Sick of it back sick of the either. So on. somehow on. (P. 8)

Beckett manages to underscore what is normally unseen: i.e., the "saying of literature," made visible by way of his "unwording," which shows the actual utterance as the impossibility of uttering anything but statements. In this sense, we see that any text is there by disappearing, but Beckett makes clear that in order to disappear (i. e., in order to be a text), there has to be the utterance of a message. In *Worstward Ho* the ontological role of enunciation is thematized, and maximally valorized, against the awareness of expressive failure:

> Said is missaid. Whenever said said said missaid. From now said alone. No more from now now said and now missaid. From now said alone. Said for missaid. For be missaid. (P. 37)

Only in the light of the fact that "from now" what is "now said" is simultaneously "now missaid" can a *pure* saying emerge: "From now said alone." Even a short sentence, like "it comes the word we're talking of words" (*How It Is,* p. 29), entails the recognition of something more than mere intertextuality or metalanguage.

When we, as readers, recall that "in the beginning was the pun," we must take into account the intrinsic duplicity of the literary word, a words that *is* coming, along and within a "talking of words." The hermeneutic cycle ignited by these texts is such that, contrary to traditional expectations, the text shows that it exceeds itself, by returning to its own statements, and subverting them radically: What *now*? What beginning? "Where *now*? Who *now*? When *now*?" (*Molloy,* p. 291; italics mine).

Therefore, only a communicative function, rather than a formal one, can define textuality in these Beckettian texts, since it is imperative to acknowledge the text as open-ended. In fact, while it is literally (in)forming, such a text is also asking: what is this word that "stirring still" *comes,* even when it is decreed absent by the talking *of* it?

Once reading has become a questioning, rather than a finding of thematic and discursive answers, it shows itself as coinciding with, rather than simply reflecting, the human experience of life, our basic "reading" of the world. (Locatelli, *Unwording*). *The Unnamable* thematizes our making-sense habits, as follows:

> Deplorable mania, when something happens, to inquire what. [. . .] There are sounds here, from time to time, let that suffice. (P. 296)

Even the rather unchallenged belief in "primary scenes," itself a psychoanalytic variation on the origin theme and myth, becomes in Beckett much less relevant than the epistemic awareness of the event-quality of textuality as ongoing communication. The epitaph of the protagonist in *First Love* well indicates the life of texts, in the present more or less:

> Hereunder lies the above who up below
> So hourly died that he lived on till now. (*Collected Shorter Prose,* p. 2)

By exceeding the self-reflective quality of the most sophisticated modern artifacts, Beckett's texts create the awareness of their self-reflexive (i.e., critical, not only self-reflective), procedural occurrence.

Therefore, a mere formal typology, on which the notion of text has rested traditionally, proves descriptively insufficient, but seems to warrant the adoption of a communicative one, as suggested by some contemporary linguists (Labov, Conte, Widdowson, Coulthard). The acceptance of a communicative principle, which does not imply immediacy nor eliminates the acknowledgment of structural delimitations, constitutes precisely the basis for this interpretation of Beckettian textuality. I believe that this approach should be extended also to other modern texts, but since there is no space here for the legitimation of such an extension, I will remain focused strictly on Beckett's works.

THE MOBILE INTERPRETANTS OF REFERENCE AGAINST TRADITIONAL REALISM

The rejection of a formalist ideology of textual immanence sustained Beckett's aesthetic quest: he pushed the limits of reference beyond description and denotation, conferring visibility to the actual utterance of texts, i.e., making the utterance part of textual reference. The opening of *Old Earth* (1974), like many other Beckettian passages (and the famous ending of *Molloy*) compels the reader to register the procedural quality of reference, due to an ongoing utterance:

> Old earth, no more lies, I've seen you, it was me, with my other's ravening eyes, too late. You'll be on me, it will be you, it will be me, it will be us, it was never us. (*Collected Shorter Prose,* p. 201)

In this sense, the mere denotative level fails "as no other dare fail," but in so doing, all Beckettian texts reveal their intrinsic communicative tension. In other words, description does not quite coincide with a descriptive message, and denotation is not exhausted by dictionary information; reference is always exceeded by its intrinsic communicative function, as the literality of the text is exceeded by its performance as text. Narration is essentially dramatic, because the meaning of the tale entails the awareness of its telling. The already mentioned concluding paragraph of *Molloy* is significant in this respect:

> Then I went back into the house and *wrote*, It is midnight, The rain is beating on the windows. It was not midnight. It was not raining. (P. 176; italics mine)

The semantic excess of Beckett's referents derives from the fact that they show that the message that contains them is an utterance. Things could not be otherwise, because the representational act and linguistic act are always inextricably connected. What changes is the referential determination produced by the interpretants, which are not totally and immutably inscribed in the letter of the text. That is why, as *The Unnamable* suggests: "Somewhere in this churn of words at last, I would still have to reconstitute the right lesson" (p. 311).

The perception of diachronic ineliminability as the constituent of the text is not simply a conceptual "message" in Beckett (since no concepts are ever predicated there, and "no symbols are intended," as Beckett himself pointed out), but the passing of time is an *ongoing* motive that, on one hand, radically modifies the traditional idea of denotation, and on the other, can shed light on the restless, ever changing, and powerful innovations that have characterized each one of the Beckettian works in time.

The denotation of life as "natural order more or less in the present more or less" indicates the direction of a radical transformation of denotation, especially in Beckett's later works, where he systematically inscribed temporality within reference, thus making denotation itself an interpretive endeavor for the reader (Locatelli, *Unwording,* pp. 180–224).

With Beckett, as with most avant-garde writers in our century, we are led to connote traditional realism as an obsolete mode of reference, cognitively insufficient, and yet, particularly with him, the reader has to admit that the relation to reality (reference) has not been abolished in literature, contrary to some vociferous but fundamentally inaccurate simplification.[5]

This is why Beckett can be fully entrusted with the authority of the "bard" of contemporary Western world; his creative "failure" allows the appropriation of a voice for subjects who have seen themselves spoken by language, and yet have learned to appropriate subject positions through actual linguistic performance, however ill-articulated representations may be. For example, if we look at the very opening of *Company*, where subject positioning is articulated, we must acknowledge both the implication of referential unverifiability and the ontology of reference, an implication usually assumed to be dichotomous in current theoretical discourse:

> A voice comes to one in the dark. Imagine. [. . .] Only a small part of what is said can be verified. As for example when he hears, You are on your back in the dark. Then he must acknowledge the truth of what is said. But by far the greater part of what is said cannot be verified. (*Company,* p. 7)

Ultimately, a text like this exposes the fact that contemporary theory lacks ways of predicating or implying that reception is already inscribed in the structural, "genetic" moment. In other words, the "voice" and the act of imagining ("Imagine") constitute the text *together*. Thus reference depends on the actualization of its interpretants.

In *Ill Seen Ill Said,* the narrator talks of "a place divided by her use of it alone" (pp. 21–22), thus eroding not only the reader's naïve assumption about objective versus subjective space but the very possibility of traditionally describing space as something given once and for all. Earlier in that passage, Beckett talks of a confusion of "Things and imaginings," naming for the reader the uneasiness of being confronted with an *unlikely* world model. Yet, as soon as this mirroring produces the assessment of confusion, the picture changes *again*:

> Already all *confusion*. Things and imaginings. As of always. *Confusion amounting to nothing*. Despite precautions. (P. 20; italics mine)

Pure negations and perfect dichotomies are made impraticable because humans are not "unalloyed" (p. 20). As early as 1932, while working on *Dream of Fair to Middling Women,* Beckett had warned us against the danger of purifying reductions: "The notion of an unqualified present—the mere 'I am'—is an ideal notion. That of an incoherent present—'I am this and that'—altogether abominable" (*Disjecta*, p. 48). It is worth noticing that self-predication in descriptive terms is qualified as a form of abominable incoherence; as a matter of fact, the "confusion" of (self)perceiver-perceived is already implied as irreducible.

Thus, ultimate realities can be imagined or conceptualized, but only from within a penultimate horizon, which should surface in conceptual representation, showing itself as the limit of representation, rather than being repressed in the name of textual coherence. Beckett clearly tells how wrong we are if we imagine the realization of a wish thus formulated: "If only all could be pure figment. Neither be nor been nor by any shift to be." In fact, as soon as the wish is expressed (whose wish?), modals and performatives remind us of the conflict of figure and concept that the wish has mapped out: "Gently gently. On. Careful" (*Ill Seen Ill Said*, 20).

The woman in *Ill Seen Ill Said* is "still without stopping. On her way without starting. Gone without going. Back without returning" (p. 19). However, the use of apotropaic discourse here serves the cause of *différance* rather than expresses the purity of perfection. In other words, here as elsewhere in Beckett, the text needs to erode itself so as to recall the figural ontology of its own making. Reference is deconstructed but not denied, necessarily not denied, in order to express the representational limits of human representation.

In *Worstward Ho* (1983) the question of what speaks in what is spoken is a referential rather than a metalinguistic question; actually, the text establishes the onto-referential context of its rhetorical questioning:

> Whose words? Ask in vain. Or not in vain if say no knowing. No saying. No words for him whose words. Him? One. No words for one whose words. One? It? No words for it whose words. Better worse so. (P. 19)

The awareness of expressive impotence underscores both the recognition and the acceptance of "language-in-use," as well as no illusion about the possibility of personal expression. The trajectory of meaning goes "from bad to worsen" (*Worstward Ho*, p. 23), i.e., away from transcendental concepts, and into the assumption of the human procedural penultimateness.

Beckett makes us aware of this textual economy because he "hampers" the realization of meaning, and by suspending reference, by witholding referential meanings (which are themselves the result of interpretation), connotes reading as a matter of interpretation rather than as a simple referential recognition. The paradox of a double negation in the following example maps out the space of interpreting reference: "And the sounds I do not yet know have not yet made themselves heard" (*Molloy*, p. 296). Even more explicitly, and again in *The Unnamable*, Beckett declares: "the topographical and anatomical information in particular is lost on me" (p. 412).

A hermeneutical code has to be found even to decode the semantics of reference, which cannot be grasped until the text has become its context of interpretation. We can say that Beckett deconstructs the very convention on which literature is based: i. e., the systematic dislocation of reference from actual utterances. By producing a symbolic order "in the present more or less" he connotes texts as acts of literature. In *Closed Space* (1975) the onto-performative value of saying is explicitly stated: "There is nothing but what is said" (*Collected Shorter Prose*, p. 199).

Already in the 1960s, and certainly in his subsequent works, he has surpassed the unchallenged complexity of his *Godot*, producing texts woven out of a lucid dismantling of conceptualization and a relentless refusal of the "empowering" idealization of experience, with the full assumption of the cogency of human weakness. Thus, the irreducible "illness" of mis-saying and mis-seeing, which, for thousands of years literature and philosophy had tried to exorcise, repress, or minimize, was brought back onto the scene of human predication, not as a mystification that would eventually be demystified but as the human condition, always marked by an ineliminable "ignorance imperative." In *Worstward Ho* the obligation to express is indeed devoid of expressive illusions:

> Know better now. Unknow better now. Know only no out of. No knowing how know only no out of. (P. 11)

> The void. How try say? How try fail? No try no fail. Say only. (P. 17)

Today the gnoseological value of Beckett's practice of impotence seems the most challenging epistemic promise one can find in a written verbal text. It implies a pressing need for a reformulation of the disciplinary boundary between philosophy and literature, without letting philosophers and literati acquiesce in a generalized mistrust.

The "poetics of indigence" and the "literature of the unword" theorized and practiced by Beckett are fascinating because they never compose a romantic iconography of renunciation, nor a rigid negation, nor a dialectical absolute.[6] Rather, the reader is called upon to hear in these texts the voice of a modern Gorgias, still challenging his own skepticism, with unprecedented, *dynamic* negations. Beckett's *via negativa* has proved effective by not letting itself be based on absolutes: it has been powerful because the impossibility of self-expression was proven (ironically) by the *assessed* impossibility of not saying, i.e., by the ineliminability of the "obligation to express."

A "Literature of the Unword" is more than an extreme exercise in oxymoronic juxtapositions; it is the declaration of the impossibility of not saying, produced, tested, and shown, by the most sophisticated exercise of resistance to saying. In other words, the "obligation to express" (which in Beckett's later works comes to coincide with the Husserlian "intentionality of thought"),[7] connotes the idealistic issue of "self-expression" as meaningless, while pointing to the duplicity of an unavoidable and inexpressive human condition, marked by the obligation to express ("Know only no out of. No knowing how know only no out of," *Worstward Ho*, p. 11). It is obvious that, with such presuppositions, the very notion of textuality is at stake, but it is interesting that textual literality has never managed to supplant the role of the speaker-reader, implied and addressed here by an impersonal imperative ("know"; "unknow").

Much more than an oxymoron, the Beckettian "obligation to express" constitutes a brilliant representation of the existential process, of the human groping with the *creation of meaning*, while the very same humans are caught in the unavoidable existential *condition of meaning* ("making sense"). Theorized in 1949, in Beckett's writings on painting, and now included in *Disjecta* (p. 139), the "obligation to express" is reformulated, in a very similar way, in *The Unnamable*:

> I have nothing to do, that is to say nothing in particular. I have to speak, whatever that means. Having nothing to say, no words but the words of others,

I have to speak. No one compels me to, there is no one, it's an accident, a fact. Nothing can ever exempt me from it, there is nothing, nothing to discover, nothing to recover, nothing that can lessen what remains to say, I have the ocean to drink, so there is an ocean then. (P. 314)

The Beckettian representation of our being in the only possible world (i.e., the one organized by human understanding), is never simplified by any reduction *ad unum,* such as the recourse to a transcendental Meaning as textual *Grund,* nor by some rhetorical reconciliation of conceptual or discursive opposites. Rather, this obligation constitutes the highly unreliable, yet unavoidable, "ground" from which any expression, any text, takes form.

In this respect, Beckett's work is neither nihilistic, nor minimalist: it is magisterially subtractive and rigorously "realistic," endowed with the same freedom of movement allowed by human mortality (a movement denied by the conceptual absolutes of "death" and "life"). His "exorbitant imagination" (as Bataille called it) is a way of thinking, literally "out of" metaphysical polarities, while tenaciously probing into the epistemic coordinates of Western civilization.

Moving along the untrodden paths of "lessness" and failure, Beckett has investigated language, time, and the subject in a way that has created an astounding nonbinary Symbolic, one in which the subject is moribund, unnamable, and logorrheic.[8] The iconism of the characters in *Worstward Ho* epitomizes human penultimateness:

In the dim void bit by bit an old man and a child. Any other would do as ill. [. . .] Any others would do as ill. Almost any. Almost as ill.

They fade. (Pp. 12–14)

Just like time, the subject is portrayed in Beckett's works as both penultimate and "interminable," knowing itself as irreversible but showing itself through repetition ("reiterate, that helps you on" (*Molloy*, p. 410).

Among the many available examples of a "myself as somewhere on a road," let us consider a passage from *The Unnamable*:

I invented it all, in the hope it would console me, help me to go on, allow me to think of myself as somewhere on a road, moving, between a beginning and an end, gaining ground, losing ground, getting lost, but somehow in the long run making headway. All lies. I have nothing to do, that is to say nothing in particular. I have to speak, whatever that means. (P. 314)

Within this Symbolic, language is always excessive, i.e., simultaneously too much and too little, at once systemic and impersonal, but "differential" as parole, and "to be uttered." In other words, language is shown as a quintessential human exercise, harboring the most perfect absence of human life as well as the human mourning of this absence (Moorjani). In fact, the visibility of this absence is produced precisely by the communicative function of texts, the only means through which the human absence from language can rigorously be spelled out, the only means that can keep us groping with lessening "traces": "Less. Less seen. Less seeing. Less seen and seeing when with words than when not" (*Worstward Ho*, p. 39)

The Dialogism of Textual Implications and Denotations

The strong intertextuality of the Beckettian texts is itself a condition for calling to our attention semiosis as a process in which the creation of meaning is the product of the dynamics of reference as interpretive performance. By conferring visibility to this "double" of meaning, Beckett also highlights the diachronic structure of his "stirring still" texts, i.e., of his self-contextualizing texts.

Furthermore, the specific inscription of the reader, that is, of the third component of the communicative model described by semiotics (Eco), in the text, points to the necessary and systematic dislocation of immediate reference in literature, literature being precisely the result of a convention (Pagnini) that decontextualizes speech acts and re-members them. It is worth noticing that this "semiotic "sliding," defined by Beckett as the "verbal oblique," is expressed thematically in his works by the virtually endless chain of an observer observing an observer, which is a constant feature of his works, and especially of *Ill Seen Ill Said*:

> To the imaginary stranger the dwelling appears deserted. Under constant watch it betrays no sign of life. The eye glued to one or the other window has nothing but black drapes for its pains. Motionless against the door he listens long. No sound. Knocks. No answer. Watches all night in vain for the least glimmer. Returns at last to his own and avows, No one. She shows herself only to her own. But she has no own. Yes she has one. And who has her. (Pp. 12–13)

The cogent movement of textual boundaries implied by Beckett's texts makes his prose truly dialogical and specularly similar to his dramatic works, where narration constitutes the subject "at play." We must remember that, strictly speaking, one cannot talk about the communicative intention of a text as if that presupposed an empirical subject. The text, however, produces tensions and is ridden with tensions, even if it cannot represent the outcome of the play of its communicative power.

Beckett's declared respect for genres has to be linked to his perception of the necessity of keeping traditional structures, in order to be able to mobilize them as the constituents of texts.[9] It is only within established conventional boundaries that he could meet the need for a broader coherence, capable of including a variety of interpretants for any given reference. *The Unnamable* invokes the presence of "walls" to protect oneself from the prison-house of language:

> nothing but this voice and the silence all round, no need of walls, yes we must have walls, good and thick, I need a prison. (P. 410)

Denotation is problematic in Beckett because predicates do not quite exhaust, nor coincide with, the problems they articulate, and yet they cannot be avoided, because their insufficiency is meant to be a component of the problem. Thus, Beckett's meanings are irreducibly dialogical, because texts push them beyond their specific semantic values, and even beyond the singularity of narrative, constative, and metanarrative functions.

We have to develop habits of reading and conceptions of texts that will no longer repress the fact that, just like Molloy, we know "How little one is at one with oneself, good God" (p. 113). We have to develop readings of difference that acknowledge the space and dynamics of difference. Beckett's practice of a thought of *différance* is the result of his diachronic wading through the main trends of Western culture: Christianity, existentialism, hermeneutics, metaphysics, and psychoanalysis. It has produced a *transversal* and *procedural* modality of identification that bypasses the canonical distinction of *substance* and *mode*, a distinction confirmed by the very idea of description in literature.[10]

Transversal rather than "posthumanist," dialogical but without the need to define the Other (or the Otherness of an "other," still confined to the role of an object), Beckett seems to have been primarily *en garde* rather than avant-garde. The unreliability of existence made him highly circumspect, and yet he devoted his extreme lucidity to the defense of our "Breath." We should not be satisfied with an understanding of Beckett's texts as mere artifacts, even if this requires conceiving new typologies of texts, no longer dependent on the separation of "phenomenological" and "linguistic" theories of interpretation. Such a separation is probably a current camouflaged form of the dichotomizing of a logocentric Symbolic Order.

Beckett's death, which he described as "Nohow naught. Nohow on" (*Worstward Ho,* p. 47), is on the unutterable side of writing, a writing that would logocenter it, and makes his Letter definitive ("Said nohow on."). However, we should not forget that it is a Letter inherently inscribed with the longing for the *Phonē*,[11] so that his texts, though a "gilded monument," still *come* to remind us that "avant-garde" is, after all, only a posthumous effect. And this, indeed, as we mourn his death, seems "enough indeed nearly enough when you come to think of it."

Notes

1. Although the definition of "text" is still subject to debate in current linguistic criticism, two main research trends ought to be taken into consideration: "Textlinguistik" and "Discourse Analysis." Because of the vastness of recent bibliography, it is impossible to be exhaustive, but I will list some seminal studies, respectively from the German and Anglo-American traditions, in the following bibliography. See in particular: Weinrich, Dressler, Ihwe, Breuer, Schmidt, De Beaugrande and Dressler, and van Dijk; and Harris, Lyons, and Sinclair and Coulthard.

2. It is impossible to discuss here, at length, the "genetic/pragmatic" methodological opposition; however, I will simply provide a list of names that should clarify my argument. Among the structuralist theoreticians we should recall the "forerunners" of the Tel Quel Group (Philippe Sollers and Jean-Pierre Faye, in particular), Julia Kristeva and Roland Barthes, and we could associate them with the "Yale Critics" and in particular to Paul de Man. As for the "pragmatic orientation" I should like to recall the "Konstanz School," well known for the development of *Rezeptionsästhetik,* and in particular the role played by Hans Robert Jauss and Wolfgang Iser, see also Suleiman and Crosman. Among the philosophers who developed a conception of meaning strongly related to the listener-speaker relationship, I recall the important (albeit diverse) contributions of Merleau-Ponty, Gadamer, Benjamin, and Grice.

3. The problem of Beckett's "humanism" has produced a lot of critical contributions; among the most recent, see Kennedy, Buning, Murphy, and Connor.

4. I will note in passing that Roland Barthes himself theorized the transition from a "genetic" (structural) conception of texts to a "phenomenological" one in his later works, particularly in "The Death of the Author," where he wrote: "the birth of the reader must be at the cost of the death of the Author" (p. 148); and in "From Work to Text" (1971), both included in *Image – Music – Text.*

5. It seems interesting to quote Nietzsche on this point: "Once we have devaluated these three categories i.e., aim, unity, and truth, the demonstration that they cannot be applied to the universe is no longer any reason for devaluating the universe" (*Will to Power,* p. 14).

6. Beckett uses the expression "Literature of the Unword" in a letter to Axel Kaun of 9 July 1937, in *Disjecta,* pp. 51–54.

7. Intentionality should not be interpreted as a psychological attitude towards the content of thought but rather as the cogency of thought itself. For further clarification see Husserl.

8. For a definition of the "Symbolic (Order)" and a rereading of Freud's "Fort! Da!" (in *Beyond the Pleasure Principle*), see Lacan, "Function and Field," pp. 30–113.

9. In a letter to Barney Rosset, his American publisher, Beckett wrote: "If we can't keep our genres more or less distinct, or extricate them from the confusion that has them where they are, we might as well go home and lie down." Quoted in Cohn, *Just Play,* p. 207.

10. For a critical discussion of traditional dualist ontology, see Whitbeck, "A Different Reality"; on the issue of "positioning the subject," see Spivak, "A Response," pp. 207–20.

11. The complex reference implied by this statement refers to J. Derrida's *Of Grammatology* and to his *Dissemination*.

Works Cited

Austin, John L. *How To Do Things With Words*. Cambridge: Harvard University Press, 1978.

Barthes, Roland. *Image – Music – Text*. Translated by S. Heath. New York: Hill and Wang, 1977.

Beckett, Samuel. *Collected Shorter Prose, 1945-1980*. London: John Calder, 1984.

———. *Company*. New York: Grove Press, 1980.

———. *Disjecta: Miscellaneous Writing and a Dramatic Fragment*. Edited by Ruby Cohn. London: John Calder, 1983.

———. *How It Is*. London: John Calder, 1964.

———. *Ill Seen Ill Said*. London: John Calder, 1982.

———. *Molloy – Malone Dies – The Unnamable*. New York: Grove Press, 1955, 1956, 1958.

———. *Worstward Ho*. London: John Calder, 1983.

Benjamin, Walter. *Illuminations*. 2 vols. New York: Schocken, 1968, 1969.

Blanchot, Maurice. "Nouvelle Revue Française" (1953). In *Samuel Beckett: The Critical Heritage,* edited by L. Graver and R. Federman. London: Henley; Boston: Routledge & Kegan Paul, 1979.

Breuer, D. *Einführung in die pragmatische Texttheorie*. München: Fink, 1973.

Buning, Marius. "Samuel Beckett's Negative Way: Intimations of the *Via Negativa* in his Late Plays." In *European Literature and Theology in the Twentieth Century,* edited by D. Jasper and C. Crowder. London: Macmillan, 1990.

Cohn, Ruby. *Just Play: Beckett's Theater*. Princeton: Princeton University Press, 1980.

Connor, Steven. *Samuel Beckett: Repetition, Theory, and Text*. London: B. Blackwell, 1988.

Conte, Maria Elisabeth. *La linguistica testuale*. Milano: Feltinelli, 1977.

Coulthard, Richard M. *An Introduction to Discourse Analysis*. London: Longman, 1977.

———. *Studies in Discourse Analysis*. London: Routledge & Kegan Paul, 1981.

De Beaugrande, R. A., and Wolfgang U. Dressler. *Einführung in die Textlinguistik*. Tübingen: Niemeyer, 1981.

de Man, Paul. *Allegories of Reading: Figural Language in Rousseau, Nietzsche, Rilke, and Proust*. New Haven: Yale University Press, 1979.

———. *Blindness and Insight: Essays in the Rhetoric of Contemporary Criticism*. New York: Oxford University Press, 1971.

———. *The Rhetoric of Romanticism*. New York: Columbia University Press, 1984.
Derrida, Jacques. *Dissemination*. Chicago: University of Chicago Press, 1981.
———. *Of Grammatology*. Baltimore: Johns Hopkins University Press, 1974,
Dressler, Wolfgang. *Einführung in die Textlinguistik*. Tübingen: Niemeyer, 1972.
Eco, Umberto. *The Role of the Reader*. Bloomington: Indiana University Press, 1979.
———. *A Theory of Semiotics*. Bloomington: Indiana University Press, 1975.
Faye, Jean Pierre. *Théorie du récit: introduction aux langages totalitaires*. Paris: Hermann, 1972.
Gadamer, Hans-Georg. "Hermeneutics of Suspicion." In *Hermeneutics: Question and Prospects,* edited by G. Shapiro and A. Sica, pp. 54–65. Amherst: University of Massachusetts Press, 1984.
———. *Philosophical Hermeneutics*. Berkeley: University of California Press, 1976.
———. *Truth and Method*. 2d rev. ed. New York: Crossroad, 1989.
Grice, Paul H. *Studies in the Way of Words*. Cambridge: Harvard University Press, 1989.
Harris, Zellig S. "Discourse Analysis." *Language* 28 (1952): 1–30.
Husserl, Edmund. *Logical Investigations*. London: Routledge & Kegan Paul, 1970.
Ihwe, Jens. *Linguistik in der Literaturwissenschaft*. München: Bayerischer Schulbuch Verlag, 1972.
Iser, Wolfgang. *The Act of Reading: A Theory of Aesthetic Response*. Baltimore: Johns Hopkins University Press, 1978.
———. *The Implied Reader: Patterns of Communication in Prose Fiction from Bunyan to Beckett*. Baltimore: Johns Hopkins University Press, 1974.
Jauss, Hans Robert. *Aesthetic Experience and Literary Hermeneutics*. Minneapolis: University of Minnesota Press, 1982.
———. *Toward an Aesthetic of Reception*. Minneapolis: University of Minnesota Press, 1982.
Kennedy, Andrew. *Samuel Beckett*. Cambridge: Cambridge University Press, 1989.
Kristeva, Julia. *Polylogue*. Paris: Seuil, 1977.
———. *Revolution in Poetic Language*. New York: Columbia University Press, 1984.
Labov, William. "The Study of Language in its Social Context." *Studium Generale* 23 (1970): 30–87.
Lacan, Jacques. "The Function and Field of Speech and Language in Psychoanalysis" (1953). In *Ecrits: A Selection*. New York: Norton, 1977.
Locatelli, Carla. *La disdetta della parola*. Bologna: Patron, 1984.
———. *Unwording the World: Samuel Beckett's Prose Works After the Nobel Prize*. Philadelphia: University of Pennsylvania Press, 1990.
Lyons, John, ed. *New Horizons in Linguistics*. Harmondsworth: Penguin, 1970.
Merleau-Ponty, Maurice. *Consciousness and the Acquisition of Language*. Evanston, Ill.: Northwestern University Press, 1973.
———. *Perception, Structure, Language*. Atlantic Highlands, N.J.: Humanities Press, 1981.
Moorjani, Angela. *The Aesthetics of Loss and Lessness*. New York: St. Martin's Press, 1992.
Murphy, Peter. *Reconstructing Beckett*. Toronto: University of Toronto Press, 1990.
Nietzsche, Friedrich. *The Will to Power*. New York: Random House, 1968.

Pagnini, Marcello. *Pragmatics of Literature*. Bloomington: Indiana University Press, 1987.

Ricoeur, Paul. *The Conflict of Interpretations: Essays on Hermeneutics*. Edited by D. Ihde. Evanston, Ill.: Northwestern University Press, 1974.

Schmidt, Siegfried J. *Texttheorie: Probleme einer Linguisik der Sprachlichen Kommunikation*. München: Fink, 1973.

Searle, John. *Speech Acts: An Essay in the Philosophy of Language*. London: Cambridge University Press, 1969.

Sinclair, John M., and Richard M. Coulthard. *Towards an Analysis of Discourse*. Oxford: Oxford University Press, 1975.

Sollers, Philippe. *Writing and the Experience of Limits*. New York: Columbia University Press, 1983.

Spivak, Gayatri. "A Response." In *The Difference Within: Feminism and Critical Theory*. Amsterdam and Philadelphia: John Benjamins, 1989.

Suleiman, Susan, and Inge Crosman, eds. *The Reader in the Text*. Princeton: Princeton University Press, 1980.

van Dijk, Teun. *Explorations in the Semantics and Pragmatics of Discourse*. London: Longman, 1977.

Weinrich, Harold. *Tempus*. Stuttgart: Kohlammer, 1964.

Whitbeck, Caroline. "A Different Reality: Feminist Ontology." In *Women, Knowledge, and Reality,* edited by A. Garry and M. Pearsall. Boston: Unwin Hyman, 1989.

Widdowson, H. G. *Teaching Language as Communication*. Oxford: Oxford University Press, 1978.

Rehearsals for the End of Time: Indeterminacy and Performance in Beckett

GERRY McCARTHY

ALAN Schneider raised the problem in 1977. If he did not place the heads in the urns in *Play* and if there was no movement for him to direct, then how was he to reply to the question: "Alan, what do you *do*?"[1] Given Beckett's scrupulous instructions for performance, what remains for creative direction? If the theatrical forms imagined by Beckett are so clear and their notation is so exact as to refuse the interventions of the director, then what remains of the directorial function? Is it not the case that Beckett's work implicitly questions that function, at least insofar as we conceive the director as being responsible for the *mise-en-scène*? And what of the actor? Where is the creative independence of a performer who must play a role circumscribed by Beckett's painful restrictions and requirements? And if both director and actor appear reduced and restricted by the careful strategies of Beckett's text, what of the collaboration and interaction of the two? What, frankly, is the purpose of rehearsal? The rote learning and execution of the dramatist's instructions?

While elsewhere in this book Robert Scanlan argues impressively for fidelity to the dramatist's theater forms, there is a widespread suspicion of a seeming purism creeping into the discussion of Beckett performance, with those who defend the integrity of the texts being represented as intellectual Luddites unable to release Beckett to float upon the creative tides of contemporary theater practice.[2] The problem goes much deeper, however, to the conception of drama that now prevails and the way in which preconceptions are challenged by Beckett's oeuvre. The problem is all the more arresting, since it is one that calls into question the practice of theater and the authority of the director on the contemporary stage. Fidelity to the text is not, however, a question of who knows best, Beckett or his director, but of how they know what they know. Beckett knew his plays as their creator, not as their critic, but additionally he understood drama as do few directors, and that understanding was grafted into the very body of his work. The dramatist was firmly anchored in the medium of performance, while the director frequently inhabits a world of theatrical impressions. The directorial function is seen as largely the presentation of a particular, and originally private, understanding of the work, with its location in spaces conceived in the minds of director and designer. The locus of such a performance is charged with the task of signing meanings to an audience that, deprived of the interpretations of the director, might fail to discern the relevance of the play to its own experiences. The director's authority and professional knowledge is a reflection of characters and their transparently clear lives, seen in his visualization and conveyed discursively to the actor. The idea of directly informed acting emanating from the exploration of the text and free of the director's explications has scant place in the structure and hierarchy of the contemporary theater.

This problem becomes clearer if one examines such a process of "interpretation" in Beckett in the context of rehearsal. This is the period during which the imagination of the director, whether an independent "vision" or an attentive response to the text, is turned into a theatrical reality. It is also, less commented, the period wherein the actor must discover the creative and professional means of performance. Here the essential integration of actor and role is forged: the sense of wholeness that is rightly called style.

Relatively little critical attention is accorded to rehearsal, and one must seek an explanation in the view that is implicitly taken of the process.[3] Whereas stagings of plays command increasing respect in critical and academic circles, it appears that rehearsal is seen as the necessary workshop in which a product is fashioned, and it is the product, as a predetermined object, that is worthy of attention. Small wonder, then, that the work of Beckett is so rebarbative; for on every side there is the conviction that the object has been predetermined not by director and cast but by a supreme and possibly unwarranted exigency in the playwright. But is this consistent with the actual processes of rehearsal and performance? And does the idea of such an "objectivity" in the construction of a *mise-en-scène* accord with the fundamentals of performance and its preparation in rehearsal? Does or can the preparation of a performance ever predetermine the actor's objectivity? And is it the case that the forms of playing can ever submit in anything other than the most external and schematic fashion to the objective interpretation of the director? One cannot help recalling Beckett's celebrated concern with the "fundamental sounds" of performance and his dismissal of the "overtones" of interpretation, and reflect on the functional relationship between the two.[4] If we are concerned with those fundamentals, rehearsal must claim a measure of our attention, for that is where they are first tackled, and it is in rehearsal that the status of interpretations appears so questionable. As ever with Beckett, practical problems call into question our lazy assumptions that we understand the processes of performance so well as to eliminate them from our critical assessment of the playwright and his work.

Rehearsal in Beckett suggests a paradox. So precise are the forms he demands, they seem to require discipline rather than sensitivity, and yet, to the critic, few actors have appeared as sensitive, even inspirational, as have Beckett's celebrated performers. (I resist, for the moment, the term "interpreters.") It is as if Diderot's paradox of the cold actor inspiring passion were revisited. Yet, as with *Le Paradoxe sur le comédien,* the contradiction may be resolved by a reexamination of experience and learning in rehearsal and performance. The question is crucial for two principal reasons. Firstly, the forms of the plays are intimately related to the indeterminate states of knowledge that characterize rehearsal, and secondly, that indeterminacy is the key to the experience of Beckett for both actor and spectator. We need then to understand rehearsal as a process whereby forms of playing are experienced before the means of their playing can be developed. For the actor this is a hard and painful process, where the sense of disintegration of the elements of performance has to be accepted as they are brought instinctively together and they achieve an organic wholeness. The internal sense that is born of the disparate elements of any performance is the ultimate goal of rehearsal. This "meaning" is manifest in performance style, and its status is reflected in the need that is felt in critical circles to examine the experience of the actor. In this respect critical feeling leads critical understanding.

It is notable that distinguished Beckett actors cannot reply to questions about the "meaning" of the texts. Because the performance is impressive, the questioner assumes that it embodies determinate reasons for the forms of acting. If you do such and such, you must "know" that it is effective and what calculations conduce to the effect. Not so. The performer knows how to act, but at no point in rehearsal was there a clear formulation of a "meaning" that was sought, nor of the appropriate means for its delivery. The critic is then rightly bemused: if there is meaning, it must be meant. Jonathan Kalb states the question when discussing Billie Whitelaw and *Rockaby:*

How could anyone, you ask yourself, create those subtleties of meaning in the taped text and the "Mores" without understanding clearly what is at stake in each of the choices?[5]

The problem lies in the understanding of "understanding." One would never say the actress fails to understand what is at stake, nor that she lacks understanding. Her performance demonstrates that *somehow* she understands the significance of what she does. The problem is not that she fails to understand, but that she cannot "tell" her meaning. The critical error lies in the assumption that the meanings of drama are ever available in discursive terms. Undoubtedly it is the business of the critic to attempt an extrapolation of the dramatic structure from the medium of action to that of discursive analysis. It is not the business of the actor to assume a discursive method in the creation of the role. To ask whether Whitelaw understands is to raise a question of the epistemology of performance. What is it that the actress knows but does not tell? How did this apparent understanding come about? The answer is that she rehearsed the play and has come to know it.

It is a commonplace in theater production that the text must be experienced before conclusions are reached, whatever the preparation and decision-making before rehearsal. There is also a good practical sense that the performance does not truncate key experiences of rehearsal, and, for the theater professional, the dividing line between preparation (rehearsal) and playing (performance) is less distinct than the rituals of the opening might suggest. Despite the impact of the audience on the prepared performance, and the realizations that that impact produces in the actor, every play needs at least a period of performance before it "beds down."[6] However complete the preparation, the acting has a life of its own.

Thus it is also the case that in rehearsal the actor may find it difficult to assimilate the guidance and interpretations of the director, as they jointly work towards the objective understanding of the performance that is to come. The actor may be convinced, say, that something is "not working." Two knowledges collide: a "knowing that" the fiction conveyed should have a particular impact; and the "knowledge how" the performance is "wrong." The response to this impasse is to "try it" another way, very often using adaptive strategies to give the actors a better feel of the role or insight into the dramatic situation. The new approach may hit upon something that supplies internal coherence in the actor, and this will confirm its validity. This restores a working hypothesis that the putative definitive account is knowable *outside* the performance: indeed *could be known*, given insight, *in advance*.

The struggles of the rehearsal room confirm the importance of the actor's "knowledge how." If the actor is unhappy, there wells up a deep certainty in him that this is not "how" to do the lines, however irritating to the superior view of the director, which is challenged on the basis of an inchoate sense of something being amiss. The difficulty is compounded by the inadequate language in which the state of mind of the actor can be represented. The chief means of conveying his unease is to fictionalize the problem and join the director's field of knowledge. Thus the actor explains what it is "right" for his character to do and not to do, and is frequently forced out of the embodiment of the role into an objective discussion of it. He offers the "knowledge that" the character "would do" something other, but never thinks to explain the disintegration *he* feels in adopting certain forms in rehearsal. So the rehearsal pursues the grail of the private knowledge of the director, which is to be generalized and shared through a "telling" in rehearsal of the fictions he imagines. This primacy of the directorial fiction is, I believe, the source of what Beckett has termed "the omnipresent massacre and abuse of directorial function."[7]

Fundamentally, rehearsal is never the exploration of the director's "known" interpretations. It is discovery: a progressive learning of an indeterminate task,[8] whereby the physical forms are established within which the play will be experienced by the player. *This* experience remains "knowledge how" and is sensible: physically felt and coherent. There is no requirement that the significance be "told," but it is evident in rehearsal that it is "sensed."

Looked at one way, Beckett's texts are tyrannical and preoccupied with detail. Alternatively, their truly permissive character can be seen in relation to the practices and experiences of rehearsal, where they can be seen to chart the playing with uncommon fastidiousness. Beckett requires long hours building up a structure of physical moves and precise efforts that in another dramatist would arise implicitly. The example of *Krapp's Last Tape* can stand here for the oeuvre. In another play stage directions might be quite general ("He takes a reel of tape from a drawer"). Here they are detailed and involve the actor in an initial concentration on *physical forms*. These moves are initially hard to learn because of their repetitive nature and the very detail of the elements that are assembled.[9] The last thing that arises is a discussion of the fiction.

Beckett characteristically exposes aspects of performance that lie buried in conventional rehearsal practice but are never unknown to the actor. Here the preoccupation with detail ensures an uncommon awareness of the physical process of performance. The progressive accumulation of elements entails a growing integration of physical forms with the objective sense of the actor. The process of selection and rejection at the opening of the play generates an attention in the actor that is no longer to the forms themselves and the contingent properties—keys, bananas, tape, etc.—but to generally experienced purposes that inhere in this physical life.

As a process of learning, this is familiar. The acquisition of a wide range of knowledge in life is grounded in the repetition of the actions of a master. Few would argue that there is an epistemological content in such practice. We speak of "knowing how" to sew, or somersault, or, indeed, peel a banana. These are intelligent, integrated, and goal-oriented. Similarly an Aristotelian account of drama stresses the "imitation" of actions wherein "knowledge" arises from "doing." This embodied knowledge is precious to every actor, but little stressed in contemporary theater practice. It is of course fundamental to choreography and mime, where the performance is directly inscribed on the dancer or mime.[10] A useful account of such embodied knowledge is provided by Michael Polanyi, who cites apprentice-learning as an example of the acquisition of performances that *then* lead to the knowledge of the master's mind.

> consider the way in which one man comes to understand the skilful performance of another man. He must try to combine mentally the movements which the performer combines practically, and he must combine them in a pattern similar to the performer's pattern of movements. Two kinds of indwelling meet here. [. . .] By such exploratory indwelling the pupil gets the feel of a master's skill and may learn to rival him.[11]

An extension of this idea allows the use of coded instructions for performances, where the skillful moves are set out in the record of a game:

> Nor is this structural kinship between subject and object, and the indwelling of one in the other, present only in the study of bodily performance. Chess players enter into a master's spirit by rehearsing the games he played, to discover what he had in mind.[12]

Similarly, the actor must rehearse the moves of Beckett's games before he can know what the playwright has in mind. In practical and theoretical terms this preempts the director's right to specify goals that can be "told" to the actor. The ends of rehearsal arise only as a function of the processes of rehearsal. The contemplation of the work *as performance* yields the tacit knowledge of what the writer had in mind. This is perhaps why Billie Whitelaw wept when she first read *Not I* and could not tell why.

Thus simple repetition and practice of the "moves of the game" in Beckett become important in the criticism of the plays, and the phenomenon of rehearsal more suggestive. In *Krapp's Last Tape* the physical forms impose themselves on the actor not only because of their extent but because they are subject to a process of redefinition (repetition or revision, which are the positive and negative replays of an action, which can never of course be replicated): from the selection of pocket contents (envelope extracted, then repocketed, etc.) through the rewinding of tape extracts, to savoring the word "spool." So difficult is this procedure in rehearsal that it is all too easy to overlook its power to circumvent some of the haphazard processes often involved in the preparation of the role. The actor has to adopt and readopt physical forms that are then reformulated at another moment.[13] McMillan and Fehsenfeld's careful description of the variations Beckett entertained in the different versions of the opening "prologue" make formidable reading enough. To an actor charged with the absorption of these moves, their explication in terms of Manichaean principles is likely to be of little practical help.[14] The moves are clearly determined, but their value to the actor remains obscure. This is expected in rehearsal, but Beckett extends the experience of indeterminacy into performance. These moves acquire a sense for the actor as they are performed, and that sense is inherent in their progressive capacity to define themselves once embodied. The use of a series of *activities*, elevated to the status of mime through the careful concentration of physical attitudes, leaves the body firmly determined in time and space while the *action* played is freely sensed within those forms. They are written on the body, but their meaning remains indeterminate, arising only at the point of playing.[15] Beckett's practice highlights the chief characteristic of the dramatic text: it is a text for learning, and the condition of knowing the mind of the master.

Polanyi notes two terms in the possession of tacit knowledge: function and phenomenon. The interplay of these allows the emergence of semantic and ontological elements: the sense of meaning and experiential value. A functional relationship exists between the forms in which skills and understanding are embedded and the objectives to which the performer attends. The phenomenal aspect expresses the feedback effect, whereby the practice of skillful performance alters sensibly the phenomena themselves and the actor's perception of the active process. This phenomenal shift is manifest as the actor learns, in a set of moves that are initially ill-coordinated and relatively ill-organized, but gradually becomes aware that the existence of the routines has bred a new sense of their nature and an enhanced condition of "indwelling" within those forms. This "feedback" effect is explained in Polanyi's analysis as a coupling of the functional and the phenomenal in which their coexistence creates the sense of the performance: the tension that is describable as meaning or significance.

In the case of Beckett's *Not I* the functional aspect of performance is very closely defined in the execution of the text as physical form. The awareness of verbalization is dangerously emphasized:

> and not alone the lips ... the cheeks ... the jaws ... the whole face ... all those— ... what? ... the tongue? ... yes ... the tongue in the mouth ... all those contortions without which ... no speech possible ... [16]

I describe this as dangerous, since in intelligent or skillful practices we attend *to* the achievement of a purpose *from* the execution of the elementary efforts of which we are aware.[17] If we overload the simple awareness of what we do, we retreat from attention to another thing and substitute attention to our detailed elementary performances. These disintegrate as they lose their tacit status and become explicit entities deprived of an integrating context. The actor would describe this experience as a loss of meaning. The efforts of speech are made and can continue, but the attention wanders and the actor is overcome with a sense of absurdity and collapses.

The threat that is contained in *Not I* is closely linked to its performance being indeterminate: a species of rehearsal for a final "performance" that will never come. Beckett keeps the actor perilously close to the conditions in which tacit knowledge is acquired from the repetition of actions. As these are integrated as a "known" entity, there arises a sense of meaning lying outside the actor as a function of her objectivity. The composition of the play then replays these processes much as one does in the practice of rehearsal by a questioning of meanings and objectives that are offered. As the search for the conclusion of a narrative proceeds, the various concluding performances are rejected. It is as though the hypothesis of the determined account, rehearsed and fixed for performance, is rejected:

> perhaps something she had to ... had to ... tell ... could that be it? ... something she had to ... tell [...] what? ... not that? ... nothing to do with that? ... nothing she could tell? all right ... nothing she could tell ... try something else [...] nothing she could think? ... all right ... nothing she could tell ... nothing she could think ... nothing she— ... what? ... who? ... no! ... she![18]

The actor's objectivity is not an interpretation. Beckett creates an action that contains its meanings embedded in performance, dependent on the tacit understandings of the performer, who night after night experiences them afresh. Their power lies in the impossibility of escaping the ontological loop whereby the greater the sense of completion the more the actor is thrown back and forced to discard explicit understandings in favor of the fundamental experience of indwelling in the action as a species of known but untellable knowledge. Thus the play always returns the actor to the first steps of rehearsal where she begins again the process of understanding the significance of her own actions.

The progress toward a conclusion of the performance of *Not I* is constantly thwarted by the construction of the play itself, which clearly posits no conclusion. Whereas in rehearsal the actor and director characteristically work upon the disintegrated or disparate elements of the play in order to reassemble them, Beckett's action requires this reintegration to be reversed and challenged in the process of each performance. In this, Beckett reveals the depth of his understanding of the process of acting and its artistic function. The plays return constantly to the basis of performance, as all great drama does, requiring the repetition of elements that must, night after night, be reintegrated by a performer trusting to the capacity of the self to assemble its own actions and reintegrate them within now-changed limits of experience. This symbolic reintegration of the personality is the fundamental characteristic of acting and can be accomplished only through bodily knowledge of the self, which anticipates the self-reflexive recollections or speculations of the human mind. The physical basis of this knowledge explains the shared experience between the actor's self and the selves of those who watch, lying as it does within the terms of all tacit learning and knowing:

> Moreover, in both these instances of our entry into the particulars of a comprehensive entity, we meet something that accounts for the coherence of the entity. In one case we meet a person cleverly using his body, in the other, a person cleverly using his mind.
>
> The recognition of a *person* in the performance of a skill or in the conduct of game of chess is intrinsic to the understanding of these matters. We must surmise that we are faced with some co-ordinated performance, before we can even try to pick out the features that are essential to the performance, with a view to the action felt to be at work in it.[19]

This is the understanding of persons that Fergusson identifies at the heart of the "histrionic sensibility," existing "before predication." It anticipates the illusions of character, which can supply dangerously speculative discussion in drama, and particularly in the works of Beckett. The recognition of the person is always contingent on the practices of the performer, not on decisions or interpretations. This "sensibility" derives from the bodily and personal basis of knowledge as it is acquired through the knowledge of the world and of other persons in the world, and accounts for the direct effect of dramatic experience:

We do in some sense perceive the shifting life of the psyche directly, before all predication, before we reach the concepts of ethics, or psychology. . . . [20]

This is nothing other than Polanyi's tacit knowledge, and Fergusson is correct when he stresses the function of acting as the enabling of a certain *direct sense* of the actor's shifting psychic life. He also raises an important question at least implicitly, since it is clear from the discussion of the rehearsal process as a condition of tacit knowledge that the life of the mind concerned is that of the actor alone, and cannot phenomenally be the mind of the character as some putative construct. This must be said despite the miasma of critical and directorial discussion that is based on the imagined individuality of this aspect of dramatic creation. The directness of this experience belies the discussions of character that bedevil the theater. For when we experience the life of the actor's psyche we share in knowing the mind of the master, the dramatist: "When we directly perceive the action which the artist intends, we can understand the objectivity of his vision, however he arrived at it. . . ."[21] The reintegration of the actor's personality becomes symbolic through being placed ingenuously at the service of the master, or, to take Fergusson's phrase, of the dramatist's objectivity. "Character" is a construct dependent on objectives emerging tacitly from the performance, and on knowledge of that objectivity, shared by actor and audience. The psychic life of the actor is a function of the tacit knowledge inhering in what he or she does, not, as the action of *Not I* confirms, in what she "tells" or "thinks." This includes what the actor thinks or tells of the character. It is significant that the objectivity to which the actress accedes should be generally felt, but impossible to achieve. Her objectivity tends to a formulation of the character's experiences as "other," whereas in fact they are always those of the actress herself. This is exactly consistent with the nature of performance, and returns us to the rehearsal and to what I have described as the personal excruciation of the performer, condemned to experience the agonizing structure of purposive action that adumbrates, but never attains, closure. The actress lives in a state of coming to know her meanings, but never, within the playing, is permitted the spurious objectivity that might liberate her from the overwhelming pressure of present time in which the self risks utter confusion and disintegration.

The dilemma of Beckett's actor is fundamentally the basic condition of drama, which balances the "known through action" against the generalized but unavoidable sense of objective where (in phenomenal terms) none is ultimately attainable. Every actor experiences to some degree the crisis of expression that is paradigmatic in Beckett. In the Aristotelian account of action and ignorance, or the Shakespearean "purposes mistook," lies the same insistence on the experience of action as the condition of knowledge in the world. This knowledge is always in tension with the impossibility of finally understanding or encompassing mentally the outcome of actions.

The realization of the primacy of what is untold in drama comes as a cold shower to the more febrile styles of contemporary direction, but it is vitally necessary if direction is to fulfill its natural function in fostering the conditions for an unmediated embodiment of the mind of the master. It is no exaggeration to identify in the work of Beckett a cause célèbre where the defense of a writer has become synonymous with the defense of the medium itself, and where criticism must respectfully but firmly contest the intellectual foundations of much contemporary theater practice.

Notes

1. Alan Schneider, "What does a director do?" *New York Theatre Review,* Spring/Summer 1977, pp. 16–17. Quoted by Jonathan Kalb, *Beckett in Performance* (Cambridge: Cambridge University Press, 1989), p. 72.

2. The recent London production of *Footfalls* with Fiona Shaw directed by Deborah Warner was such an example, where the text was treated as a classic and reinterpreted with the relative freedom the director had assumed with Shakespeare or Ibsen. Shaw's intelligent defense of the production on BBC radio's Kaleidoscope refused the stagnation she alleged could overcome a dramatist treated with exaggerated respect. It will be clear I regard such arguments as being ill-founded, if understandable.

3. Subsequent to the first drafts of this article, I have seen the publication of Shomit Mitter's *Systems of Rehearsal* (London: Routledge, 1992).

4. Letter to Alan Schneider, 29 December 1957, published in *Disjecta* (London: John Calder, 1983), p. 109.

5. *Beckett in Performance,* p. 17.

6. A short series of "preview performances" is now a commercial necessity, as is sometimes the out-of-town tour. Although the rehearsals are over, the play continues to evolve.

7. *Beckett in Performance,* p. 1.

8. When Louis Jouvet describes the rehearsal of Molière he asserts that the text contains a rhythm, and that rhythm cannot be determined but must be discovered. I discuss Jouvet's rehearsal in "Jouvet and the Playing of Molière," *Nottingham French Studies* 33, no. 2 (Autumn 1994): 1–9.

9. In *Beckett in the Theatre* (London: John Calder, 1988), Dougald McMillan and Martha Fehsenfeld record Beckett's meticulous work as director of *Krapp's Last Tape,* where his notes list *jeux écoute,* further developing the playing of Krapp as he listens to the tape. As they suggest, writing and directing are here bound together: "The choices Beckett made in giving structure to this plot and in finding gestures to express it were as much acts of playwriting as direction. No other aspect occupied him more in arriving at the new version of Krapp finally seen on the stage in Berlin" (pp. 269).

10. *Krapp's Last Tape* started life as the *Mime du rêveur* A. See *Beckett in the Theatre,* pp. 241–42. Beckett's interest in mime is evident.

11. Michael Polanyi, *The Tacit Dimension* (London: Routledge & Kegan Paul, 1966), pp. 29–30. The reader may enquire how physical movements are mentally represented. The relevance to acting and the operations of empathy is clear.

12. *The Tacit Dimension*, p. 30.

13. Beckett's fondness for the effect is well known. Winnie's reprise of the toothbrush sequence in *Happy Days* is typical. The structure of *What Where* is built out of the progressive redefinition of action through a process of replays. Reprise and replay are crucial to the forms of rehearsal.

14. Beckett's sources in Manichaean theology are detailed by McMillan and Fehsenfeld (*Beckett in the Theatre,* chap. 5). Their discussion relates the oppositions of light and dark in the philosophical inspiration of the theatrical image within which the actor performs.

15. McMillan and Fehsefeld publish a short account by Ernst Schroeder of his work with Beckett on *Endspiel* at the *Schiller Theater Werkstatt* in 1967. "'You can do what you want now, the script belongs to you, the structure's set.' I couldn't do what I wanted—outside the fact that that wasn't what I had in mind—all I could do was what was musically correct . . ." (p. 238). Schroeder's disquiet had to do with character and psychology, on which the "taciturn" Beckett refused to be drawn. The account is interesting for the record of Beckett's idea of the freedom of the actor. Schroeder seems to think that a "musically correct" performance was somehow constrained. A musician might take a different point of view. It is ironic that for all his protests Schroeder was not minded to do something that lay beyond the limits of the text. Ultimately, through all the trials, he affirms that he came to "know" Hamm like an old acquaintance. One sees the problems that beset the description of professional performance.

16. *Collected Shorter Plays* (London: Faber, 1984), p. 219.
17. *The Tacit Dimension*, p. 10.
18. *Collected Shorter Plays*, pp. 221–22.
19. *The Tacit Dimension*, p. 30.
20. Francis Ferguson, *The Idea of a Theatre* (New York: Doubleday, n.d.), p. 255.
21. Ibid.

The Proper Handling of Beckett's Plays

ROBERT SCANLAN

Artworks are artifacts, and this includes those complex artifacts we call "plays." Beckett's plays, in particular, have provoked debate over acceptable leeway in interpreting his work in the theater. We all know that Beckett was always uneasy with the necessity of policing his formal achievements in the theater. He was reluctant to show serious artists the disrespect of constraining their creative work and he had a long track record of permitting certain projects that pained him. In 1986 he wrote to me, on the subject of stage adaptations of his prose texts, three unambiguous sentences in a row: "Je suis contre. Je me suis laissé faire. Je n'aurais pas dû." From this and from correlative conversations with Beckett over many years, I have no doubt how firmly Beckett wanted his formal stagings respected. I have spoken and written in other places about insuperable problems of genre-jumping with Beckett—i.e., staging his prose. Today I want to write about acceptable latitude in staging his plays.

We cannot hope, now that Beckett is gone, to base authoritative strictures solely on those things he said or wrote to us while he was alive. There is a paradox here, and a painful one: it is Beckett himself who cemented my own convictions about his work; this is a deeply personal matter, and it has *everything* to do with his authority. Nevertheless, I do not think we who had contact with Beckett can hope to pass on his authority as though we were disciples or high priests of his work. It is a ridiculous role none of us wants to play.

What do we do, then, with the *convictions* Beckett planted in us? I can think of only two courses: stage the plays from time to time, and from time to time present persuasive, self-sustaining arguments on the authority of the work itself. There are reasons other than "Beckett wanted it so" for respecting his formal constraints on the proper staging of his plays.

And here, I can only describe the outcome of my work and hope that it is persuasive.

Beckett's characteristic mark as an artist is his *constitutive* use of the formal constraints that define the various media (and genres) in which he worked: page, stage, radio, television, film. The Beckett "matière" found continual renewal in the various formal "nests" Beckett wove for the intractable problem of locating a voice—or a seat of being. In the theater works, this question of voices and the "locus" of possible "beings" is far more important than the number of actors we need to stage the play. As a stage director, what I usually learn from a cast of characters, I learn in a Beckett play from a "locus-of-being" analysis.

There is, in each work, a finite number (usually three or four) of such loci, and the *play* is woven variously from strands of speech or "text" and stage "presences" of various kinds—either generating, witnessing, or interrupting strands of "text." This can be swiftly illustrated by *Not I*, which requires only two performers but is formally a quartet played among four "locus-of-being" sites: (1) mouth, who spouts the text; (2) listener, who "receives" the text helplessly; (3) "She," whose being is the *subject* of the text; and (4) the interrogator, who interrupts mouth's text and prompts her to say "I." All four coexist in the performance of the play, whose action is to locate, among the four loci, a stable habitation for the Self.

The fugal pattern of *Not I* is its fundamental *identity* as a work of art. If the situation of the play (or the circumstances of its staging) are changed, then the meaning of the play is profoundly altered—the play is swiftly denatured. This is not true in less strictly controlled forms, and what is true of the meticulous artifacts Beckett devised for the stage, especially since *Not I*, is not widely applicable as a rule to looser, more conventional work.

I am aware that purist arguments advocating proper interpretation of Beckett's plays strike many theater artists, especially young ones, as deadeningly constraining: they feel urged toward a dreary, mechanical obedience to the Master's every meticulous wish; little seems left to the talent and imagination of the performing artist. This is an exaggeration of the actual situation "purists" (like myself) advocate in the rehearsal hall. It is true that the fidelity to form that I advocate does not "allow" so-called artistic latitude to performers in a "proper" staging of one of Beckett's pieces for the theater. But instead of this curtailed "freedom," Beckett's pieces *require* artists to perform at the highest pitch of their capacities. Beckett's pieces are comparable to Bach's *Well-Tempered Klavier* books or to Scarlatti's feverish sonatas, or to Beethoven's late quartets. For the performers, the *required* artistry far outweighs any "allowed" artistic freedom. They are all extremely difficult to perform "correctly." The extraordinary aspect of their performance, however, is the undreamt-of liberation experienced *because of* the arduously controlled formal strictures. This is the experience and lasting example of artistic mastery—it is worth, in the balance, any amount of "artistic freedom."

Let me conclude by returning to my remarks about the *constitutive* use of formal constraints in Beckett's work. I mean by this that Beckett discovered in every genre a medium in which he composed the *defining* limitation of the form and then lodged his subject there—at the difficult *boundaries* of the medium. I disagree with those who claim that Beckett always contrived to find an impasse. In his recent book on Beckett, *Samuel Beckett: Repetition, Theory and Text*, Steve Connor writes something about the plays that strikes me as exactly wrong:

> Although Beckett has frequently indicated that he turned to the theatre as a form of relief from the impasse that the writing of fiction had led him to, it seems as though his project in the drama is really to find new avenues of approach to the same impasse.[1]

This formulation, "to find new avenues of approach to the same impasse," seems to me opposite to the action of the plays. Beckett *did* find relief in the theater. The nature of his enterprise—an invariant seeking for a sufficient habitation for the Self—is that it *lodges* itself in the boundaries of the artistic medium. It is an impasse only if you are trying to get out. Beckett's creatures are not trying to get out; they are only trying to inhabit the appropriate place. That place is at the formal boundaries of the medium. It is like misinterpreting the movement of lice seeking the seams of a garment: they are not trying to get out . . .

Analytical engineers employ a useful concept when they devise mathematical models of physical systems. It is the concept of *boundary conditions*. These are applicable by analogy to Beckett's formal artifacts. In the mathematical depiction of real things, like buildings and bridges and aircraft flying at high altitudes, the "boundary conditions" are those stipulated constraints that *determine* the nature of an actual reality modeled conceptually by mathematical equations. The solution of equations of motion, or load distributions in a structure, is possible only through the stipulation of *actual* constraints (or "boundary conditions) on the theoretical system. These points of constraint can be understood as the liaison points between unlimited (and therefore insoluble) theoretical possibilities and individual examples in reality "expressible" mathematically once their contact points with the real world are specified.

Beckett's stage plays create analogous "real cases" for a generalized and unlimited problem. Each play of Beckett's maturity creates a meticulously specified set of boundary conditions within which the *formal* problem of "sufficient habitation" finds its unique and exact solution. It is like a patient with a specific pain finding the exact configuration of minimal suffering each time the attending nurse adjusts the bed. Each new set of constraints determines a new work—on the identical *principle* as the last. Each new configuration of "loci of being" has a determined state of minimal sufficient habitation. The plays are "about" their boundaries: seeking them, reaching them, using them, "living" within them. The Beckett creatures all seem to say, "Set me the conditions, I will construct you the life . . . I will show you, like a potted plant, the limits of the possible." All subsequent relations *within* each work depend on the initial boundary conditions.

It is for this reason that any variations in Beckett's found "solutions" completely disrupts the raison d'être of the formal structure. Beckett's formal plays are completely analogous to "solved" equations in mathematics: there is no meaning whatsoever to errors in mathematical problems. Changing the theatrical parameters of his plays makes nonsense of his "situation" of the problem of being on the stage.

As I have said elsewhere: it is possible to do Beckett wrong, and it matters. The surest way to do the stage plays wrong is to alter their parameters—or boundary conditions—and play the unchanged text helplessly into physical situations undreamt-of by Beckett. It makes what is admittedly hard ridiculous instead—and that smacks more of invidious license than of artistic freedom.

Notes

1. Steven Connor, *Samuel Beckett: Repetition, Theory and Text* (Oxford: Basil Blackwell, 1988), p. 2.

Au Contraire: The Question of Beckett's Bilingual Text

DAVID J. GORDON

ASKED if he considered himself an English writer, Beckett replied simply, "Au contraire." The wit is delicious, coming from an Irishman writing in French. An Irishman may well understand himself as the contrary of an Englishman, but the French language is the contrary of the English language for Samuel Beckett alone, who chose to write now in one, now in the other, an idiosyncratic choice that he highlights by answering a question in English with a phrase in French.

His bilingualism was more than a matter of alternating the language of original composition. Not only did Beckett switch over in 1945 from English to French, and switch back again from time to time, but he also established himself as a systematic and imaginative self-translator. With negligible exceptions, Colin Duckworth's 1966 description of Beckett's practice remained accurate throughout his career: "he has translated (occasionally in collaboration) all his French works into English and his English ones into French with such complete command of style that only a bibliographical list will reveal the secret of which language any particular work was conceived in" (*En attendant Godot,* p. xvii). Historically, this is a "possibly unique phenomenon" (Cockerham, "Bilingual Playwright," p. 143), but it raises fascinating theoretical questions of broad bearing. What is the status of self-translations that must be considered "texts in their own right" (Fitch, *Beckett and Babel,* p. viii)? More generally, what is the status of *any* text that comes to us in multiple versions bearing equal authority, none of which can make unequivocal claim to being the single *best* text?

We cannot assign a superior textual authority to either the French or the English version of one of Beckett's works. To put it another way, principles that might be invoked to support the superior authority of one or the other cancel each other out. If we try to argue that one version is more authoritative because it is the original, then we face the argument that a reworking by the author should take precedence because it embodies his more recent intention. But if we try to argue on that basis that the revised version is better, then we face the objection that translation even by the author is intended to supplement rather than replace the original composition. In dealing with versioned texts, we cannot say that intention is unitary, for it evolves in phases over time. Therefore it cannot serve as the specific criterion for deciding whether an earlier or later version has greater authority. Whether priority should be given to the more original or the more recent form of an author's intention must remain a puzzle, one wittily dramatized by Oscar Wilde, whose Gwendolyn claims Ernest as her fiancé because her diary proves that he proposed to her *first,* whereas Cecily claims Ernest because the *later* proposal in her diary proves that he has since then changed his mind.

The theoretical questions raised by Beckett's bilingual texts are greatly enriched if we place them in the context of recent developments in the fast-growing field of textual criticism, a field now much influenced by developments in literary theory generally. According to D. C. Greetham, a leading student of this field, "[B]y the third quarter of the twentieth century, it would be fair to say that the dominant mode of Anglo-American textual criticism," led by W. W. Greg and his disciple Fredson Bowers, adopted an essentialist view of the text (like the New Criticism, whose spirit it shared), and sought "to produce a reading clear-text whose features were a fulfillment of authorial intentions," a text that was necessarily eclectic in form, a composite of an author's intentions (*Textual Scholarship,* pp. 334–35). The Greg-Bowers school understood that, when versions of a text existed, a single version could not accomplish this purpose, and so it repudiated the influential editorial principle, laid down earlier by R. B. McKerrow and others, that held that the best text was the last one published in an author's lifetime. Because its eclectic method *constructed* authorial intention, its text "became known as the 'text that never was' . . . but . . . *ought* to have been" (p. 334). Greg-Bowers thus avoided the ambiguity of "intention" in multiple text situations, but clung still to the idea of an author-based, *overall* intention that could be fulfilled in an ideal, *definitive* text.

During the last decade or two, Greetham reports, "the concept of a definitive edition has been largely abandoned by the editorial community" ("Total Utterance," p. 400). Influenced by widely discussed literary theories concerned with indeterminacy and the social construction of meaning, a number of contemporary editors endorse the independent authority of versions of a text, however variant and even contradictory they may be, "instead of postulating a single, consistent, authorially-sponsored text" (*Textual*

Scholarship, p. 341). Some critics have argued, for example, that the two versions of *King Lear* represent different phases of Shakespeare's intention and so should be treated as autonomous units. Editions of Shakespeare have usually conflated the two versions for the sake of providing readers and students with a single text that combines what the editor takes to be the best of each. But this conflation is ideal, a non-Shakesperean concoction. And such an approach to definitiveness, problematic enough in the case of Shakespeare, is of course totally out of the question in the case of Beckett's bilingual texts, where we have two versions that are lexically discrepant at every point. Conflation is not even imaginable, and therefore any single text we use is inevitably haunted by a sense of its own incomplete authority.

I have thus far assumed for convenience that a Beckettian text—let us choose *En attendant Godot/Waiting for Godot* to focus our discussion—exists in *two* versions of equal authority. That is enough to guarantee permanent textual instability, to be sure, but the textual situation is actually *more* complex than this, making the problem before us more glaring and harder to ignore.

What we have taken to be the definitive French *Godot* is actually the second edition of 1952. And what we have taken to be the definitive English edition, published by Grove Press in 1954, makes authorial changes in the script used for the 1955 Criterion Theatre production of the play and published by Faber and Faber in 1956. Duckworth counts "two hundred and sixty-seven examples of variation in meaning or tone in [Faber] compared with the second French edition," among which are (just to start with) adding the word "tragicomedy" on the title page, seating Estragon on a "low mound" instead of "par terre," and introducing an "immediate contrast, lacking in the French, between the highly literate speech of the two tramps and their physical condition" (*En attendant Godot,* p. 91). As for Grove compared with Faber, it restores deletions "made to satisfy the requirements of the Lord Chamberlain," such as the talk of getting an erection and of a mother in a family called Gozzo who "had the clap" (changed to "had warts" in Faber [ibid., pp., 91–94]). In subsequent years, Beckett supervised the Royal Court production of 1964–65 (which also restored the deletions of the Faber text) and in 1975 directed the important Schiller-Theater production of *Warten auf Godot*. His director's notebook *(Regiebuch)* offers, according to McMillan and Fehsenfeld (*Beckett in the Theatre,* p. 87), "an unusually detailed indication of how Beckett sees *Godot.*" In addition, the altered English text that emerged from the Schiller-Theater production, rather than the Grove text, was brought to Brooklyn by Walter Asmus, who duplicated Beckett's changes, e.g., the oddly piquant addition " . . . or red" to Vladimir's question about Godot's beard—"Fair or . . . *(he hesitates)* . . .

black?"—and the restoration of some not unimportant lines from the French, such as those describing the comfortable night Didi and Gogo hope to spend in Godot's loft. With Beckett's approval, Asmus made a few further changes for an American audience (e.g., Macon and Cackon to Napa and Crappa).[1]

The claim to authority of the German translation itself, dating back to 1952, cannot be disregarded. It was undertaken by Elmar Tophoven, but Beckett went over the manuscript carefully and, by Tophoven's report, made a number of very meticulous changes, resulting in a first trilingual text published in 1963 and a second trilingual version (following the Schiller-Theater production) published in 1976.[2] This is a collaborative situation one can hardly distinguish from that of Patrick Bowles working with Beckett on the English translation of *Molloy*, an important text whose authority is not debated. Indeed, in 1975 Beckett used the German translation to make some changes that brought the English text into closer alignment with the French and German, for example on six occasions changing Estragon's "Ah!" to "Ah, yes," catching more closely the connotation of the German "Ach, ja" and the French "C'est vrai." This new English text, or rather the Suhrkamp's second trilingual edition of which it is part, is really the last edition of the play published during the author's lifetime and thus the most authoritative copytext by McKerrow's by no means forgotten editorial principle.[3]

Finally, if we are granting authority to textual changes made at different times because they reflect changes in the author's idea of his text, why should the original French *manuscript* of *Godot* not be put into the series as well? Or the Prompt Script for the groundbreaking Paris production of 1953? They simply represent earlier rather than later ideas of the text, and so, one could argue, should take their place in a sequence of phases that, taken together, express the whole of Beckett's changing intentions, equivalent to what Hershel Parker calls the work's "full intentionality" (*Textual Scholarship*, p. 340).

Such complication of the question of Beckett's "bilingual" text is not frivolous, for there are new but increasingly reputable editorial principles to support the authority of all of these versions of *Godot*, not only the second French and Grove editions. These two texts have had the most influence on readers and audiences over the years, and so their authority remains important even if we shift from an author-based criterion of "best" text to a reader-based criterion of "influential" text. But the Faber edition, by this standard, also has textual authority, since it served as the basis for a production that made a significant if incalculable first impact on an English audience. It is part of the history of the work's reception. Editorial principles based on reception are highly regarded today—for example, Jerome J. McGann's promotion of a "hypertext" that takes into editorial account the entire social history of the text, Donald Pizer's idea that an influential censored version of a text (like that of *Sister Carrie*) must be granted textual authority (and Beckett did in effect censor the Faber text), and even Edward Mendelson's argument that the base text for an edition of W. H. Auden should be chosen not from "the earliest moment of composition" but from "a point in the history of a work when it achieved a state suitable to be offered for readers" (Greetham, "Total Utterance," p. 408). The privileged position of Grove and the second French edition is also challenged forcefully, as we have seen, by the second Suhrkamp trilingual edition of 1976, all the more because manuscripts carefully recording Beckett's numerous changes have been studied and discussed by scholars, and are part of the ongoing discourse concerning *Godot*. Indeed, the German text served as a kind of normalizing version for changes in those texts, and the whole edition comes closer than any other to embodying its author's "final intention," a principle still respected even if the idea of a definitive text has been put into question. Finally, there are textual theorists ready to claim the original manuscript of a work as one of its versions, part of a palimpsest and no less important than the published text. Brenda R. Silver and Susan Stanford Friedman take this view of Virginia Woolf's manuscripts, arguing that the line between her self-editing and self-censoring can be very fine (Greetham, "Total Utterance," p. 410). This may seem inapplicable to Beckett, but, then again, the script of a produced *play* is peculiarly sensitive to the opinions of those involved in the production, and it is really impossible in most cases to distinguish between self-editing and self-censoring in the fact of Beckett's acquiescence to the suggestions of others.

One might expect that Beckett scholars would welcome a situation so rich in instability and indeterminacy. But there is a difference between uncertainty as an aspect of theme or representation and uncertainty in the status of the material text itself, for the latter rumbles the ground under *any* interpretation. It is not surprising, therefore, that, when they take account of the textual situation, even Beckettians try to stabilize the ground. Colin Duckworth, for example, described the second French edition of 1952 as the "edition de base" (*En attendant Godot,* p. 91)—a phrase that must strike us, in the context of my discussion, as overconfident. In using quotation marks to describe Beckett's *Regiebuch* for *Warten auf Godot* as part of a "definitive" version, McMillan and Fehsenfeld are, I think, being defensive, backing off from a claim they *do* want to make (not, of course, without some reason) but know is questionable. And there is Elmar Tophoven, who takes an understandable but unduly modest view of this same "definitive" version, consistently calling it a *translation* in contrast to the French and English *originals* of presumably superior authority (McMillan and Fehsenfeld, *Beckett in the Theatre,* pp. 317–24), as if the English itself is not a translation or as if *Warten auf Godot* is not, like *Molloy*, a collaboration with the author. Our very talk about Beckett's *bilingual* text, though meant to problematize the monolingual text that is usually studied, really works toward containing the text, as if to prevent it from becoming *tri*lingual and *multi*versioned to boot—that is, out of control.

Some critics who appear to take a quite radical view of the textual situation created by Beckett's bilingualism are still denying, I think, its inherent instability. Brian Fitch asserts that the bilingualism of Beckett's text is "tantamount to the work's possessing no text at all" (*Beckett and Babel,* p. 165). He approvingly quotes Olga Ostrovsky: "Double works remain suspended over a linguistic abyss, creating a bridge leading to nowhere, creating a neutral zone in which language is nullified" (p. 158 n). And he might have quoted Richard Coe, who wrote that Beckett turned to French "because in the gap between one language and another there may reside that non-language which it is Beckett's final aim to realize" ("Beckett's English," p. 41). But a double text, I would argue, is not the same as a nontext. Nor is language nullifed in Beckett, however much "nothingness" or "silence" is evoked through a certain use of language. Nor can we speak unequivocally of his "final aim," as if his intention were consistent all along. Fitch, Ostrovsky, and Coe are all assuming a unitary if text-consuming intention. They are assuming, in other words, that there is one resolving truth of negation rather than two material texts that cannot be fused into one or reduced to none by *any* means.

Beckett's own well-attested insistence that productions of his play follow the text exactly might be thought to be yet another case—an especially impressive one—of hankering for textual definitiveness. But I don't think this is what it means. If, on the one hand, "Sam was most emphatic" that performers should follow exactly a particular text (refusing, for example, to allow the first line of the play to be changed into "It's no good" or "Nothing doing" [McMillan and Fehsenfeld, *Beckett in the Theatre,* p. 47; Duckworth, *En attendant Godot,* p. 91]), on the other hand, we have the equally well-attested image of Beckett the practical man who allowed his experience at rehearsals and the suggestions of others more experienced in the theater to prompt certain changes of wording, gesture, and staging. If on the one hand the trilingual edition attempts to bring three texts into greater semantic harmony, yet on the other no exclusionary claim is made, there is no denial that *Godot* as text is a palimpsest, versioned over a period of thirty years.

Beckett's own practice might serve as a model of the practical problem we must face when we decide—as editors, teachers, students, critics—which text to use. The practical requirements involved in dealing with a text—and these include laziness and expense along with the unquestionable needs of these groups of readers—will restrict our wide-open theoretical consideration. Greetham admits that, in spite of the definitive text's fall from grace, "intentionalist editions are still being produced more often than any other form" (*Textual Scholarship,* p. 341). His explanation is that "it will take some time for practice to catch up with theory," but I would say that practice will *never* catch up with theory, because the one is by its nature restricted, the other not. Even so sophisticated a palimpsestic edition as Hans Walter Gabler's genetic text of *Ulysses* prints an ideal, clear-text, after all, on the recto side. Otherwise it would be quite unusable by teachers, students, and (if there are any) common readers. But critical reading can admit the instability of the textual situation up to a point and allow itself to be influenced by the textual theory brought to bear upon it.

Practically, this probably means (in Anglophonic forums) dealing with the 1954 English text supplemented by some consideration of the second 1952 French text. And since a bilingual text provides instability enough, I would like at this point to consider some specific differences between these versions and comment briefly on what they imply.

Are these differences, after all, significant? No one would claim that Beckett altered his play so radically as to create a markedly different overall impression in subsequent versions. But it's hard to say exactly at what point the accumulation of smaller changes becomes significant—hard to say because the answer might well be different for different readers. McMillan and Fehsenfeld offer a list of differences under the headings of cuts, additions, and alterations, headings which perhaps make the differences sound more mechanical than they are. Because Beckett is working *across languages*, the changes appear motivated much less by a desire simply to improve the wording of a text (as in revising a text in the same language) than by a desire to find phrasing that works, that seems most idiomatic and most vigorous in the other language. To suggest that there is no way, after all, to *close* the gap, I make my list under the headings of "Nuance" and "Free Translation," as well as "Insertions/Deletions." It is surprising, by the way, and quite worth noting, that no two lists—whether comprehensive like Duckworth's and McMillan/Fehsenfeld's or samplings like Lawrence Graver's and mine—have quite the same feel or merely duplicate their examples. I infer that, since "difference" *permeates* the text, even lists made without a particular agenda will turn out to look different, one from another.

Nuance

It has often been pointed out that, although "Waiting for Godot" is a plausible translation of "En attendant Godot," it misses the participial effect of the French: *while* waiting. But it is equally true that the French phrase, implying a process, misses an effect of the English phrase, which implies a state. And both a process and a state of waiting are connotations pertinent to our understanding of the work in either version.

Sometimes a nuance is lost from French to English, at other times it is gained. The opening words of the play, "Rien à faire," contain two relevant meanings in French—"nothing to be done," also "nothing to do"—while the English version only preserves the first. The French wording is also more nuanced in the following:

(1a)   ESTRAGON. —Qui a pété?
           VLADIMIR. —C'est Pozzo.
           POZZO. —C'est moi! C'est moi! Pitié!
           ESTRAGON. —C'est dégoutant.

           ESTRAGON: *(recoiling)* Who farted?
           VLADIMIR: Pozzo.
           POZZO: Here! Here! Pity!
           ESTRAGON: It's revolting.

The English loses the humor of Pozzo's unwitting acknowledgment, by means of the repetition of "C'est" (Vladimir's "C'est Pozzo," followed by Pozzo's "C'est moi"), of responsibility for the fart, although Pozzo presumably intends only to direct attention to his own desperate plight.

But at times the English text is richer in nuance:

(1b)   VLADIMIR. —Qu'est-ce que tu fais?
           ESTRAGON. —Je fais comme toi, je regarde la blafarde.

           VLADIMIR: What are you doing?
           ESTRAGON: Pale for weariness.
           VLADIMIR: Eh?
           ESTRAGON: Of climbing heaven and gazing on the likes of us.

The translator has discovered an opportunity in "la blafarde" (the pale moon) to charge the English translation with an allusion to Shelley's fragment "To the Moon" ("Art thou pale for weariness / Of climbing heaven and gazing on the earth"), an allusion whose poignance is turned by Estragon, once a poet by his own report, into mordant wit.

Another added nuance in the English emerges when Vladimir and Estragon wonder about their role in relation to Godot:

(1c) ESTRAGON. —Quel est notre rôle là-dedans?
VLADIMIR. —Notre rôle?
ESTRAGON. —Prends ton temps.
VLADIMIR. —Notre rôle? Celui de suppliant.

ESTRAGON: Where do we come in?
VLADIMIR: Come in?
ESTRAGON: Take your time.
VLADIMIR: Come in? On our hands and knees.

Translating "Quel est notre rôle là-dedans?" as "Where do we come in?" allows Beckett (or was devised by him to make possible) the image of the suppliant literally reduced to a humiliating crawling posture.

Finally, one of the subtlest nuances added to the English results from Pozzo's consistent use of the word "on" where the French may use "vite," "plus vite" or "en avant." His first words are, "*(en coulisse)* Plus vite!" In English the stage direction is "*off*" and the command is "On!" Here is added not only a pleasant jest for the play*reader* but also a resonance deriving from Beckett's other work, including the famous last words of *The Unnamable* (not yet translated) where the French "continuer" becomes the English "go on." Beckett's use of the word "on" throughout his oeuvre may well be intended, as H. Porter Abbott keenly suggests, to mock the earnest Victorian trope of onwardness in the political and social rhetoric of progress that modernist texts did so much to undermine ("Late Modernism," pp. 77–83).[4]

Free Translation

While preserving in English a vaguely French provenance (with references to the Eiffel Tower, francs rather than pounds, etc.), Beckett changes place names and other proper nouns into more familiar forms for the new audience (Voltaire becomes Berkeley, Normandie Connemara, etc.) and also tries to find alternative puns. But his principal motive for taking liberties in translation appears to be to maximize in each version the idiomatic strength of the language in question. A professional translator would also seek to be idiomatic, of course, but would hardly dare to reimagine the wording as Beckett does:

(2a) VLADIMIR. —Pour jeter le doute, à toi le pompon.
VLADIMIR: Nothing is certain when you're about.

(2b) ESTRAGON. —Ma foi, la tu m'en demandes trop.
ESTRAGON: I'm not a historian.

One might have reasonably rendered the French of *2a* as "When it comes to doubting, you take the cake" and the French of *2b* as "Good heavens, you're asking [or that's asking] too much" or even "That's the last straw." But the wry quality of the responses in Beckett's translation is inventive, not merely resourceful.

Some of the free translations in *Godot* perceptibly intensify the bleakness of the tone of the play:

(2c) VLADIMIR. —C'est long, mais ce sera bon.
VLADIMIR: Hope deferred maketh the something sick.

(2d) VLADIMIR. —On ne t'a pas battu?
ESTRAGON. —Si . . . pas trop.

VLADIMIR: And they didn't beat you?
ESTRAGON: Beat me? Certainly they beat me.

In the French of *2c,* Vladimir's sense of deferred hope is expressed rather earnestly; in the English, by way of blurring a biblical quotation, a more sardonic note is struck. In the French of *2d,* similarly, Estragon is more reticent, less angry, about his beating than in the English.

Insertions/Deletions

Many of these were probably the fruit of the playwright's experience with the first production of the play or simply the result of the translator's close inspection of his own work and consequent wish to make little improvements as he proceeded, clarifying this or touching up that. Thus it doesn't make much sense for the blind Pozzo, when he bumps into Lucky, to say "who cried out?" So the English has him say, "who is it?" Similarly, Beckett omits in translation a little passage in which Vladimir wonders if Pozzo is really blind, probably as a result of realizing that the point is not whether Pozzo is blind but the relation between his blindness and his sense of time. Again, the irony is nicely improved when Pozzo *"puts on his glasses"* between "Yes, gentlemen, I cannot go for long without the society of my likes" and "even when the likeness is an imperfect one."

But some insertions and deletions (for example, the insertion of the word "dying" amid the enumerated sports in Lucky's tirade) also suggest more darkness in the English, and others suggest as well more pathos in the tenderness between the two friends:

(3a) VLADIMIR. —Où allez-vous de ce pas?
POZZO. —Je ne m'occupe pas de ça.
VLADIMIR. —Comme vous avez changé!
Lucky, chargé des bagages, vient se placer devant Pozzo.
VLADIMIR. —Where do you go from here?
POZZO. —On.
(Lucky, laden down, takes his place before Pozzo.)

The simple word "On" instead of "Je ne m'occupe pas de ça" and "Comme vous avez changé" makes Pozzo a bit more stark and mysterious in the English text, a figure about whom Vladimir cannot even exclaim, "How you've changed!"

(3b) ESTRAGON. —Non, rien n'est sûr.
VLADIMIR. —On peut toujours se quitter, si tu crois que ça vaut mieux.

ESTRAGON: No, nothing is certain.
Vladimir slowly crosses the stage and sits down beside Estragon.
VLADIMIR: We can still part, if you think it would be better.

(3c) VLADIMIR. — ... Gogo! *(Silence. Il se met à arpenter la scene presque en courant. Estragon rentre précipitamment essoufflé, court vers Vladimir. Ils s'arrêtent à quelques pas l'un de l'autre.)* Te revoilà enfin!

VLADIMIR: ... Gogo! Come back! *(Vladimir runs to extreme left, scans the horizon. Enter Estragon right, he hastens toward Vladimir, falls into his arms.)* There you are again!

The inserted stage direction in *3b* (*Vladimir slowly crosses the stage and sits down beside Estragon*) and the added touches in *3c* (especially "Come back!" and *"falls into his arms"*) clearly contribute a warmer coloring, and hence a further poignance, to this desperate friendship.

We should not exaggerate these differences in tone, for Lawrence Graver is right enough, I think, in saying that Beckett's main concern in Englishing *Godot* was actability, but we cannot ignore them or feel that they are trivial. One alteration not yet mentioned epitomizes for me our need to hold on to *both* texts at the same time. I quote from Duckworth: "[Estragon] calls himself 'Catulle' in the published French version, 'Catullus' in the Faber English edition—no doubt in sarcastic reference to his status as an impoverished poet. In the Grove Press edition, however, he replies 'Adam' instead of 'Catullus'.... [Beckett's] explanation to me was this: 'We got fed up with "Catullus".'" If this were the only reason, one could justifiably take the author of *Godot* to task for indulging in deliberate mystification" (pp. lxiii–lxiv). Well, yes, Beckett's explanation is somewhat disingenuous. Adam is a name, like Cain, Abel, and Godot itself, so highly charged with symbolic potentiality that the effect of using it in this wide-open way is to *empty* it of meaning and let the void show through. This is a tactic so characteristic of Beckett's work in this period that it must surely be counted as deliberate. Yet one misses the sarcastic reference to Estragon's status as an impoverished poet (for Duckworth is surely right about that). Social context is kept vague in *Godot,* but it is not quite removed—Estragon's role in particular carries a reminiscence of the fact that he was named Levy almost until publication. One wants to preserve in *Godot* both its metaphysical drift and its social undertone, and this single difference between the French and English versions helps one to do so—*if* both names are held simultaneously in mind.

From this too brief sampling and from my argument about the status of the bilingual text, we may conclude as follows. Although Beckett's authority is felt in either the French or English *Godot* by virtue of the precision and finesse of the language, it loses the unitary strength of a consistent intention when we stand back and consider the two texts together, and even more when we consider the textual variations that developed over several decades. "Meaning," then, seems to *hover* between or among texts, to become unstable in a sense not covered by the application of the concept of indeterminacy to the theme or form of a single text. Theoretically, we can no longer defend the idea of a definitive text. But although for practical purposes we are probably obliged to privilege a single text, textual theory can inform our use of it, helping us surrender the dream of a stable text and thus encouraging a constant awareness of alternative wording. A two-text situation is unstable in a very concrete sense, for we cannot take refuge in the idea of the annihilation of meaning. Rather, we must move between this and that, between two particularities that cannot be reduced. Interpretation of Beckett's work is doubtless difficult enough if a single, stable text is assumed. But a full recognition of this new dimension adds a welcome complexity, because it leads practical criticism in a direction that is as richly ambiguous as it is irreducibly concrete.

Notes

1. These manuscripts include Beckett's *Regiebuch*, two versions the German translation known as Suhrkamp *Warten auf Godot 1* and Suhrkamp *Warten auf Godot 2*, and Walter Asmus's Green Notebook—all deposited in the Reading University Beckett Archives. They are expected to be published soon as part of the series called *The Theatrical Notebooks of Samuel Beckett*, two volumes of which (on *Endgame* and *Krapp's Last Tape*) have already been published. A full discussion of these manuscripts may be found in *Beckett in the Theatre* by Dougald McMillan and Martha Fehsenfeld (1988).

2. A sample passage from Tophoven's record of Beckett's help in this translation will give some idea of the author's collaborative involvement: "My first experience of working directly with Beckett was in Karlsruhe in 1952 when we went over my translation of *En attendant Godot*. Then later I went during several afternoons to his little studio in the *rue des Favorites*. I read my translation aloud to him and he pointed out what needed changing. At one place Gogo suggests that Pozzo's watch '*ist stehengeblieben*' (' . . . it has stopped'); earlier Didi had said '*Die Zeit steht* ('Time has stopped'). Beckett wanted the two verbs to coincide: either "'*Die Uhr ist stehengeblieben*,' '*Die Zeit ist stehengeblieben*' or '*Die Uhr steht*'; '*Die Zeit steht*.' There are twenty pages between those two passages in the text. . . ." (McMillan and Fehsenfeld, *Beckett in the Theatre*, p. 317).

3. This editorial principle, known as that of the author's final intention, governs for example Richard J. Finneran's 1983 edition of W. B. Yeats's poems, and Greetham himself argues that "if there *is* a demonstrable final intention to the work," this is probably the best basis for a clear-text edition (*Textual Scholarship*, p. 368).

4. However, the textual alignments made in the trilingual edition include at one point Beckett's adding the word "faster" after "on" and, at another, replacing "On! On!" (spoken by Pozzo) by "Faster!" (spoken first by Estragon and then by Vladimir). See McMillan and Fehsenfeld, *Beckett in the Theatre*, pp. 156, 159.

Works Cited

Abbott, H. Porter. "Late Modernism: Samuel Beckett and the Art of the Oeuvre." In *Around the Absurd: Essays on Modern and Postmodern Drama,* edited by Ruby Cohn and Enoch Brater, 73–96. Ann Arbor: University of Michigan Press, 1990.

Beckett, Samuel. *En attendant Godot: Pièce en deux actes*. Paris: Les Editions de Minuit, 1952.

———. *The Theatrical Notebooks of Samuel Beckett: "Endgame."* Edited by S. E. Gontarski. New York: Grove Press, 1992.

———. *The Theatrical Notebooks of Samuel Beckett: "Krapp's Last Tape."* Edited by James Knowlson. New York: Grove Press, 1992.

———. *Waiting for Godot: A Tragicomedy in Two Acts*. New York: Grove Press, 1954.

———. *Warten auf Godot. En attendant Godot. Waiting for Godot*. Deutsche Übertragung von Elmar Tophoven. Vorwort von Joachim Kaiser. Frankfurt am Main: Suhrkamp, 1963.

———. *Warten auf Godot*. Dreisprachig. Übersetzung von Elmar Tophoven. Frankfurt am Main: Suhrkamp, 1976.

Cockerham, Harry. "Bilingual Playwright." In *Beckett the Shape Changer*, edited by Katharine Worth, 139–59. London and Boston: Routledge and Kegan Paul, 1975.

Coe, Richard N. "Beckett's English." In *Samuel Beckett: Humanistic Perspectives*, edited by Morris Beja, Pierre Austier, and S. G. Gontarski, 36–57. Columbus: Ohio State University Press, 1982.

Duckworth, Colin, ed. *En attendant Godot: Pièce en deux actes*, by Samuel Beckett. Foreword by Harold Hobson. London: Harrap, 1966.

Fitch, Brian T. *Beckett and Babel: An Investigation into the Status of the Bilingual Work*. Toronto: University of Toronto Press, 1988.

Graver, Lawrence. *Beckett's "Waiting for Godot."* Landmarks of World Literature. Cambridge: Cambridge University Press, 1989.

Greetham, D. C. *Textual Scholarship: An Introduction*. New York and London: Garland, 1992.

———. "Total Utterance and the Modernist Voice." Review of *Representing Modernist Texts: Editing as Interpretation*, edited by George Bernstein. In *Yeats: An Annual of Critical and Textual Studies*, edited by Richard J. Finneran and James W. Flannery, 400–412. Ann Arbor, Mich., 1992.

Kiberd, Declan. Script of "Silence to Silence." WNET TV (1990). Sponsored by the Irish Tourist Board and Aer Lingus.

McMillan, Dougald, and Martha Fehsenfeld. *Beckett in the Theatre*. London: John Calder, 1988.

"A Voice from Elsewhere": Impossible Survivals and the Annihilating Power of Language in Beckett's Fiction

HARRY VANDERVLIST

THE dilemma of obligation and impossibility, which critics have long recognized as a crucial element in all Beckett's writing, merely receives its most famous formulation in the much-quoted passage from the trilogy: "you must go on, I can't go on, I'll go on" (p. 179). In fact this central tension suffuses all of Beckett's early writing. Starting with a profound suspicion of the means and materials of the writer's art—language and human memory—Beckett perceives the artist's task as impossible. Out of the perception that it is of this very impossibility that art is obligated to speak, he creates a fiction that embodies this founding idea with increasing sureness: a fiction speaking of its own "impossibility." Gradually the application of this aesthetic idea is broadened, until it can encompass statements about not just the artist's difficulties in constructing characters and narratives but the difficulties human beings face in trying to accommodate the contradictory sense that the "I" of whom we speak in language—that character in a narrative—is both "I" and "not I."

In his 1928 essay *Proust*, Beckett defines literary art and its possibilities so narrowly as to make that art virtually impossible.[1] Everything feasible is scorned in Proust, as if to anticipate the famous remark, in Beckett's *Three Dialogues* of 1949, that art must depart from "the plane of the feasible" and thus the artist must "fail, as no other dare fail." This absurd stance is owed partly to the presentation of "Beckett" as a cranky and distracted participant in the *Three Dialogues,* and of his viewpoint as an eccentric one. Yet the idea that art might turn away from doing "the possible" and consider "the impossible" as a potential arena is really pursued seriously in Beckett's novels. Beckett's development of his own view of time in the essay on Proust stresses the annihilation of personality's "permanent reality, if any," by the "unceasing modification" of Time (p. 15). The antidote to this corrosion of self can only be memory; yet Beckett carefully withdraws any hope of such aid by dividing memory into two kinds, one voluntary but also habitual and unauthentic, the other "real" and "adequate" but triggered only by chance stimuli. Neither kind of memory is subject to "the least control" by the artists's, or the self's, conscious will.

It is from this impossible position, in which to possess the will is by definition to lack the means, that the (Beckettian) writer must work. Yet it took several attempts for Beckett to discover how to put such a rigorously limited aesthetic into practice. The 1934 collection *More Pricks than Kicks*, like its contradictory protagonist, is openly exasperated with its own procedures. Unsure how to work within the dilemma of obligation and impossibility that suffuses Beckett's later writing, the stories project this tension onto the protagonist, from whom we are distanced by a third-person narrator. The narrator's implied attitude, in its turn, is disturbingly unresolved, creating an overall feeling of "uneasiness" or "prickliness." J. E. Dearlove touches on this aspect of the stories, describing them as "a comedy of manners without an acceptable social norm," one that displays "an almost decadent dependence upon the forms it debunks" (*Chaos,* p. 22). Beckett's 1938 novel *Murphy* might be similarly described.

It is in *Watt* (1942), Beckett's last novel to be written in English, that the aesthetic of impossibility is applied to the novel's use of language. Where *Proust* and *More Pricks than Kicks* stressed the fragmentation of the self at the center of the work, *Watt* challenges the very idea that consciously arranged language, or the novel as a genre, can "serve" the representation of a protagonist. In this way the dialectic of obligation and impossibility is more clearly embodied in the narrative itself. In *Watt* our knowledge of the novel's central subject is interfered with, postponed, and dismissed as not worth the effort. Finally the novel undermines even Watt's sense that he might gain reassurance of his identity, "semantic succour," through words. Separated from those who would "use" it, language has become an autonomous, closed system. Language in *Watt* is much like Mr. Knott's house: one is either in it, in which case there is nothing else *but* language, or one is out of it, in which case one cannot speak, one cannot give voice to the self that is after all merely a "retrospective hypothesis," forged out of memory and words. And in the terrible dilemma by which Beckett has defined his fictional territory, both memory and language must be unauthentic if serving as instruments, yet inaccessible to the artist's will if functioning autonomously rather than instrumentally.

This situation is presented most clearly in the trilogy *Molloy, Malone*

Dies, The Unnamable. In both *Molloy* and *Malone Dies* the spectacle of compulsory narratives-being-composed demonstrates the use of narrative to actively evade the very thing the novels' titles seemed to offer: knowledge about Molloy and Malone. Part 1 of *Molloy* makes it plain that its narrative is "a contrivance," a narrative that is made up as it goes along. The benefits of composition and revision are alien to this compulsory writing. Not trusting himself to be consistent as he writes, Molloy warns the reader that "if I speak of the stars it is by mistake" (p. 15). Similarly, he admits that he might forget the infirmities he has attributed to himself in his writing, so that it is important for the reader to understand that "If I ever stoop, it will not be me, but another" (p. 36). In fact although he may appear to be telling "his story," Molloy prefers naked invention to reminiscence, even warning us that "perhaps I'm remembering things" (p. 8). Finally, he abandons the half-hearted pretext of telling his story, or any continuous story, in favor of a fabric of digressions: "And as to saying what became of me, and where I went, in the months and perhaps the years that followed, no. For I weary of these inventions and others beckon to me" (p. 68).

The issue of the unreality and triviality of *Molloy*'s fictional world is pressed, with a great deal of humor, throughout the text. The "condition of Molloy," then, or the "world of Molloy," is one in which many of the novel's conventional means for satisfying readers have been given up. Yet the restraints of the novel have disappeared as well. Molloy, and *Molloy*, can do as they wish. One of the novel's bleakest passages comments on this "freedom":

> [F]ree to do what, to do nothing, to know, but what, the laws of the mind perhaps, of my mind, that for example water rises in proportion as it drowns you and that you would do better, at least no worse, to obliterate texts than to blacken margins, to fill in the holes of words till all is blank and flat and the whole ghastly business looks like what it is, senseless, speechless, issueless misery. (P. 13)

Throughout *Molloy*, words are presented as *material*. Silence is a space they can fill, and their function is a negative one: to fill up, blacken, block out. Molloy says that "to restore silence is the role of objects" (p. 13). But as in *Watt*, words have themselves *become* objects: independent, autonomous, distant, and unknowable. The novel, *Molloy*, becomes from this point of view a series of blackened pages, a "something gone wrong with the silence."

The stories Malone tells himself in *Malone Dies* resemble the stories in *Molloy* in that they are explicitly in the process of being composed and in that their characters are puppets, pure inanimate convention. The comical arbitrariness of one of these—Sapo's story-in-the-process-of-composition—is clear from the start, and we can almost hear pure automatism take over, interrupted by the exasperated narrator's interjections, as the story begins to rattle on:

> Sapo had no friends—no, that won't do.
> Sapo was on good terms with his little friends, though they did not exactly love him. The dolt is seldom solitary. He boxed and wrestled well, was fleet of foot, sneered at his teachers, and sometimes even gave them impertinent answers. Fleet of foot? Well well. (Pp. 12–13)

Farcically, "Sapo's life" is something that Malone will finally lack the energy to finish inventing: "The peasants. His visits to. I can't" (p. 19). Finally Malone makes a parting gesture that recalls the addenda to *Watt*: "There is a choice of images," notes Malone wearily.

The trilogy's concluding novel, *The Unnamable*, designates by its very title an exploration of something that lies *beyond* language. The contempt for language in its usual sense as a bearer of meaning, and of the novel as a constructor of a plausible world, moves further here than in any of the previous novels. Conscious of the previous novels' arbitrariness ("the old trick worn to a thread," p. 33), of the extent to which they sought to narrate "any old thing" (p. 53), the narrator acknowledges how easy it is to elicit "reams of discourse" (p. 24). Now, the narrator of *The Unnamable* recognizes more clearly than ever that to speak at all has been to fall into a trap: "But it seems impossible to speak and yet say nothing, you think you have succeeded, but you always overlook something, a little yes, a little no, enough to exterminate a regiment of dragoons" (p. 20). The annihilating power of language is at the fore here, because this narrator-protagonist actually seeks something that he hopes can survive the act of "saying nothing"—this residue is the "I" that seems to begin to emerge at the end of *The Unnamable*. "Shall I be able to speak of me and this place without putting an end to us?" asks the narrator, implying that language annihilates but also that there may be something that survives the act of "speaking and saying nothing." In *The Unnamable*, the discourse of the novel seems to be envisioned as a kind of radiation therapy that will purge language itself and the "self" inherent in language, and expose something *beyond* that self. This "something beyond" is elusive and difficult to perceive, the narrator concedes:

> [W]hile unfolding my facetiae, the last time that happened to me, or to the other that passes for me, I was not inattentive. And it seemed to me then that

> I heard a murmur telling of another and less unpleasant method of ending my troubles and that I even succeeded in catching, without ceasing for an instant to emit my he said, and he said to himself, and he answered, a certain number of highly promising formulae.... But it has all gone clean from my head. For it is difficult to speak, even any old rubbish, and at the same time focus one's attention on another point, where one's true interest lies, as fitfully defined by a feeble murmur seeming to apologize for not being dead. (P. 27)

This "other that passes for me," it appears here, refers to the trilogy's narrating voice. Where *The Unnamable*'s "true interest lies," however, is with another "I," held in reserve, who has felt the difference between "the other that passes for me" and "me," which the narrator ventures to call "the true at last, the last at last" (p. 28). This apparent faith in an "authentic" self or one "beyond the discourse" seems to contradict much of what the previous fiction implied about the selves evoked there, and their inextricability from language, their lack of any self-sufficient being that would permit them to "use" their discourse rather than be spoken by it.

Yet it is clear that this narrator does struggle against whatever external compulsion forces him to take up a place in language. If indeed the speaker can succeed in overcoming his original "childish" insertion into language via birth and naming, such escape will be short-lived and difficult to grasp: "they will devise another means, less childish, of getting me to admit, or pretend to admit, that I am he whose name they call me by, and no other" (p. 89). The *Unnamable* seeks to evoke something best understood in terms of "the Unconscious itself, as the reality of the subject which has been alienated and repressed through the very process by which, in receiving a name, it is transformed into a representation of itself" (Jameson, "Imaginary Symbolic," p. 363). The previous two novels of the trilogy, if described in such terms, might be said to have evoked the pain of representing oneself while continually perceiving one's difference from that representation. Those novels portrayed a reluctant and painful awareness of the way in which the narrator-protagonist, wishing to see itself as self-sufficient, tries to repudiate its own interconnection with others, while sensing the *lack* of self-sufficiency that contradicts its continual assertion of control. Thus the earlier narrator-protagonists fled from the occasional insight into their constructed status by turning to substitute narratives such as the story of Sapo. Yet finally in *The Unnamable* the text will confess that "it's not me" speaking. Paradoxically, this will allow a previously repressed "I" (the "everlasting third party" [p. 123] now become first person) at least to be indicated behind the "pretexts" that formed the substance of all the previous narrations.

In *The Unnamable*, what is perhaps a new conception of the subject in Beckett's novels emerges. This conception is described in Lacan's *Seminar I*:

> [T]he complete restitution of the subject's history is the element that is essential, constitutive and structural for analytic progress. . . . The path of restitution of the subject's history takes the form of a quest for the restitution of the past. (Pp. 12–14)

Such a quest formed the basis for *Molloy*, for instance, but the quest for Molloy's "true history" was an impossible one, partly for the reason that agency, desire, and, for Beckett, voluntary memory are all questioned once the discursive construction of the subject is accepted. However, Lacan goes on to say:

> the fact that the subject relives, comes to remember . . . the formative events of his existence, is not in itself so very important. What matters is what he reconstructs of it . . . what is involved is a reading, a qualified and skilled translation of the cryptogram representing what the subject is conscious of at the moment. (*Seminar I*, pp. 12–14)

"Cryptogram" is an apt term for the "cryptic" and "deathlike" images of later Beckett narrator-protagonists, as they narrate from the vases, rooms, mines, or graves in which they are trapped. But the more important aspect of Lacan's observation is that despite the inaccessibility of the subject's "true history," it remains possible to approach what he calls "reconstitution," which in *The Unnamable* is perhaps the moment when "I" begins to speak at the end, a moment that recalls Lacan's description of psychoanalytic healing: "The realization of the subject through a speech which comes from elsewhere, traversing it" (*Seminar II*, p. 232).

The speech that comes from elsewhere, once a tormenting proof of the narrator's unessential quality, now becomes an instrument of reconstitution. How can this be? As Lacan might put it, Beckett's narrators, looking for themselves in the place where they are not, have been both right and wrong. The difference lies in accepting that the self and others are intertwined, so that instead of looking for himself somewhere others could not penetrate—in silence, in nothingness—the narrator of *The Unnamable* simply listens more closely to the self within the other's voice. In losing the autonomous selfhood that earlier Beckett narrators hoped to claim, *The Unnamable*'s narrator finds something close to such a self. As Malone proleptically observes, "[O]n the threshold of being no more, I succeed in being another" (*Malone Dies*, p. 17).

In order for the "voice from elsewhere" to be perceived in this new way, the narrator of *The Unnamable* must accept, to a much greater degree than the previous narrators, the fact that "I'm in words, made of words, others' words" (p. 139). Now this "I," different but indistinguishable (thanks to the indeterminacy of pronouns) from the "I" that speaks at the novel's end, is certainly the subject that inheres in discourse, the "other that passes for me," as the narrator put it earlier. However, the "murmur" that this "I" hears behind his own speech is *another* voice, Lacan's "speech which comes from elsewhere," and which embodies the realization that upon entry into language, something was repressed, which still survives, though "apologizing for not being dead."

This realization places the narrator upon a threshold that represents a place unattained in the previous novels:

> [P]erhaps that's what I feel, an outside and an inside and me in the middle, perhaps that's what I am, the thing that divides the world in two ... that can be as thin as foil, I'm neither one side nor the other, I'm in the middle, I'm the partition, I've two surfaces and no thickness, perhaps that's what I feel, myself vibrating, I'm the tympanum, on the one hand the mind, on the other the world, I don't belong to either, it's not to me they're talking, it's not of me they're talking. (*The Unnamable,* p. 134)

This sense of equilibrium, of a self-sufficiency beyond the distinctions that plagued Murphy (the world versus the mind) and beyond speech, compels us to recognize a change in *The Unnamable*. Something previously repressed emerges in the final section of the trilogy:

> No doubt something which isn't expressed doesn't exist. But the repressed is always there, insisting, and demanding to be. The fundamental relation of man to this symbolic order is very precisely what founds the symbolic order itself—the relation of non-being to being .... The end of the symbolic process is that non-being comes to be, because it has spoken. (Lacan, *Seminar II*, pp. 307–8)

The final pages of *The Unnamable* are as close as Beckett's fiction comes to the moment when the repressed emerges and comes into being, as when the narrator begins to marvel, "I'm something quite different, a different thing, a wordless thing in an empty place" (p. 139). The narrator even hazards the idea that "Perhaps I've said the thing that had to be said, that gives me the right to be done with speech, done with hearing, without my knowing it" (p. 150).

However, if something has momentarily come into being that had not been present in the earlier works, then from that moment it becomes subject to the conditions of those earlier works. The narrator admits that "the next time I won't go to such pains... I'll know that no matter what I say the result is the same, that I'll never be silent, never at peace" (p. 150). If in *The Unnamable*, for a moment, a solution to Molloy's quest is glimpsed, then it also vanishes just as quickly, as soon as it is named. Then the "other that passes for me" reasserts itself. The closing phrases of *The Unnamable* return to the situation of *Molloy*, in which discourse is endlessly extorted by some external force, despite its being founded upon the repression of the "I" that spoke so briefly.

In the trilogy as a whole it is made clear that, as Andrew Kennedy observes:

> The central importance of language in all modernist writing becomes, in Beckett, a dangerous immersion in language as a creative/destructive element, language as the stuff that makes up, or else annihilates, the world and the self. (*Samuel Beckett*, p. 2)

Kennedy's "or else," with its implication that there are alternatives and choices, ought to be replaced with "and also." This substitution brings us back to the idea of simultaneous obligation and impossibility. Language is *both* the medium in which the narrator-protagonists of the trilogy have their being *and* the instrument of their torment, as they are forced to "go on" and on and on. They must continue to speak, and thus construct themselves in language, even after it becomes clear to them that language may conceal something silenced, something outside naming and outside intersubjectivity. The image of such a transcendence of the closed system haunted Murphy, and reemerges in *The Unnamable*, showing that the idea never entirely leaves Beckett's early and middle fiction. This tension between two sides of a paradox—words that are all surface, or simply objects in a closed system, versus words that might contain "a voice from elsewhere"—is what generates the movement of the trilogy.

Notes

1. Nicholas Zurbrugg points out that although Beckett pretends to offer an "analysis of the values of Proust" the essay succeeds better in "adumbrating the antithetical values of Beckett" (*Beckett and Proust*, p. 170).

Works Cited

References to Beckett's fiction are to the Grove editions.

Beckett, Samuel. *Proust and Three Dialogues with Georges Duthuit*. London: John Calder, 1965.

Dearlove, Joyce E. *Accommodating the Chaos: Samuel Beckett's Non-Relational Art*. Durham, N.C.: Duke University Press, 1982.

Jameson, Fredric. "Imaginary and Symbolic in Lacan: Marxism, Psychoanalytic Criticism, and the Problem of the Subject." *Yale French Studies* 55–56 (1977): 338–95.

Kennedy, Andrew K. *Samuel Beckett*. Cambridge: Cambridge University Press, 1989.

Lacan, Jacques. *Seminar I (1953–54): Freud's Papers on Technique*. Translated by Jacques-Alain Miller. New York: Norton, 1988.

———. *Seminar II (1954–55): The Ego in Freud's Theory and in the Technique of Psychoanalysis*. Translated by Jacques-Alain Miller. New York: Norton, 1988.

Zurbrugg, Nicholas. *Beckett and Proust*. Gerrards Cross, Buckinghamshire: Colin Smythe, 1988.

Dramatizing Silence: Beckett's Shorter Plays

DOROTHEE OSTMEIER

In Beckett's play entitled *Play*, the phrases spoken by one figure could just as easily be the phrases of another figure. Nevertheless, the voices and faces of the speakers continually alternate. What is the relation, then, between speakers and speech? Is speech an expression of the speakers, or are the speakers theatrical, visual expressions of their speech?

Recent criticism addresses these questions in different ways. In her discussion of the play Ruby Cohn suggests an analogical relation between linguistic patterns and extralinguistic, nontheatrical processes of life. She views the repetitive structures of *Play* as a reflection of Beckett's concept of life as repetition.[1] Other criticism turns bluntly against such mimetic readings by pointing to the antimimetic setup of Beckett's plays. Anna McMullan's title "Mimicking Mimesis" points straight in this direction: The plays resist interpretative strategies that address theater as representation.[2] Steven Connor reads Beckett's later theater as an examination of the opposition of speech and writing. He associates repetition and mechanical structures of speech with the process of writing itself. Beckett's theatrical languages seem to illustrate the discrepancy between speech acts and written signs as analyzed and thematized by Derrida.[3] Whereas Karen Laughlin rejects dialogues as a dramatic basis for the later plays in general,[4] Paul Lawley focuses on the theatrical structure of *Play* as a parody of basic theatrical elements: dialogues are dehumanized to an exchange between bodiless voices and theatrical props.[5]

S. Connor, P. Lawley, A. McMullan, K. L. Laughlin, and others view Beckett's plays as challenges for their own criticism. These pieces reflect on and explore the modes of theatrical production, the modes of presenting and representing, on one hand, and of perceiving, on the other. Especially the problems of perception have to be addressed in order to confront perceptional habits and traditions of readership and audience, rather than to rely on them. This is why Connor, Lawley, and McMullan concentrate on relations established between the visual and acoustical elements of the plays. Different theatrical languages are struggling with each other. Whereas words appeal to rational understanding, visual elements—the space of the stage, for example—appeal to sensual perceptions. This essay will focus on the theatrical events mediating between these different theatrical spheres. By analyzing the status of expressions in *Play* and in two of Beckett's other shorter plays, *Krapp's Last Tape* and *Rockaby*, it will inquire into the range of processes revealing the in-between of theatrical languages that could be called in acoustic terms "silence," and in visual terms "invisibility."

It is true that the alternation of voices and of their spotlighted faces in *Play* distinguishes the speeches of the two figures, W1 and W2, from each other, but it is also true that the spoken words themselves seem to be interchangeable. Even as they denigrate each other, these two figures present one type of speech:

> W1: When I was satisfied it was all over I went to have a gloat. Just a common tart. What he could have found in her when he had me—
> [Spot from W1 to W2]
> W2: When he came again we had it out. I felt like death. He went on about why he had to tell her. Too risky and so on. That meant he had gone back to her. Back to that!
> [Spot from W2 to W1]
> W1: Pudding face, puffy, spots, blubber mouth, jowls, no neck, dugs you could—
> [Spot from W1 to W2]
> W2: He went on and on. I could hear a mower. . . .
> W1: Calves like a flunkey—[6]

The stage directions give no names to the two voices; they are simply referred to by the letter W and minimally distinguished by the numbers one and two. Their sentences flow into each other: W1 runs her competitor down, W2 complains about her lover's handling of his two love affairs. Nevertheless, W1's portrait of her competitor could also be read as W2's disparaging of her lover's other beloved. Each W talks about the other only in subversive metonymies, reducing the other to the demonstrative pronoun "that" or to derisively named body parts: "Pudding face, puffy, spots, blubber mouth, jowls, no neck." The figures are not distinguished by the language they speak. Differences in thematics are superseded by the way they talk. All figures produce their words mechanically, without any personal involvement, individual breathing, or speaking rhythms. The stage directions read: "Faces impassive throughout. Voices toneless except where an expression is indicated. Rapid tempo throughout."[7]

Theatrical gesture and movement are reduced to accelerated articulation, which produces mechanical sounds and exposes speech to a kind of automatic production and reproduction. W2 thematizes this mechanism of speech when she compares M's speaking with "dragging a great roller" and its noise with that of "an old hand mower." For her, his speech presents nothing but disturbing mechanical noise. With their toneless voices, rapid tempos, and repetitions, each speaker performs what he or she describes. Words, phrases, and sentences that function first as acoustic signs gradually evade their signifying potentialities throughout the play. This is very obvious when W1 arranges a sequence of words according to the play of their explosives and fricatives (*P-, F-* and *B*-sounds) in the line "Pudding face, puffy spots, blubber mouth . . ." *(P-dd-f, p-ff-p-t, b-bb-th)*. The semantic distortion of the face goes hand in hand with the fascination of the play. Unable to interrupt the flow of speech, the figures seem to be possessed by it. Herein lies their tragic paradox: Although they try to withdraw from speech, they are repeatedly drawn into its presence. Already in the beginning of the play, when the voices are still fused in the simultaneous sound of a choir, all of them are faint, and in the repeat they are "breathless" from the start. In W1's and M's lines one hears the longing for an end, for "all still," "all over," "all wiped out," "all out,"[8] although it is not clear what is left from the past to be wiped out.

The beginning, the narrative part of the play,[9] is dominated by memories, often by literal quotations of dialogical fragments indicated by such phrases as "I said to him," "she screamed," "she said." As A. McMullan points out, "[T]here is no chronological order in the figures' 'discourse' or the relation of the narrative, so that the text shifts forwards and backwards in time . . . making it very difficult to piece together into a 'whole'."[10] Later the figures try to compensate for their obsessions with the past on an imaginary level, but in vain: M himself rejects his dreams about a peaceful union of the three struggling with each other in "a little dinghy" as "such fantasies,"[11] noticing the gap that splits him as speaker from the imaginary level of his speech. The motoric mechanism, the rapid tempo of the speech, enforces its autonomy from such references. Moreover, the gap between the semantics and acoustics of language opens up a series of fissures between different theatrical elements: between the visual presence of the speakers faces, the movement of their speech apparatus, and speech. It is striking that the faces themselves are constructed and set apart. The stage directions artificially separate the faces from the voices: "faces so lost to age and aspect as to seem almost part of urns" are opposed to "the toneless voices" that Beckett dictates should be spoken with "rapid tempo throughout."[12] A paradox is inscribed into these faces: on one hand, they are stiff as in death; on the other, they are forced to perform extremely fast movements of articulation. In fact, a reversal seems to take place: The speaker does not control the speech, but speech itself takes over the functions of his or her physical speech apparatus. The "impassive faces" are only moved by the motor of speech that—as the stage directions read—is controlled "by a spotlight projected on faces alone. The transfer of light from one face to another is immediate."[13] The spotlight interrupts one speech and provokes another, isolating different parts from their original context in order to assemble the different fragments anew. The spotlight takes over this torturing initiative.[14] Beckett calls it "a unique inquisitor";[15] M addresses it as "mere eye" and "you."[16] With this anthropomorphization they transform the operational function of theater technology: instead of only supporting the play "behind the scenes," it takes an active, indeed a dominant, part. It is the mobile spotlight that silences one speaker and prompts the other to speak. The light subdues the speakers to its control: it makes them visible and audible, and thereby presents the representational functions of theater. But as McMullan points out, the light, now in the position of authorship, fails "to make an ordered, meaningful narrative out of the fragmented phrases and images";[17] it is subjected to ambiguous controls itself.

Addressed as a "you," the spotlight is ascribed the role of a partner in dialogue. But it also resists this role by not reacting dialogically. The "you" remains anonymously silent and leaves the speakers brutally isolated in their attempts to establish a dialogic relation. It thwarts every communicative intention and reduces the spoken language to unproductive motoric generations of sounds, words, and sentences. The dialogue turns into a confrontation of the visual and acoustic elements of theater, isolating them from each other. Thus the visual scene overpowers the acoustic one, interrogating the speeches/speakers under its control. Through this kind of inquisition, speech can materialize only as a relic left over from a past life, without affecting any presence. And this is why, in Beckett's scene, it issues from the mouths of urns.

> From each a head protrudes, the neck held fast in the urn's mouth. . . . Faces so lost to age and aspect as to seem almost parts of urns. But no masks.[18]

With urns one associates death, ashes, and the silence of the grave. But here the muteness—that is, death—starts to speak. How does one understand death here? Has someone or something died? The theatrical languages themselves? As theatrical props, urns and spotlights take over the play, superseding its characters. Because these characters are only actively present in their reliclike speech, they are reduced to maneuverable stage properties. In other words, once the visual elements, spotlight and urns, step out of their anonymous background function into the center of the play, the characters are pushed into anonymity. This detachment alienates the different theatrical processes from each of them, confusing all conventions of acoustical perceptions. K. L. Laughlin[19] points in Paul Klee's terms to the necessity of the audience's multidimensional attention toward the clashes between word and image. This "clashing between" will become the focus of this essay's further investigations of Beckett's texts.

In his early philosophical work on language, Benjamin distinguishes carefully between the very different aspects of language—of the divine, the human, and the language of things—by pointing toward their paradoxical relations to one another. His essay "Über Sprache überhaupt und über die Sprache des Menschen" distinguishes between "Lampe" and "Sprach-Lampe," an actual lamp from a lamp present in language, existing as a name.[20] Things by themselves are mute; according to Benjamin's reading of and speculations about Gen. 1, they are silent expressions of an original divine language. But by being named they are drawn into the presence of human language. By naming the things, this language breaks away from its origin. The actual presence of words points only indirectly through the broad range of semantic connotations to the language of the divine as well as to the language of the things. As Benjamin suggests in his essay about the task of the translator, a word or a text needs numerous translations into other languages in order to gain access to its hidden implications. Benjamin calls the language between all actual languages "die reine Sprache,"[21] the pure language. With this term he conceptualizes that which can never be present, which presents itself paradoxically only through its absence.

In Beckett's *Play* language itself becomes a mere thing. Although words—because they are spoken—appear as a part of language, they are at the same time separated from it. How can one understand this self-division of language? Benjamin says: "Das sprachliche Wesen des Menschen ist seine Sprache" [The linguistic being of the human is his language].[22] In Beckett's *Play*, however, this human language is reduced to the function of a stage property and thereby assumes the object character of a mechanical technicality. It becomes detached from its appearance as human expression and separated from its speakers and references; by becoming afunctional it discloses its inhuman aspects and functions as language of the mute thing itself. We have to consider here an intriguing and inversive shift: while language becomes detached from its speakers and reduced to acoustic stage properties, unnamed conventional—in this case, mainly visual—

stage properties assert themselves and take over designating and determining functions. This fragmentation of the speech act deprives it radically of all semantic connotations. Although stage properties and language seem to exchange their functions, it is obvious that neither can take over the naming function, nor can language be completely divested of it. By subverting the distinctions between conventionally defined theatrical orders, *Play* opens up an enigmatic realm between them and leaves each theatrical element in an inverted relation to itself. Although language still appears as language, it is reduced to a relic of itself, having lost all its attributes: its naming, calling, and communicating functions.

Because the figures of Beckett's *Play* are trapped within the accelerated and motorized presence of their past language and are withdrawn from any dialogic exchange, they become figures for the death of language as actual human expression. The speaking heads protrude out of the mouth of urns and can only lend their voices to the relics of life. But in contrast to the radical silence of the urns' ashes, the eccentric motoric talk offers no prospect of tranquility or untroubled commemoration. Silence itself is absent, and although the figures desire dialogue, they remain excluded from it. Referring obsessively to a tormented past, endlessly reciting their tortured jealousies, their monologic speech is unable to achieve anything other than the reproduction of its signifying process. This penetrative speech strips itself of its semantics, empties itself out, and so takes over the qualities of silence without being silent. At one point W1 considers overcoming speech by biting off her tongue, swallowing it, and spitting it out. With this attempt to castrate her own speech apparatus, W1 resists being penetrated by the driving forces of speech. But she does not gain any control, and her speech remains simply an expression of the apparatus's motoric functions—a mere prop.

In contrast, the figures in *Krapp's Last Tape* and *Rockaby* exercise a silence that moves towards a stillness beyond the reach of language. They encircle a silence that is excluded in *Play*. By staging the processes either of listening or of speaking, these scenes examine the relation of speaker or listener to an already established language by exploring the possibility of moving beyond the limits of their own experiences with it. The figures listen to recordings of their own voices until the recordings run out. This transition from silence to stillness distinguishes two modes of quietness. How does this distinction come about and which function does it serve?

Listening to old recordings is intended to stimulate Krapp to the production of new ones, relating the narrations and reflections of a distant past to the present. But because he throws away the only text he actually records, he remains restricted to listening to his preserved speeches, never finding an actual language that could be appropriated for his recording. Krapp's alternating but very repetitive and mechanized autoerotical habits—eating, walking back and forth, listening, relistening, and speaking—break off finally after he has listened for the third time to one special part of his recording. As an introduction to this scene, he quotes a sentence from the recording but changes its past tense into an imperative: He transforms the sentence "I lay down across her" into "Lie down across her." But instead of pragmatically reacting to this self-imposed imperative and leaving his room in order to visit his girlfriend, he remains seated in front of the recorder, rewinds it, and replays the same old report again, melancholically bound to his familiar linguistic patterns.

> KRAPP: . . . Be again, be again. [Pause.] All that old misery. [Pause] One wasn't enough for you. [Pause.] Lie down across her. [Long pause. He suddenly bends over machine, switches off, wrenches off tape, throws it away, puts on the other, winds it forward to the passage he wants, switches on, listens staring front.]
> TAPE: . . . I asked her to look at me and after a few moments – (Pause.) – after a few moments she did, but the eyes just slits, because of the glare. I bent over to get them in the shadow and they opened. (Pause. Low) Let me in. (Pause) We drifted in among the flags and stuck. The way they went down, sighing, before the stem! (Pause.) I lay down across her with my face in her breasts and my hand on her. We lay there without moving. But under us all moved, and moved us, gently, up and down, and from side to side. [Pause. Krapp's lips move. No sound.]
> Past midnight. Never knew such silence. The earth might be uninhabited.[23]

Two scenes of silencing are placed one upon the other: one occurs in the poetic imagination of Krapp's taped memory and the other in his experience as a listener. The listening becomes the stage for erotic fantasies. Since the listener does not speak again, he exposes himself to this sexual arousal as an act of silence. The imperative "Lie down across her" results finally in "Krapp motionless staring before him. The tape runs on in silence," suggesting the ongoing "up and down" and "side to side" movement in and of his fantasies, instead of "a post-coital emptiness" as Gontarski suggests.[24] Normally, Krapp would interrupt his listening, rewind the tape, get up, and eat or drink, but this time he is not only silenced but also physically immobilized. His quiet reception leads him to a radical withdrawal from language and an urge for repetition in general. Whereas the silence following sexual ecstasy is disrupted again by daily routines and speech patterns, the silence while listening to the recorded silence no longer turns into speech. It is ongoing and overruns the borders within which any speech about silence remains compressed. The change from one silence into the other is presented as an autoerotic, self-touching process: "Krapp's lips move. No sound."[25]

The thematization of silence can never recapture the actual experience, because it always interrupts it. The acoustic presence of language per se contradicts its theoretically postulated absence. Krapp surrenders to the silence about which he says: "Never knew such silence. The earth might be uninhabited."[26] This observation leaves open the question of whether Krapp will ever start to speak again. Does his silence tear away from language in order to block any further contact with it?

As long as he speaks, Krapp refers to his speech as a paradox, as a speech that has nothing to say. "Nothing to say, not a squeak,"[27] he says. This nothingness allows him an enthusiastic play with the word "spool."

> Ah! [. . .] Box . . . thrree . . . spool . . . five [. . .] Spool! (Pause) Spooool! (Happy smile. Pause. He bends over table, starts peering and poking at the boxes.) Box . . . thrree . . . thrree . . . four . . . two . . . (with surprise) nine! good God! . . . seven . . . ah! the little rascal! [. . .] Spool . . . (he peers at ledger) . . . five . . . (he peers at spools) . . . five . . . five . . . ah! the little scoundrel! [. . .]Spool five[. . .] Box thrree, Spool five.[. . .] Box thrree, spool five.[. . .] Spooool! . . .[28]

This play with sounds that transforms speech into a musical playground introduces Krapp as speaker and inspires—as he implies—the various levels of the scene. As presentation of the letter *o* the turning tape visualizes and automates the letter's graphic shape. These graphic-theatrical associations are related to acoustical ones. Transferring linguistic musicality to visual theatricality, the play with the material manifestations of words creates a logic of sounds and shapes that undermines conventional semantics. Assonances between the words "spool" and "stool" relate physical digestive processes to processes of memory, marking memory as excrement, as something to expunge rather than as a productive process of working through remembrances in Freud's sense.[29] In becoming freed not only from psychological and physical connotations, the word "spool" does not lead to any comprehensive reflections but to fun with its tone, to the "Happiest moment of the past half million."

> The sour cud and the iron stool. (Pause) Revelled in the word spool. (With relish) Spooool! Happiest moment of the past half million.[30]

The tape recorder isolates the spoken words from the speaker and from all extra-audible conditions of speech. It dehumanizes the spoken words by reducing them to magnetically preserved data that become independent from sensual physical production and consciousness. Thus the tape recorder abstracts technically from all those linguistic elements from which Krapp tries to escape and presents that what Krapp is looking for: sound.

But as a machine, the tape recorder presents another quality: although it can record and reproduce speech, in itself it is speechless and soundless. The precondition for possible recordings lies in its technically produced silence. Whenever it runs quietly without reproducing anything, it confronts Krapp with an extranatural, extrahuman, and extralinguistic silence. Therefore we can distinguish two modes of silence: that technically produced and the caesura that separates one linguistic expression from the other. As the spotlight in *Play*, the tape recorder does not function any more as an anonymous requisite. From the very beginning it becomes the center for the action. The new medium offers access to a tranquility that cannot turn into speaking. But this tranquility does not imply a standstill or stagnation. The wheels go on turning around and guarantee the continuity of silence. Whereas all earlier quiet moments interfered with the desire to speak and to confront memories, this silence has its source in the relaxed play with the linguistic sounds and their presentation in smooth mechanical turning movements, distancing speaker and listener from all intentional and referential functions of speech.

Krapp's final stillness seems to break off with a series of interruptions. Throughout his play, pauses rhythmically separate one action from another—eating from drinking, listening from speaking, and so on. But the final pause no longer mediates between two actions. It does not allow itself to be interrupted again; instead, it replaces all theatrical actions by radical silence and the associated motionlessness. When the voice of the tape breaks off, the silence of the listener encounters the silence of the speaker without interrupting it. Indeed, it is as if silence listens and speaks to silence, and moves thereby beyond the reach of conventional expression. Does this process hint at the beginning of a new language that can only be present through its absence, a language that Benjamin called "pure language"? This play does not only try "to transcend the compulsion of language by the greater . . . use of visual imagery," as Martin Esslin[31] claims for Beckett's stage work in general, but at the same time it transcends the visual imagery by narrowing in on a scene of silence listening to silence. It evokes a between from which the theater of words and images might originate or into which it might collapse. One could read it as the theatrical presentation of Krapp's utterance, "Nothing to say, not a squeak."

In *Rockaby*[32] a woman is made to listen to her taped voice and to be moved by her mechanically rocking chair. The rocking movement and the rhythms of speech, with its repetitions and rhyming assonances, are so tuned to each other that they seem to present a continuous, ongoing process. The only tension occurs when the rocking and voice come to a rest, threatening her with an "end," the "close of a long day," a stopping of time, and death. With the one word "more," the woman resists this interruption three times; then she gives in and allows herself to be rocked off, silently accepting nursery rhyme rhythms as the rhythms of her death rattles. Turning to articulation and speech, to her word "more," allows her to remain in time and its circular movement; it is the only escape from the threat of the unknown in pauses and interruptions, which always imply the possibility of the radical end of all familiar moments of time and of all presentations.

In *Play*, speech is reduced to maneuverable stage properties; it figures silence through mechanized speech. As long as this figuration of silence takes place, silence is still bound to the function of expression. In *Krapp's Last Tape* and *Rockaby*, the voice of the main figure is split into two: into the taped one and the "live" one, the preserved and the actual. These two voices merge in the end, in the culmination of all pauses and interruptions: the final pause of silence never ends. Listening and speaking are bound together in this silence: in the one language of (comprising) all absent languages.

The rocker in *Rockaby* has long been identified as the rocker of the woman's dying mother. The voice says:

> down the steep stair . . .
> right down
> into the old rocker
> mother rocker
> where mother rocked[33]

Taking over the position of the mother suggests her return to the womb. S. Connor has pointed to the shifting pronouns that "bring about a merging of identity between the mother and the daughter who replicates her life and death."[34] In ceasing the rock and coming to the "fade-out" of the scene the voice withdraws from acoustical and, finally, visual presence. Lois Oppenheim suggests removing the discussion of the play's end from any discourse on gender, implying that Beckett conceives of a language that is free "from the political and ideological functioning of a masculine or feminine discourse."[35] This theoretical speculation—inspired by Heidegger's philosophy of being and language—is on target, within its limits; but it amounts to not taking the actions and images of the stage seriously. The voice in *Rockaby* knows that she is able to gain access to the hidden "pure language" only through the physical reappropriation of the mother's position. Krapp in *Krapp's Last Tape* gains such access through fantasizing about a sexual encounter. In both of these stage productions Beckett seems to examine different ways for overcoming the psychological, social, political, or ideological constraints of language. Only by living intensely up to such limits is there the hope for breaking through them: socially in *Play,* where the vivacious discourse of the past turns into a monotonous memento of speech, in *Krapp's Last Tape,* where the male artistic monologue silences itself by being drawn into the imaginary away from the stress of its production, and in *Rockaby* where the female figure physically rocks herself off into the spheres of the dead and the unborn.

Notes

1. "In *Play* Beckett uses his habitual doublets and triplets, but conceals them by variation or distance. Calling marked attention to itself, however, is the repetition of the whole play, with its intimation not only that life is repetitive play, but so is any conceivable afterlife." Ruby Cohn, "The Churn of Stale Words: Repetitions," in *Just Play: Beckett's Theatre* (Princeton: Princeton University Press, 1980), pp. 96–139, 127.

2. Anna McMullan, "Mimicking Mimesis," in *Theater on Trial: Samuel Beckett's Later Drama* (New York: Routledge, 1993), p. 15.

3. Steven Connor, *Samuel Beckett: Repetition, Theory and Text* (New York: Blackwell, 1988), p. 126. Connor focuses here especially on *Krapp's Last Tape, Ohio Impromptu, Rockaby,* and *That Time.*

4. Karen L. Laughlin, "Seeing is Perceiving: Beckett's Later Plays and the Theory of Audience Response," in R. J. Davis and L. Butler, eds., *"Make sense who may": Essays on Samuel Beckett's Later Works* (Gerrards Cross, U.K.: Colin Smythe, 1988), pp. 20–29.

5. Paul Lawley, "Beckett's Dramatic Counterpoint: A Reading of *Play,*" *Journal of Beckett Studies* 9 (1984): 25–41.

6. Samuel Beckett, *Play,* in *The Collected Shorter Plays of Samuel Beckett* (New York: Grove Weidenfeld, 1984), p. 150.

7. Ibid.

8. Hersh Zeifman addresses such desires for an end in theological terms as desire for "redemption" and identifies—perhaps too quickly—the addressed "you" as the conventional Christian God who punishes for sins; see Hersh Zeifman, "Being and Non-Being: Samuel Beckett's Not I," *Modern Drama* 19 (1976): 35.

9. Martin Esslin divides the text, according to a discussion with Beckett, into three parts: chorus, narration, and meditation. See Martin Esslin, "Samuel Beckett and the Art of Broadcasting," *Encounter,* September 1975, 44; see also Lawley, "Beckett's Dramatic Counterpoint," p. 31 n. 5.

10. Anna McMullan, *Theatre on Trial: Samuel Beckett's Later Drama* (New York: Routledge, 1993), p. 22.

11. Beckett, *Play,* p. 156.

12. Ibid., p. 147.

13. Ibid.

14. Paul Lawley ("Beckett's Dramatic Counterpoint," p. 36) speaks here of the "light torture."
15. Beckett, *Play*, p. 158.
16. Ibid., pp. 156–57.
17. McMullan, *Theatre on Trial*, p. 22.
18. Beckett, *Play*, p. 147.
19. Laughlin, "Seeing is Perceiving," p. 27.
20. Walter Benjamin, "Über Sprache überhaupt und über die Sprache des Menschen," in Rolf Tiedemann and Hermann Schweppenhauser, eds., *Gesammelte Schriften*, vol. 2 (Frankfurt a.M.: Suhrkamp, 1980), pp. 140-57.
21. Walter Benjamin, "Die Aufgabe des Übersetzers," in Tillman Rexroth, ed., *Gesammelte Schriften*, vol. 4 (Frankfurt, 1980), p. 13.
22. See Benjamin, "Über Sprache," pp. 140–57; 142.
23. Samuel Beckett, *Krapp's Last Tape*, in *The Collected Shorter Plays*, pp. 53–63; 63.
24. S. E. Gontarski, "The Making of *Krapp's Last Tape*," in James Knowlson, ed., *Krapp's Last Tape* (London: Brutus Books, 1980), p. 19.
25. Beckett, *Krapp's Last Tape*, p. 63.
26. Ibid.
27. Ibid., p. 62.
28. Ibid., p. 56.
29. Sigmund Freud, "Erinnern, Wiederholen und Durcharbeiten," in *Schriften zur Behandlungstechnik*. Studienausgabe, Ergänzungsband. (Frankfurt: Fischer, 1975), pp. 205–15.
30. Beckett, *Krapps Last Tape*, p. 62.
31. Martin Esslin, "Telling It How It Is: Beckett and the Mass Media," in Joseph H. Smith, ed., *The World of Samuel Beckett* (Baltimore: Johns Hopkins University Press, 1991), p. 212.
32. Samuel Beckett, *Rockaby*, in *The Collected Shorter Plays* (New York: Grove Weidenfeld, 1984), p. 272.
33. Ibid., p. 280.
34. Steven Connor, *Samuel Beckett: Repetition, Theory and Text* (Oxford: Basil Blackwell, 1988), p. 134.
35. Lois Oppenheim, "Anonymity and Individuation," in R. J. Davis and L. Butler, eds., *"Make Sense Who May": Essays On Samuel Beckett's Later Works* (Gerrards Cross, U.K.: Colin Smythe, 1988), p. 45.

Undoing and Doing:
Allegories of Writing in the *Trilogy*

LI-LING TSENG

Suspicious of philosophy as he is, Samuel Beckett is nonetheless unable to avoid the influence of Western philosophy, in particular, Cartesian philosophy. Since his first major novel *Murphy* (1938), about which he stated to Georges Reavey that "the wild and unreal dialogues . . . are the comic exaggeration of . . . the Hermeticism of the spirit,"[1] Beckett has been wrestling with the issue of the Cartesian cogito, its consolation as well as problematics. The Cartesian model prescribes the prior (hence superior) contamination-free, enclosed subjective (hence reflective) consciousness whose self-sameness and certainty is ontologically guaranteed. "[T]here is nothing which is easier for me to know than my own mind," claimed Descartes.[2] By regimenting radical doubt as its method, the thinking "I" is in a position to disinfect the realm of world and things considered cognitively unviable by Western epistemological tradition,[3] and thus to achieve mathematical certitude concerning it.

Cartesian doubt institutes substantive dualism by creating a "dramatic dehiscence" and driving a wedge between the subjective and the objective realms; "mind and world" thereby come "asunder in irreparable dissociation."[4] Since the world of matter is considered indirect, unreliable, uncertain, and unavailable to subjective cognition, the Cartesian dichotomic hierarchy privileges the mind in the dyads. Similarly, we find in Beckett, as early as in *Proust* (1931): "Nor is there any direct and purely experimental contact possible between the subject and object, because they are automatically separated by the subject's consciousness of perception and the object loses its purity and becomes a mere intellectual pretext or motive."[5]

Beckett's fiction is, to be sure, swarming with Cartesian thinking heroes. The *Trilogy* is the peak work not only of Beckett's creative career but also of his digestion (or rather, indigestion) of the Cartesian philosophy.

According to the Cartesian dicta, nature, namely, an extension of the Cartesian mind, is "dehumanized" and "despiritualized."[6] The four serial-narrators of the *Trilogy* tend to alienate themselves from this spiritless, external world of matter, even their own bodies. Immobile in bed, Molloy, Malone, and the Unnamable all feel apart from their own physical bodies. Molloy characteristically concludes that the confines of his room, bed, and even his own body are as remote as those of the Molloy country: "when I see my hands, on the sheet . . . they are not mine, even less than ever mine, I have no arms, they are a couple."[7]

This subject-object schism naturally affects the thinking self's representation of the outside world. Moran tends to feel that the outside world is remote from his inner mind. When Gaber comes to announce the chief's command, Moran's close-up, analytic, or even clinical, dissection of Gaber's feet crushing his daisies (p. 86) is symptomatic of Moran's acute sense of alienation from the outside. He has also initiated his son's young "mind" into the "horror of the body and its function" (p. 108). Recalling in his report a man inquiring if he had seen an old man with a stick pass by in the forest, Moran can see in the narrative present the man's hand still thrusting at him. He perceives that it is "coming towards [him], pallid, opening and closing. As if self-propelled." It is because of this sense of alienation and menace from the outside world experienced by the thinking ego that Moran next struck him on the head without even being conscious of his act (p. 139).

The outside world, as registered in the Unnamable's mind, is even more abstracted and cognitively impermissible than that of his predecessors'. Not only what has happened but also his own meaning escape him (p. 269). The world is polarized into two alternatives, both inaccessible: a void or a "plenum," a world infused with "matter" (p. 275). Faced with extreme uncertainty, the Unnamable desperately reasserts his identity by saying that it is he who writes, in the same breath as saying that he cannot even raise his own hand from his knee, let alone write (p. 276). His body suffers enormous deterioration and dismemberment, so much so that his subjective identity is also in great peril. In short, polarized from his thinking mind is an unintelligible and obscure world.

In contrast to the hermetic thinking mind of the Cartesian sort, the outside world of matter is radically "other"—all that the subject is not. This otherness comes in concrete forms of human figures whom the narrators encounter and who seem at the same time to be others and to resemble them: A and C in *Molloy*; Malone and Sapo; the great gang of the Unnamable's masters/creatures. Or it is dramatized by the Sartrean gaze of the other: the "watchful gaze" of the traffic policeman who stops Molloy (p. 22); the gaze of the policemen and jailers at the police station (p. 25);

the "other eyes" that Malone feels close behind his own closed eyes when he is in the heat of inventing his stories (p. 180).

In the midst of the unavailability, unreliability, and otherness of the outside world of matter, however, the narrators and characters of the *Trilogy* occasionally derive a consolation from the Cartesian thinking model; namely, their thinking subject lays claim to an indubitably superior status. It detaches itself or even triumphantly retreats from the messy world of matter. Moreover, its self-enclosed purity and monadlike self-sufficiency facilitate and guarantee its being the absolute origin of knowledge. For example, Molloy announces that he will be "over with this world" (p. 10), asserting the mind's superior distinctness from matter. Specifically, he claims that his feet will not take him to his mother unless his mind tells them to (p. 29). He has an intuition that he was "not merely physical" (p. 79)—affirming the substance of the mind in its own right, as Descartes had done when he distinguished the two independent substances of the mind and the matter.[8] In the same vein, Moll in *Malone Dies* also instructs Macmann that "the flesh is not the end-all" (p. 240). Malone prides himself in the statement that "All the things I was always with in spirit. In body no. Not such a fool" (p. 246). The Unnamable consoles himself that his soul, unlike his body, is immune from deterioration and dismemberment (p. 303). He exhibits contempt for the unruly outside world and maintains the source of speech within himself, because "anything is preferable to the consciousness of third parties and . . . of an outer world" (p. 359).

The *Trilogy* is packed with the idiomatic phrase "no matter" in sentences such as "no matter, let us go on" (p. 15); "no matter, let's leave it, no harking" (p. 356); "no matter, I've shut my doors against them, I'm not at home to anything, my doors are shut against them" (p. 360). The phrase "no matter," meaning nonimportant, is in fact a figure of speech. It can, however, literally refer to the narrators' incantative rejection of the world of matter. Here deconstructive maneuver may render fruitful discovery in accounting for Beckett's Cartesian concerns in the *Trilogy*. In developing a "rhetorical" type of deconstruction,[9] Paul de Man proposes in *Allegories of Reading* the constitutive blurring of the "literal" and "figurative" levels of meaning, whose clear demarcation has been accused by Jacques Derrida of characterizing the perpetual priority of Western philosophy. De Man discovers that the literal, or referential, meaning of language is always contaminated with figurality; it is already a figure of figures, a trope of tropes. Hence, not only a sharp distinction between the two levels of meaning ceases to be maintained but also any discourse *must* (notice the obligatory nature of the condition, see J. Hillis Miller's rendition of de Man's idea) invite both literal and rhetorical readings at once.[10] Therefore, many phrases and sentences in the *Trilogy* may be read in this alternative literal way and hence unexpectedly reinstate the narrators' preoccupation with the disinfected superiority of the Cartesian thinking mind.

This hermetic or even solipsistic enclosure of the reflective mind vies against "the incoherence, the multiplicity, and the complexity"[11] of the given world and hence guarantees an a priori sureness of cognition for the *Trilogy* narrators. They locate the ultimate source of knowledge in their thinking cogito. The ultimate issue is in the head or, to use Molloy's words, in the "heart of hearts" (p. 57). Molloy, Malone, and the Unnamable all make reference to their shut-up head to which they owe their existence (p. 203). The point is to "know the laws of the mind" (p. 14), which, according to Descartes, cannot be easier and more reassuring. The Unnamable best encapsulates the narrators' common aspiration and confidence: he identifies the sole possible "hierarchy" in the "subject" itself[12] and aspires to be endowed with a "mind" in order to know a pain in the neck "once and for all" (p. 325). The mind, therefore, undoes the remoteness and alienation of bodily sensation and information, because it is the "self-causing cause."[13]

Although he is obviously fascinated by the "Hermeticism of the spirit" safeguarded by the Cartesian cogito, Beckett fails to embrace wholeheartedly the optimism with which the sealed Cartesian subject seems to brace itself. More often than not, his characters are left chilled and haunted by the unresolved and failing aspects of the Cartesian solution. Truer to the case, the Beckettian characters in the *Trilogy* are, at most, Cartesian *manqués*. The "regime of systematic doubt" prescribed by Descartes, with which he dismisses the unreliable external world and fortifies deception-free subjective reflection, proves inadequate and just as inert as the object that such a method aims at unraveling.[14] After successfully quitting Lousse's house, Molloy comments on the absurd hilarity derived from his awkward way of moving with crutches:

> There is rapture, or there should be, in the motion crutches give. It is a series of little flights, skimming the ground. You take off, you land, through the thronging sound in wind and limb, who have to fasten one foot to the ground before they dare lift up the other. And even their most joyous hastenings is [*sic*] less aerial than my hobble. But these are reasonings, based on analysis. (P. 60)

The final line of self-comment on his preceding manner of analytic reasoning seems to suggest that it fails to capture the essence of the experience that his legs render. He then continues to explain why the same old "care," the intent of going to his mother, now becomes "less" in the same mode of reasoning:

> because these were ancient cares and the mind cannot always brood on the same cares, but needs fresh cares from time to time, so as to revert with renewed vigour, when the time comes, to ancient cares. But can one speak here of fresh and ancient cares? I think not. . . . What I can assert without fear of—without fear, is that I gradually lost interest in knowing, among other things, what town I was in and if I should soon find my mother and settle the matter between us. And even the nature of that matter grew dim, for me, without however vanishing completely. For it was no small matter and I was bent on it. All my life, I think, I had been bent on it. . . . I had been bent on settling this matter between my mother and me, but had never succeeded. (P. 60)

This passage, like the "no matter" example, may fall within the de Mannian vector with its two complementary but destabilizing, literal and rhetorical, pointers. The words "think" and "matter" may likewise be read in the literally Cartesian context, thereby destabilizing the surface meaning that Molloy intends. Derrida elaborates that the "spacing" that "constitutes the written sign" separates the sign from all intended authorial closure; moreover, the sign is always subject to an "open possibility of extraction and grafting."[15] Hence, in deconstructive reading, the pause of the sentence, or the literal space "between" (i.e., Derrida's *entre*), is bound to be enforced:[16] the Cartesian narrator/hero acknowledges that his existence hinges on mental reflection—"All my life, I think." Typical of a Cartesian, his greatest concern is with the "matter" that is "no small." Likewise, by the same deconstructive reading strategy, he self-defeatingly confesses that he "gradually lost interest in knowing," admitting to the failing problematics of the thinking faculty, and that he never succeeded in settling the "matter," whose nature grows "dim." Employing de Man's proposed model of reading, we find that both rhetorical and literal readings, if taken together, generate a multiplicity of meanings, all of which may be successfully contextualized in the anti-Cartesian dialectics.

Knowing he is dying, Malone is indecisive about his designed program of telling stories or speaking of his possessions. He questions himself in an inner colloquy with himself:

> Would it not then be better for me to speak of my possessions without further delay? Would not that be wiser? And then if necessary at the last moment correct any inaccuracies. That is what reason counsels. *But reason has*

not much hold on me just now. All things run together to encourage me. But can I really resign myself to the possibility of my dying without leaving an inventory behind? There I am back at my old quibbles. (P. 167; emphasis added)

Neither does reason have hold on Malone's creature, Sapo, who "was sorry he had not learnt the art of thinking . . . and sorry he could make no meaning of the babel raging in his head, the doubts, desires, imaginings and dreads" (p. 177). Uninitiated as he is, Sapo resembles the Cartesian-oriented Malone to a great extent: "Nothing is less like me than this patient, reasonable child, struggling all alone for year to shed a little light upon himself, and of the last gleam, a stranger to the joys of darkness" (p. 178). Like his Cartesian creator/master, Sapo is concerned with seeping the "light" of the mind through the "murk" and "darkness" of the external world of phenomena, but obviously to no avail (cf. Descartes's preference for using the image of light for reason).[17]

Moran, too, possesses a distinctively Cartesian rationalism that is gradually swallowed by the incommensurability of mind and matter. The Molloy case, of which he is put in charge, thickens into a chameleon-like puzzle to the extent that he laments "How little one is at one with oneself" (p. 104). This passage requires no de Mannian conversion from the rhetorical to literal reading to be understood in the Cartesian context. Moran's comment on the self demonstrates the Cartesian problematic, turning it inside out. The self-same, self-identical Cartesian cogito's enclosed totality is here deconstructed. "One" and "oneself," more often than not, fail to coincide. Malone also confesses in his writing that "the subject falls far from the verb and the object lands somewhere in the void" (p. 215). The Unnamable is so greatly confused by the inter- and intrapersonal voices he hears that he desperately claims that "the subject doesn't matter, there is none" (p. 331). When located in de Man's two-dimensional radius vector with the literal and rhetorical readings as its two separate poles, this exclamation at once affirms the thinking subject's distinctness from "matter" and the former's failure to settle the question of the latter. The Unnamable fails to be a true Cartesian, because he is always short of "me" (p. 313).

Indeed, Molloy, Malone, and the Unnamable tend to forget their "selves." The metaphors Molloy uses in describing this hermetic subjectivity are symptomatic of his failed Cartesianism: "I was no longer that sealed jar to which I owed by being so well preserved, but a wall gave way and I filled with roots and tame stems for example" (p. 46). The image of the well-preserved "sealed jar" recurs in the condition of Mahood and Worm, the Unnamable's creatures. They owe their existence literally to the jar in which

Mahood and even Worm find themselves stuck. Like the wall, this image is a good visual transcription of the sealed Cartesian mind. The thinking I's hermetic purity is safeguarded by a mental wall that screens off, though registering at the same time, the outside world. However, neither Molloy's metaphoric jar nor Mahood's literal jar succeeds in preserving the self intact from the encroachment of the outside. None of these *Trilogy* characters maintains the integral self-identity of his thinking subject, which, instead, gives way to the material world of things and others. They inherit the Cartesian model of thinking; they are all unable, however, to digest its qualifications wholesale.

Not only are the characters failed Cartesians, but Beckett intentionally exposes the failings of the Cartesian method and problematizes Cartesian logocentrism. John Pilling summarizes that "The whole of Beckett's . . . philosophical thinking is determined by his acceptance of Descartes's methods and rejection of Descartes's consolations."[18] Martin Esslin comments that the entire Beckettian oeuvre never ceases to "dismantle and deconstruct the Cartesian *cogito ergo sum*."[19]

Descartes's famous method of systematic enumeration is parodied in Malone's finding his possessions conveniently "divided into five," but he soon questions himself, "Into five what? I don't know. Everything divides into itself, I suppose." He then admonishes himself, "If I start trying to think again I shall make a mess of my decease" (p. 168). Later he dismisses the head as the "seat of all the shit and misery" (p. 245). The famous Cartesian doubt is mere "pretext," among other of his inventions, for "not coming to the point" (p. 254). The Unnamable goes further, employing disrespectful, excremental imagery: his masters have taught him "love, intelligence, to count, and reason" and "Some of this rubbish has come in handy on occasions . . . I use it still, to scratch my arse with" (p. 273). Thinking and its accessories—reasoning, doubting, and making logical hypotheses—are openly acknowledged as "lies" (pp. 378, 379). The Unnamable cautions himself: "I must not try to think, simply utter" (p. 274). Thinking proves to be symptomatic of the "excess" *(de trop)* of the Sartrean consciousness, or the for-itself, forever "differed" and "displaced" from the "lack" *(manque)* in the in-itself.[20] In imagining the sadomasochistic struggle between a group of masters torturing his own creature (Mahood) in fervent dialogues between them, the Unnamable makes apparent this paradoxical "excess" in his "incompetent" Cartesian thinking: "No one asks him to think, simply to suffer, always in the same way, without hope of diminution, without hope of dissolution, it's no more complicated than that. No need to think in order to despair" (p. 338). Inasmuch as the existential anguish plagues the identity-unknown narrator, the rational mode of thinking proves *both* inadequate *and* superfluous. The Unnamable is immensely drawn by the two-headed carriage of anti-Cartesian inclinations. On the one hand, the desire for possessing a clear mind to know the "pain in the neck once and for all" is urgently expressed. On the other, the thread of undoing that desire is pulling in the opposite direction.

In spite of the strenuous effort to get at and to clearly define the "I" of the thinking self, none of the *Trilogy* narrators achieves an affinity to it; they are forever fallen behind it. Malone confesses to the disparate "distance" between him and his "self," saying, "I shall hear myself talking, afar off, from my far mind, talking of the Lamberts, talking of my myself, my mind wandering, far from here, among its ruins" (pp. 198–99). In the final delirium, the Unnamable, too, has an insight into his failed self: "I say I, knowing it's not I, I am far, far" (p. 372). Excessive abstraction results from the narrators' Cartesian doubting apparatus, so much so that the Unnamable's disembodiment and dismemberment ironically configure the model's problematics. He is not equipped with a mouth, an ear, or even a head. Not even an abstract "mind" may be located for his keeping: "I don't feel a body on me . . . it's not yet my turn . . . to have a body, complete with head, to be able to understand" (p. 379). He becomes like Derrida's "entre," or the "between": "that's what I feel, an outside and inside and me in the middle . . . I'm the tympanum, on the one hand the mind, on the other the world, I don't belong to either" (p. 352).

The Unnamable's radical dismemberment, achieving sure knowledge of neither the body nor even the mind, suggests Beckett's intentional undoing of Cartesianism. He not only exposes but acts out its entangled problematics. A conscientious postmodern writer, Beckett undoes not only philosophy but, more importantly, literature's referential and signifying system. Combined with the failure to achieve the centrality of the Cartesian ego, the self-sameness of the authorial intention and its coincidence with the verbal expression are also undone. Both Molloy and the Unnamable experience a dislocation of things and their names (pp. 31, 375). Molloy surrenders his failed subjective control to the objective "words" that create, independently of the creating consciousness, undesirable "worlds" alien to the former: he knows only "what the words know," even though he thinks he is the one who invents his story; he clearly knows he invents nothing but stammers out the "lesson" he already learned, "the remnants of a pensum" (p. 31). In other words, the originative source of utterance supposedly attributed to the speaking subject is now decentered by alien words that, when uttered, merely repeat the same old thing.

Derrida demonstrates that there is no self-same repetition. Written signs rely on their reiterability to be transmitted across persons and time. The word, however, draws an "alterity" to itself, for "iter" in Sanskrit, as Derrida explains, means means "other."[21] Susceptible to endlessly new contexts, the written sign must veer farther away from the original speaking situation. So it is with Molloy's discovery of his own condition. Not only is the boredom and tedium of having to repeat the same lesson unbearable, but the first-person subject's repetitions turn out to be about "Not I."

The lack of guarantee of a return to the signifying and referential origin occurs in Molloy's daily conversations with others. He detests having conversations with others, for other people's words are heard "as pure sounds, free of all meaning" (p. 47). This blocked return to the original self is again concretized in Malone's inability to fully control his Sapo story. The Unnamable even literally mouths alien words whose origin and meaning escape his understanding: "where do these words come from that pour out of my mouth, and what do they mean" (p. 340).

The more desperately the *Trilogy* characters attempt to be one with their own "selves," the more disparate seems the correspondence. The Unnamable's repeatedly failing efforts to "get born" by implanting within himself a name-complete and identity-complete configuration are a good allegory for the undone Cartesian subject's exile from itself, a movement characterized by Derrida's *différance,* namely, perpetually differing and deferring from the origin. The Unnamable desperately wants to be any of the personages he himself actually creates, but he is unable to make up his "mind" about the certitude of Mahood or Worm or even the surreptitious appearances of other characters, including Watt and Jones (pp. 311–12). This entangled identity problem breaks open the closed Cartesian "circuit of ipsemosity."[22] It allegorizes the centrality of the self deconstructed by "self-division into a confrontation with its other"; the self splits into a series of "simulacra."[23] The logocentric Cartesian system in *The Unnamable* is hence rendered "weightless" and becomes nothing but "a gigantic simulacrum . . . exchanging in itself, in an uninterrupted circuit without reference or circumference."[24] Indeed, the *Trilogy* can self-reflexively serve as an allegory for Beckett's entire oeuvre, weaving in and out these "brandips, beginning with Murphy" (p. 359), and staging a "furious progression of deictic masks" that tell and act out story lines "one inside the other in an infinite regression."[25]

In truth, the Unnamable already undoes the attempt to return to the a priori origin at the opening of the novel: "Where now? Who now? When now? Unquestioning. . . . Keep going, going on, call that going, call that on" (p. 267), supplanting it with the actional "going on" of the late Wittgensteinian sort, departing from the hunt for "saying" and its referential absolutes.[26] From the fully embodied Moran, to Molloy, who gradually disintegrates physically, to Malone, who is radically dismembered, to the Unnamable, who is both bodiless and mindless, Beckett has undone in stages the single, unique Cartesian self and supplanted it with the differing play characterized by Derridean *écriture*.

Indeed, the obligation to submit in writing or to be submitted to write is the ur-condition facing all *Trilogy* narrators. Western philosophers, according to Derrida's analysis, tend to dismiss writing for its susceptibility to contamination and abuse, thereby destroying authoritarian Truth.[27] Because of the repeatability of written signs, writing, for Derrida, is the means and the symptom of self-division and plurality in the self.[28] In the *Trilogy*, writing, indeed, is susceptible to deconstructing the clear distinction between signifier and signified and subverting the conventionally prior speaking subject. The written words, or writing in the guise of speech, distance themselves from a fixed meaning or reference. Molloy likes to call his mother Mag, for the letter g seems to abolish the preceding two letters (p. 18). The other *Trilogy* narrators are also wary of the self-stultifying movement inherent in writing. The Unnamable's situation is typical. He is confronted head-on with the nonreference of his words: "Perhaps that is how it began. . . . No matter how it happened. It, say it, not knowing what" (p. 267). The self-styled questioning of the obvious pronoun "it" spells out the problematics of the correspondence between word signs and their referents. Similar trouble from pronouns can be seen in one of his final desperate statements, wherein he struggles to come to terms with the crippled referential system of his own use of language: "There's no name for me, no pronoun for me, all the trouble comes from that, that, it's a kind of pronoun too . . . I'm not that either, let us leave all that, forget about all that" (p. 372). Meaning, pronounces Derrida, is choicelessly disposed to difference from itself.[29]

Writing often has an inaugural, autoconstitutional quality that upsets the centrality of the writing or speaking self. The Unnamable is twice pleasantly surprised by the autoformation of unexpected wor(l)ds in his storytelling. He describes Worm's eagerness to depart toward his master, "and his long shadow will follow him, across the desert, it's a desert, that's news" (p. 337). The Unnamable is no more in full control of his stories than Malone of his Sapo story. Speaking of his own condition and his struggle with "them," the Unnamable is surprised by his account: "they must have taught me believing too . . . I've always been here, here there was never anyone but me, never, always, me, no one, old slush to be churned everlastingly, now it's slush, a minute ago it was dust, it must have rained" (p. 371). He seems to fall behind his words; his oral speech now seems to take on a *différant* tendency, comparable to that of writing.

In conclusion, the *Trilogy* enacts important Derridean grammatological issues. On the one hand, its characters find themselves in the midst of "voices," guaranteeing nearness to the speaking presence; on the other, they all gravitate toward muteness, aphony, and silence, undoing that presence of speech. Like many of the deconstructed dichotomies in the *Trilogy*—such as mind/body, male/female (i.e., Lousse and Ruth), fundamental/accidental (p. 74), *de trop/manqué* (p. 33), narrator/narratee, teller/told (p. 284, 346)—this one between presence and absence, voice and silence, is further upset. Indeed, the narrators' desire for restoring the presence of speech and voices "originally" theirs suggests the narrators'—or even, one can argue, Beckett's own—conservative endeavors to return to a logocentric priority and holism. In fact, their undecided maneuver demonstrates that their critical efforts to be disengaged from metaphysics in their writings are never easy or complete. Such undecidability ultimately must also apply to the readers' (such as my own) like-minded metacritical maneuver. Reflecting upon the given metaphysical tradition, neither Beckett's characters, Beckett himself, nor I, in other words, can avoid repeating the very same tradition from which we want to dissociate our "selves," and this by resorting time and again to the issue of the Cartesian self and by being susceptible to an ironic fixation on presenting Beckett's anti-Cartesian endeavors in a totalizing and hence unexpectedly logocentric way. (Here one can recall de Man's model of reading, which never fails to produce unexpected but nevertheless legitimate meanings.)

One must not forget, however, that it is the "literature of the Unword" that is most impressively and distinctively demonstrated in the *Trilogy*[30] (Beckett's first hero, Murphy, had undone the biblical logos cunningly:[31] "In the beginning was the pun.") The narrators' attempt to restore intact the superiority of the Cartesian subject must be ruthlessly displaced by the problematic that accompanies it. Their commitment is identical with what Beckett, greatly influenced by Schopenhauer, had envisaged in *Proust* as the ultimate objective of art: namely, the world as Idea, rather than the world as will or matter.[32] Beckett's *Trilogy*, however, achieves neither the middle path of Schopenhauer—in closing the gap between world and mind, between the solipsistic Cartesian cogito and the objective world of things[33]—nor, a great step further, the essentialist, transcendental consciousness of Husserl, accomplished by the method of *epochē*,[34] though both are anti-Cartesian.

The problematic inherent in the nostalgic restoration of origin and Beckett's subsequent self-styled act of undoing coincides with that of grammatology. Just as his narrators have their authorship usurped as writers of their own life-accounts, so Beckett, entangled with anti-Cartesian dialectics, perpetuates himself in the self-defeating cycle of undoing and doing. Plunging into the Cartesian problematic, he fails to escape its influence intact. He is "less writer than written" into the already "inscribed" Western intellectual tradition of which he struggles desperately to strip himself.[35] The *Trilogy*, rather than the narrators' *auto*-biographies, is composed of enigmatic biographies of texts and *écriture*. That is to say, they are dynamic, self-reflexive, allegories of writing—critical, like Beckett's fiction, as well as metacritical, like this critical work of mine.

Notes

1. Samuel Beckett, *Disjecta* (London: John Calder, 1983), p. 103.
2. René Descartes, *The Philosophical Works of Descartes,* trans. Elizabeth S. Haldane and G. R. T. Ross (Cambridge: Cambridge University Press, 1978), 1:157.
3. Robert Denoon Cumming, ed., *The Philosophy of Jean-Paul Sartre* (New York: Random House, 1956), p. 14.
4. Beckett, *Disjecta,* p. 82.
5. Samuel Beckett, *Proust and Three Dialogues* (London: Calder & Boyars, 1931), p. 74.
6. Robert Smith, *Studies in the Cartesian Philosophy* (New York: Russell & Russell, 1962), p. 12.
7. Samuel Beckett, *The Beckett Trilogy* (London: Picador, 1983), p. 61. All subsequent references to the *Trilogy* are from this edition and page numbers are given in parentheses in my text.
8. In "Discourse IV" in *The Philosophical Works of Descartes,* 1:101, Descartes clarifies his substantive dualism as "I was a substance the whole essence or nature of which is to think, and that for its existence there is no need of any place, nor does it depend on any material thing; so that this 'me', that is to say, the soul by which I am what I am, is entirely distinct from body...." See also Reinhardt Grossman, *Phenomenology and Existentialism* (New York: Routledge & Kegan Paul, 1984), p. 172.
9. Raman Selden, *A Reader's Guide to Contemporary Literary Theory* (Sussex: Harvester Press, 1985), p. 91.
10. Paul de Man, *Allegories of Reading* (New Haven: Yale University Press, 1979), pp. 9–58, 270; J. Hillis Miller, *The Ethics of Reading* (New York: Columbia University Press, 1987).
11. Paul Valéry, *The Living Thoughts of Descartes* (London: Cassell, 1948), p. 32.
12. Beckett, *Proust and Three Dialogues,* p. 84.
13. Richard Kearney, *Modern Movements in European Philosophy* (Manchester: Manchester University Press, 1986), p. 122.
14. Steven Connor, *Samuel Beckett: Repetition, Theory, and Text* (Oxford: Basil Blackwell, 1988), p. 122.
15. Jacques Derrida, "Signature Event Context," in *Margins of Philosophy* (Chicago: University of Chicago Press, 1982), pp. 309–30.
16. Jacques Derrida, "The Double Session," in *Dissemination* (Chicago: University of Chicago Press, 1981), p. 177.
17. Descartes is fond of using the Platonic dark cave image to illustrate illustory human

perceptions and cognitive blind spots. He compares his philosophical endeavors to beams of light that penetrate undesirable darkness: "as though I threw open the windows and caused daylight to enter the cave" ("Discourse VI," in *Philosophical Works of Descartes,* 1:125.). The phrase "the light of nature" also occurs several times in *Meditations* (1:176, 1:192). See also Dalia Judovitz, *Subjectivity and Representation in Descartes: The Origins of Modernity* (Cambridge: Cambridge University Press, 1988), p. 44.

18. John Pilling, *Samuel Beckett* (London: Routledge & Kegan Paul, 1976), p. 114.

19. "Modernity and Drama," in Monique Chefdor et al., *Modernism: Challenges and Perspectives* (Urbana: University of Illinois Press, 1986), p. 59.

20. Dominick LaCapra, *A Preface to Sartre* (Ithaca: Cornell University Press, 1978), p. 126.

21. Derrida, "Signature, Event, Context," p. 315.

22. Eugene Kaelin, *The Unhappy Consciousness: The Poetic Plight of Samuel Beckett* (Dordrecht: Reidel, 1981), p. 21.

23. Connor, *Samuel Beckett,* pp. 60, 50.

24. Jean Baudrillard, *Simulations,* trans. Paul Foss et al. (New York: Semiotext(e), 1983), pp. 10–11.

25. Angela Moorjani, "Beckett's Devious Deictics," in Lance St. John Butler and Robin J. Davies, eds., *Rethinking Beckett: A Collection of Critical Essays* (London: Macmillan, 1990), pp. 24, 25.

26. Charles L. Creegan, *Wittgenstein and Kierkegaard: Religion, Individuality, and Philosophical Method* (London: Routledge & Kegan Paul, 1989), p. 62.

27. Selden, *Reader's Guide,* p. 86.

28. Jacques Derrida, "The End of the Book and the Beginning of Writing," in *Of Grammatology* (Baltimore: Johns Hopkins University Press, 1977), pp. 6–26.

29. Jacques Derrida, "Force and Signification," in *Writing and Difference* (Chicago: University of Chicago Press, 1978), pp. 11–12.

30. Beckett, *Disjecta,* p. 135.

31. Samuel Beckett, *Murphy* (London: Picador, 1973), p. 41.

32. Beckett, *Proust and Three Dialogues,* p. 90.

33. Patrick Gardiner, *Schopenhauer* (London: Penguin, 1963), p. 150.

34. Sylvia Debevic Henning, *Beckett's Critical Complicity: Carnival, Contestatio, and Tradition* (Lexington: University Press of Kentucky, 1988), p. 20.

35. Stanley Gontarski, *The Intent of Undoing in Beckett's Dramatic Texts* (Bloomington: Indiana University Press, 1985), p. 6.

Beckett's Dramatic Vision and Classical Taoism

KIRILL O. THOMPSON

Moved deeply by Beckett's literature, we yearn to comprehend the philosophic vision behind it. Beckett, however, expressed his views through literature because he deemed it impossible to render his sense of things in the expository language of philosophy.[1] He intended his literary works—his drama in particular—to *show* and intimate, rather than to *assert* and proclaim, some deep-felt intuitions about existence. Thus, attempts to get at the philosophy behind Beckett's art tend to founder upon this dilemma: philosophic assertion requires clarity, precision, and objectivity, but Beckett's basal intuition of world and self was that they are at root opaque, inchoate, subjectively determined, and resistant to analytical inquiry. Springing from a similar intuition and outlook, classical Chinese Taoist thought can perhaps provide some insight into the Beckettian philosophy.

Because of his absurdism and prolonged immersion in the Parisian cultural milieu, Beckett is frequently characterized as existential in temperament and outlook. This characterization must be qualified, however, for Beckett couldn't "understand" Sartre and Heidegger's crucial distinction between being and existence.[2] Moreover, he was skeptical regarding the being of objects as well as of selves, in contrast to the existentialists, who focused on the nothingness of personal existence. Thus, he doubted a key link in the existential project of self-creation. Other critics dwell upon Beckett's interest in Cartesian doubt and radical skepticism of the sort first argued for by the Sophist Gorgias (483–375 B.C.).[3] Still, whereas Cartesian doubt is methodological, an intellectual exercise intended to justify rational knowledge and support Christian doctrine, Beckett felt his doubt to be real and insurmountable. He accepted Gorgias's skeptical deduction:[4]

1. There is nothing which has any real existence.
2. That even if anything did exist, it could not be known.
3. That supposing real existence to be knowable, the knowledge would be incommunicable.

This argument conditions but still leaves open the character and tone of Beckett's philosophic vision.

Others offer mystical Christian accounts of Beckett's works, but these are deeply inconsistent with his stated views.[5] They do, however, signal the positive element in his message: we need to be constantly reminded that we are dying, so that we will remain more intent on our living.

Inasmuch as the classical Taoist texts *Lao Tzu* and *Chuang Tzu* portray human life and death in a discernibly Beckettian landscape, it is instructive to explore some salient parallels between Beckett's philosophic vision and classical Taoism.[6]

The Fundamental Intuition

Beckett's distinctive intuitions about world and self began to grip him and shape his art about when he turned forty. At that time, he began to shed the modernist faith in the positive possibilities of knowledge and linguistic expression he had inherited from James Joyce and others.

From that point, Beckett remained impressed that existence is fundamentally chaotic and does not sustain the facts and truths upon which human life is premised. In incessant flux, it remains free of the grip of our most basic concepts, categories, and beliefs. Haunted thus by the impression that our life is, in essence, a muddle through the void, he felt obliged as artist to depict this sense of life through displays of humanity groping in the darkness in a state of unknowingness and impotence.[7]

Taoist thought, too, issues from an intimation of the uncertainty of facts and truths and includes notions of nonknowledge and nonaction. The experience of Tao (the Way) itself is a profound intuition of the inner identification of all things that encompasses the unity of subject and object, the identity of multiplicities, and the identity of opposites.[8] A salient consequence of this experience of identity is the realization that nothing—neither self, nor other, nor world—possesses a fixed self-nature or persisting identity; it is the understanding that everything, including man, is relationally structured, a reflection of its environment, which conditions and eventually absorbs it, but against which we identify it by means of language.[9]

As noted, Beckett denied the possibility of expressing his intuition of life in the assertoric language of philosophy. Taoists observe that, because of the rigid form of propositional language, our dependence on language—for such purposes as identification, definition, assertion, and information—misleads us into thinking the world itself consists of hard facts and definite truths. They sense that language foists a procrustean impress of order and fact upon a fundamentally chaotic, recalcitrant world. To counter the perception that the world indeed reflects the form of linguistic propositions and to support their intuition of identity, the *Lao Tzu* and *Chuang Tzu* attempt in various ways to show that even seemingly unassailable truth claims and value judgments must inevitably break down. The Taoist position is that, cognitively, nothing holds fast; man ultimately dwells in a state of nonknowing and best proceeds in life by nonaction.[10]

Nothing to be Known or Done

In *Waiting for Godot* Vladimir, thinker, attempts to verify certain facts or truths, a project in which Estragon, poet, takes little interest. Notably, Vladimir questions a discrepancy in the Gospels concerning personal salvation and inquires about their putative savior Godot. The discrepancy in the Gospels is irresolvable, and Godot remains a fleeting hope throughout the tragicomedy; thus, these hapless characters are destined to remain suspended in limbo until Godot at last deigns to appear and assign them their titles and their missions.[11]

In Beckett's world, not only are the distant past and the imminent future uncertain, but Vladimir and Estragon cannot distinguish between yesterday and the day before; and even though Krapp has a taped record of past stages in his own life, he is no longer able to recall or grasp their original significance. Ultimately, the Beckettian present is as uncertain as the past and future.

In a similar spirit, the *Chuang Tzu* contains many stories about Confucius and the ancient sage kings of China that undermine their status as authority figures: they are depicted as frequently changing their minds, renouncing the truths attributed to them, or just admitting that they lack enlightenment.[12] "Confucius," for example, "has been going along for sixty years and he has changed sixty times. What at the beginning he used to call right he has ended up calling wrong."[13] Moreover, Taoist sages and hermits are depicted in the *Chuang Tzu* as responding to the queries of truth-seekers with nonsense and paradox intended to undermine the idea that there is a definite truth or way of life and to indicate a nondirective life orientation.

As with the wait for Godot, the more keenly one attempts to experience Tao, the more elusive it becomes.

The Beckettian World

The Beckettian world depicted in *Godot* is a barren, silent landscape betwixt heaven and earth, rent by a meandering path, punctuated by a scruffy tree and a dark rock, at dusk. The lack of definite landmarks indicates that the world ultimately lacks a definite order or frame of reference, that space and time are adrift and but tentatively marked and registered. Mankind initially cuts paths through the land and devises calendars according to habit and need, but later treats these directions and markers as absolutes. (Thus the shred of poignancy in Pozzo and Lucky's purposeful marches through "their" countryside, a landscape that has reverted to an amorphous primal condition.) The world is in motion and insubstantial. The cosmos bodies forth forces of light and dark that give rise to heaven and earth and are reflected in terrestrial phenomena, such as the tree groping skyward and the rock squatting on the soil. Though the scene in the play is always at dusk, that the revolutions of heaven and earth produce cycles of days, seasons, years, and lives is implied.[14] These compose the rhythm of life (and death) with which man seeks to attune himself, within and without.[15]

Taoist landscapes also reflect the interplay of complementary forces, such as yin, yang, and the five phases,[16] which give rise to heaven and earth, in the midst of which the myriad things arise. Revolving in open-ended cycles, the world has no beginning or end, direction or purpose. Here space and time are relative: Tao engenders and embraces heaven, earth, and the myriad things by virtue of its nothingness. It is at once the open ground in which things exist, the emptiness at their core, and the void to which they finally revert.

Man, according to Taoism, spontaneously articulates his world—i.e., he creates paths by walking, language by communicating, and customs by acting—but he eventually sanctifies these paths, signs, and customs into official roads, real names, and sacred rites. In time, these venerable roads and capitals make him imagine there are real directions and destinations; the names, that there are actual meanings and verities; and the rites, that there is a right way to conduct life. Man thereby forges an artificial world in the image of these spontaneous creations and thus deviates from Tao in thought and practice. Lucky's dance and speech make a shrill mockery of quests for meaning and significance in divinity, nature, and humanity. They give vivid expression to the chaotic, nonteleological, nonredemptive character of the

Beckettian world, wherein man's lot is to "shrink on an impossible earth under an indifferent heaven."[17] In sum, it is a place in which our life is a dog's life.[18] Taoism, too, doubts the viability of quests for transcendent meaning and purpose in heaven, earth, or humanity, and stresses the purposelessness and indifference of the universe. *Lao Tzu*, chapter 5, for example, reads:[19]

> Heaven and earth are not benevolent;
> They treat the ten thousand things indifferently
>   [lit., as straw dogs].
> The wise is not benevolent;
> He treats man indifferently [as straw dogs].
> The entire cosmos is basically void, . . .

Beckettian People

Usually written off as modernist or absurdist curiosities, Beckett's motley crew—the cripples, the infirm elders, the mindless gossips, and the tramps—are essential to his philosophic vision: only outsiders skittering along the precipice have had glimpses into the reality of the void.[20] They occupy a primitive, unvarnished world into which most of us can only cast a brief, wary glimpse. Cushioned by our personal devotions and relationships, most of us have no occasion to face the problem of the inner vacuity of life and death until perhaps finally driven to it by time and circumstance; then there "is a despair that comes out of that reality that cannot be simulated."[21]

The *Lao Tzu* characterizes the man of Tao by contrast to ordinary people. He is like an innocent baby—dark, dull, obscure, blunt, solitary, tranquil—that stays close to the mother.[22] And, unique in Chinese literature, the *Chuang Tzu* makes heroes of cripples, beggars, hermits, criminals, and other fringe figures who have been cast out of or have renounced society, its ways, and its trappings.[23] Liberated from the narrow range of facts and values recognized and insisted upon by society, these characters turn inward and experience the void variously. They thus reach various levels of insight into self, world, and life. But there is little prospect for any widespread realization of Tao, because anxious clan and social authorities seek to conceal the emptiness, purposelessness, and aimlessness of existence by breeding the young to concentrate on cultivating a firm self concept and seeking merit, fame,[24] wealth, and power.[25] Taken as verities as they are, these concerns blind all but a reflective few to the Way and inner potency *(te)* of self and world, which are at root empty.[26]

Beckett's characters, too, have strayed from their social milieu and have had glimpses into the chaos and emptiness of existence. Increasingly aware of, yet unwilling to surrender to, the void that permeates life, Vladimir and Estragon continue to wait for Godot; Pozzo and Lucky continue to seek to reestablish their earthly estate, Winnie continues to chatter on, and Krapp goes on reviewing his past. In fact, they display courage in pressing on in spite of the gnawing sense of emptiness that haunts them. And Beckett of course deemed it a point of artistic integrity not to offer his characters any escape from their predicament. The only authentic way was to leave them muddling along their adopted paths toward a shadowy terminus.[27]

Language and Paradox

Beckett averred that because the world is basically chaotic, empty, and formless, it neither corresponds to nor sustains our truth claims and value judgments; any such claims and judgments are inherently paradoxical. Consequently, in *Waiting for Godot*, the quest for certain facts and reliable judgments yields only paradox and deeper uncertainty, culminating in the soliloquies of the blind Pozzo and the awakening Vladimir.

The Taoist authors share this attitude toward truth claims and value judgments, and parallels can be drawn between the uses of assertion and paradox that appear in Beckett's works and the Taoist texts. On the basic level, since simple assertions of fact and value are always subject to negation and collapse, they prove to be paradoxical vis-à-vis subjective experience. This is a recurring motif in *Waiting for Godot*, which climaxes in Lucky's dance and speech. The *Lao Tzu* and the *Chuang Tzu* both recognize paradoxes of fact and value and propose various explanations. For instance, the *Chuang Tzu* argues the perspectival point that every "this" is also a "that" and every "that" is also a "this," and thus that the instant someone makes an assertion (from his perspective), others will counter it (from their perspective). By extension, rational disputes ultimately prove to be unresolvable, for there can be no final, transperspectival adjudicator. There can be no last word; therefore, the Taoist sage attempts to embrace and transcend all sides.

On another level, paradoxes are themselves affirmed as truths that reflect the imperfect fit of language (as well as of human thought and aspiration) to recalcitrant reality and, thus, are taken as evocative of the basic problematic of the human condition. For instance, Pozzo proclaims:

One day we were born, one day we shall die, the same day, the same second, is that enough for you. (*Calmer*) They give birth astride a grave, the light gleams an instant, then it's night once more.[28]

The *Chuang Tzu* contains countless parallel laments:

Man's life between heaven and earth is like a white colt passing a chink in the wall, in a moment it is gone. . . . By a transformation, you are born, by another you die. . . .[29]

The sun at noon is the sun setting. The thing born is the thing dying.[30]

But where there is birth, there is death; where there is death there must be life.[31] On reflection, paradoxes of this sort turn out to be more or less straightforward negations of our commonsense thoughts, beliefs, and aspirations about life, but they do not of themselves impart a much more sufficient view.

Nor are such negative paradoxes treated as definitive by Beckett or the authors of the *Lao Tzu* and the *Chuang Tzu*, who attempt to break through this impasse of linguistic expression by evoking their deepest intuitions about life in poetry rather than assertion; for their basic intuitions are aesthetic and meditative and thus require a more holistic mode of expression than direct assertion, negation, or paradox. Accordingly, the epiphanies in act 2 of *Waiting for Godot*, such as the litany to the dead, Estragon's allusion to Shelley's plaintive "To the Moon," and Vladimir's last soliloquy, are surprisingly poetic. Krapp's reveries also wax highly poetic and poignant. Taoist philosophy also is fundamentally poetic and meditative in character. The *Lao Tzu* consists mostly of rhymed verse, and the *Chuang Tzu* breaks into verse whenever the circle of assertion, argument, and paradox collapses and the path has been cleared for the poetic evocation of the intuition of the Tao:

What shall we think noble, what shall we think base? This is called drifting back to the Source. Don't fix a sphere for your intent, Or you'll become too lame to walk the Way.

The Way has no end and no start, There are things which died, things which are born. Can't be sure of the prime of life. Now they are empty, now they are full. There's no reserve seat for their shapes. The years cannot be warded off, Times cannot be made to stop. Dwindling and growing, filling and emptying, Whatever is an end is about to start.[32]

And,

> Within yourself, no fixed positions: Things as they take shape disclose themselves. Moving, be like water. Still, be like a mirror. Respond, like an echo. Blank! as though absent. Quiescent! as though transparent . . .[33]

Such poetic evocations are holistic and meditative and thus not nearly so sharp and abrupt as the negative paradoxes listed above. As Vladimir muses, "astride of a grave and a difficult birth. Down in the hole, lingeringly, the grave-digger puts on the forceps. *We have time to grow old.* The air is full of our cries."[34] We exist, though tentatively and conditionally: what more can we know? How are we to carry on? How are we to manage our share of the suffering?

The rigor of Beckett's art is thus a reflection of his grasp of the "logic" of the medium, which he turned back on itself to express the senselessness, the illogicality, and the vacuity that underscore our lives. *Chuang Tzu* also deftly wielded the sword of logic upon itself to dismember claims of common sense and paradoxical denial alike in numerous remarkable passages:

> Knowledge journeyed northward and met Do-Nothing and Say-Nothing. Of him he asked: "How must we think in order to come to a knowledge of *Tao*? How is it approached? How do we pursue and attain it? Do-Nothing and Say-Nothing answered not a word because he could not. Knowledge then traveled southward and met All-in-Extremes and put the identical questions to him. "I know," All-in-Extremes answered. And he started to tell him but immediately forgot what he was going to say. So Knowledge went to the Yellow Emperor and put his questions to him. The Yellow Emperor replied: "*Tao* may be known by no thoughts, no reflections. It may be approached by resting in nothingness, by following nothing, pursuing nothing. The sage teaches a doctrine that does not find expression in words."[35]

Life and Death

Beckett frequently focuses on "being toward death" in his art, on characters whose lives are basically spent and who now are to some limited extent seeking meaningful closure. Beckett permits them no closure, however, for he discerns no objective religico-metaphysical solution, nor does he countenance the possibility that a subject can experience its own closure or termination. Subjectively, one just carries on in a cycle of habitual motions.[36] Composed during the bloody, drawn-out Warring States period (480–222 B.C.), the Taoist texts identify death as man's great dread. And death is their underlying problematic, to which they offer an intriguing "nonsolution."[37]

Taoists discuss the problem of death from a variety of perspectives.

Basically, they view life and death as a natural process, as stages in a cycle much like yin and yang, growth and decline, night and day, the four seasons, and the reverse movement of the Tao.[38] Decline and death mark one's "return to the Tao," whence one's remains are thrown back into the mix to participate in the formation of new life forms. In this respect, a person's death is a natural transformation and an event to be celebrated rather than mourned. To those yet fearful of crossing the great divide, the *Chuang Tzu* offers the suggestion that death perchance will not be any worse than life; for now freed from the petty designs and pursuits of the ego and no longer subject to injuries and illnesses of the body, the spirit should be at ease and contented, a condition that approximates enlightenment.

Ultimately, the Taoist sage embraces and transcends the opposition of life and death, just as he embraces all oppositions. This effort is complicated because the ego constitutes a psychologically potent "this" in contrast to the various thats—"this" self in contrast to "that" thing, "that" person, even "that" cosmos. The sage, however, succeeds in embracing and transcending these oppositions by virtue of his transformative Tao experience, which frees him completely from attachment to his subjective ego and opens him up to totality. This is a practical corollary of the Taoist thesis that things, including human beings, are relationally structured and codependent; they are not independent, self-existing entities. That is, Taoists regard persons and things as fleeting images of time and circumstance that inevitably dissolve, whether from internal dissipation or external pressure.

Parallel insights animate Beckett's philosophic vision and art. The dependent nature of the Beckettian character has been noted by Jennifer Birkett:

> In Beckett's book no such beast exists [as discrete, atomic individuals] . . . the subject "I," . . . seems to dominate action. . . . But it is also passive, subject-ed, depending for its whole existence. . . . Our sense of self is structured, constituted, and invented by language. . . .[39]

Language produces the human speaker and not the other way round. And whether we look for our identity in the past or in the future, hoping all the time to find something different, we never find anything but the same patterns we are living in the present. Estragon and Vladimir in act 2 come to realize that it is through their daily round of clowning and cantering that they grasp and maintain, to some limited extent, their sense of their own existence and persistence: "Estragon: We always find something, eh Didi, to give us the impression we exist? Vladimir: Yes, yes, we're magicians. But let us persevere in what we have resolved, before we forget."[40]

One who experiences Tao identifies with totality (the great self). He is no longer confined to the narrow, subjective perspective of the ego; his mind has expanded to the all-embracing vantage of Tao. At this level, thoughts of personal death lose their sting, for it is realized that the ego is at root a fleeting reflection of totality, with which he now fully identifies:

> Lieh Tzu was on a trip and was eating by the roadside when he saw a hundred-year-old skull. Pulling away the weeds and pointing his finger, he said, "Only you and I know that you have never died and you have never lived. Are you really unhappy? Am I really enjoying myself?"[41]

This is the profound Taoist (non)solution to liberation from the great anxiety of life—death. In light of this insight, Taoists considered the attitude a person takes toward death to be a measure of his wisdom and courage.[42]

"Closure"

Parallels reverberate between Beckett's philosophic vision and classical Taoism. The Taoist classics thus open new paths for coming to grips with Beckett's fundamental intuition and his ideas concerning human existence. They underscore the coherence of his vision and suggest ways to think through his art.

At the same time, Beckett and the Taoists push their conclusions in different directions. Beckett above all feels the suffering;[43] as the premises of our lives and the tenets of our civilizations prove to be illusions and our worlds unravel and go awry, he depicts us as having naught to do but to stay the habitual course, disencumbered by illusion and false expectation. For the Taoists, the suffering is real and irreducible; still, while the sage stays the habitual course, his mind is freed from the perspective of a limited ego and earthly estate and he identifies with the cosmos itself, a source of primordial joy. The Taoist sage thus walks two paths at once.[44]

Beckett at forty shed his intellectual attachments and began to look directly to his roiling emotions within.[45] Although his art depicts man at the impasse, brave perhaps but bewildered and at a loss, Beckett's artistic genius and devotion indicate that he walked the "two paths"—his joy exhibited in his artistic creations and the catharsis and realization they inspire. To depict man at the impasse is to stir every man to dream anew, each in his own way.

Notes

I wish to express my appreciation to Martha Fehsenfeld, Harry White, and Daniel Lamb for their encouragement and comments on this paper.

1. "If I could have expressed the subject of [my art] in philosophical terms," Beckett once said, "I wouldn't have had any reason to write [it]." From a 1961 interview with Gabriel D'Aubarède. See Lawrence Graver, *Samuel Beckett: Waiting for Godot* (Cambridge: Cambridge University Press, 1989), p. 23.
2. Ibid., p. 219.
3. Ruby Cohn, "Philosophical Fragments in the Works of Samuel Beckett," and A. J. Leventhal, "The Beckett Hero," in Martin Esslin, ed., *Samuel Beckett: A Collection of Critical Essays* (Englewood Cliffs, N.J.: Prentice-Hall, 1985).
4. Leventhal, "The Beckett Hero," p. 46. Beckett himself noted that, were he a scholar, he would commence his enquiry with two quotations: "Nothing is more real than nothing" (Democritus) and "Where you are worth nothing, there you should want nothing" (Geulincx). (Mentioned on the motto page of Richard W. Seaver, ed., *A Samuel Beckett Reader* [New York: Grove Weidenfeld, 1976].)
5. Hélène Baldwin, *Samuel Beckett's Real Silence* (University Park: Pennsylvania State University Press, 1981), and G. S. Fraser, *"Waiting for Godot,"* in Cohn, ed., *Casebook* (New York: Grove Press, 1967), pp. 133–37. For criticism, see Hersh Zeifman, "Religious Imagery in the Plays of Samuel Beckett," in Ruby Cohn, ed., *Samuel Beckett: A Collection of Criticism* (New York: McGraw-Hill, 1975), pp. 93–94.
6. These texts are attributed to Lao Tzu (6th cent. B.C.) and Chuang Tzu (4th cent. B.C.). Good English translations include: Chang Chung-yuan, trans., *Tao: A New Way of Thinking* (New York: Harper & Row, 1975); D. C. Lau, trans., *Lao Tzu: Tao Te Ching* (Harmondsworth: Penguin Books, 1983); and Burton Watson, trans., *The Complete Works of Chuang Tzu* (New York: Columbia University Press, 1968). For an absorbing account of Taoist philosophy, see Chang Chung-yuan, *Creativity and Taoism: A Study of Chinese Philosophy, Art and Poetry* (New York: Julian Press, 1983).
7. Graver and Federman, *Critical Heritage*, p. 148.
8. Chang, *Tao,* pp. xv–xvii, and *Creativity,* pp. 20, 30–40.
9. The Taoist notion of world order thus is aesthetic rather than logical in character. See Roger Ames and David Hall, *Thinking Through Confucius* (Albany: State University of New York Press, 1987), pp. 16, 131–38, 307.
10. See A. C. Graham, trans., *Chuang Tzu: The Inner Chapters* (London: George Allen & Unwin, 1981), pp. 9–14; and Chang, *Tao*, chap. 2. On the doctrine of nonaction, or nonintentional action, see A. C. Graham, *Disputers of the Tao: Philosophical Argument in Ancient China* (La Salle, Ill.: Open Court, 1980), pp. 232–34. See also Chang, *Tao,* pp. 8–20.
11. Man needs a Christ, a Confucius, or a perhaps a Hollywood agent to assign him a nature and a destiny—a soul and a final purpose.
12. On Confucius and Ch'ü Po-yü, see Graham, *Chuang Tzu,* p. 102. On the sage kings Yao and Shun, see Graham, *Chuang Tzu,* pp. 45–46, and on the sage king Yü, see p. 175.
13. *Chuang Tzu*, chap. 27; Watson, *Complete Works of Chuang Tzu*, p. 305.
14. Graver, *Samuel Beckett,* pp. 26–27: "Vladimir and Estragon . . . exist in other sets of circles: living organisms subject to the cycles of time, on a round planet, orbiting the sun. . . ."

Martha Fehsenfeld kindly referred me to Beckett's list of Manichaean emblems of light and dark on p. 43 of his director's notebook for *Das Letzte Band*, 1969, reproduced in Douglas McMillan and Martha Fehsenfeld, *Beckett in the Theatre: The Author as Practical Playwright and Director* (London: John Calder, 1988), p. 280; see pp. 258–61 for discussion.

15. Such as by yoga, breathing exercises, and meditation, as hinted at in the "Let's do the tree" routine, *Waiting for Godot*, p. 49. Murphy practices a yoga of sorts. Yogic practices are essential to experiencing Tao; see Chang, *Creativity and Taoism*, pp. 123–68, and *Tao*, pp. 21–24, 32–34, 47–49, 131–33. The *Chuang Tzu* contains innumerable references to yoga: notably chap. 2 opens with a character meditating and then discussing the experience.

16. According to traditional Chinese cosmology, the world is composed of *ch'i* (cosmic vapor), which has complementary interactive aspects, yin and yang, whose intercourse gives rise to five phases—earth, wood, fire, water, metal—which in turn engender the world. The paradigmatic account of this conception is given in "Explanation of the Supreme Ultimate" by Chou Tun-i (1017–73 C.E.). For English translations with commentaries, see Wing-tsit Chan, *A Source Book in Chinese Philosophy* (Princeton: Princeton University Press, 1963), pp. 463–65, and Fung Yu-lan, *A History of Chinese Philosophy* (Princeton: Princeton University Press, 1952), 5:435–41. What is fundamental to this conception and what distinguishes it from classical Greek atomism is that yin, yang, and the five phases are not regarded as immutable elements with fixed natures; they are conceived of as fluid, interconvertible phases in the processes of *ch'i* transformation.

17. Graver, *Samuel Beckett*, p. 50. See also John J. Sheedy, "The Net," in Cohn, *A Casebook*, pp. 159–66.

18. Graver, *Samuel Beckett*, p. 50, and *Waiting for Godot*, pp. 37–39.

19. Chang, *Tao*, pp. 18–19. And Lau, *Tao Te Ching*, p. 9.

20. "Vladimir: And where were we yesterday evening according to you? Estragon: How would I know? In another compartment. There's no lack of void" (*Waiting for Godot*, p. 42). The term "nothing" punctuates the play from the first to the last line and the sense of silence grows ever more persuasive as the play proceeds.

21. Carol Fennelly of the Center for Creative Non-Violence on a recent Smithsonian Institution exhibit entitled "Etiquette of the Undercaste."

22. *Lao Tzu*, chaps. 20 and 55.

23. Graham, *Chuang Tzu*, p. 4. Watson, *Complete Works*, pp. 67–68.

24. *Chuang Tzu*, chap. 1; Watson, *Complete Works*, p. 32.

25. *Lao Tzu*, chaps. 13, 44, 46.

26. Ibid., chap. 12.

27. Although Murphy dies, it is more that he is blasted into the dark third zone of reality than that he passes simply from life into death. Beckett does seem to intimate a mist-shrouded closure in the very personal poem, "my way is flowing into the sand":

> my way is in the sand flowing
> between the shingle and the dune
> the summer rain rains on my life
> on me my life harrying fleeing
> to its beginning to its end
>
> my peace is there in the receding mist
> when I may cease from treading these longshifting
>   thresholds

> and live the space of a door
> that opens and shuts

From *Collected Poems, 1930–1978* (London: John Calder, 1984), p. 39. Discussed by Hugh Kenner in *A Reader's Guide to Samuel Beckett* (London: Thames and Hudson, 1973), pp. 47–48. The courage of Beckett's woebegone characters, pressing on in spite of the void, is discussed by David McCandless in "Beckett and Tillich: Courage and Existence in *Waiting for Godot*," *Philosophy and Literature* 12, no. 1 (April 1988): 48–57.

28. *Waiting for Godot*, p. 52.

29. *Complete Works of Chuang Tzu*, chap. 22; Graham, *Chuang Tzu*, p. 133. Such ruminations were not alien to the old English tradition. Interestingly, a counselor to Northumbria's King Edwin gave the following speech to persuade him to convert to Christianity in 827:

> Your Majesty, when we compare the present life of man on earth with the time of which we have no knowledge, it seems to me like the swift flight of a single sparrow through the banqueting-hall. . . . In the midst there is a comforting fire to warm the hall; outside, the storms of winter rain or snow are raging. The sparrow flies swiftly in through one door of the hall, and out through another. While he is inside, he is safe from the winter storms; but after a few moments of comfort, he vanishes from sight into the wintry world whence he came. Even so, man appears on earth for a little while; but of what went before this life or of what follows, we know nothing. Therefore, if this new teaching has brought any more certain knowledge, it seems only right that we should follow it.

From Bede, *A History of the English Church and People*, trans. and ed. Leo Shirley-Price, rev. R. E. Latham (Harmondsworth: Penguin, 1968), p. 127. Beckett would surely have viewed this with irony and sympathy.

30. *Chuang Tzu*, chap. 33; Watson, *Complete Works*, p. 374, Graham, *Chuang Tzu*, p. 283.

31. *Chuang Tzu*, chap. 2, Watson, *Complete Works*, p. 39. Graham renders this passage: "'Simultaneously with being alive one is dead', simultaneously with dying one is alive." (*Chuang Tzu*, p. 52)

32. See chap. 17; Graham, *Chuang Tzu*, pp. 147–48.

33. See chap. 33; Graham, *Chuang Tzu*, p. 281.

34. *Waiting for Godot*, p. 58; italics added.

35. Chap. 22; Watson, *Complete Works*, p. 244.

36. This is reflected in the litany to the voices of the dead in act 2 in *Waiting for Godot*. Beckett heightens the tragedy of his dramas by not permitting his characters to die—understanding that their death would allow the audience to sentimentalize; in his rigorous thought, even death is not a closure and there is no exit. This idea is perhaps hinted at in the obscure conclusion to *Lao Tzu*, chap. 18, which in Chang Chung-yuan's translation reads: "Even when the body dies, it is not the end." (*Tao*, p. 47)

37. Graham, *Chuang Tzu*, p. 24; Chang, *Tao*, pp. 180–200.

38. On reversal as the movement of the *Tao*, see *Lao Tzu*, chap. 40; Chang, *Tao*, pp. 112–14.

39. Beckett, *Waiting for Godot*, Macmillan Master Guides (London: Macmillan, 1987), p. 5. The *Chuang Tzu* presents the idea of dependency broadly in light of a philosophy of universal codetermination, as illustrated in the following dialogue:

Penumbra said to the Shadow, "A little while ago you were walking and now you are standing still; a little while ago you were sitting and now you are standing up. Why this lack of independent action?" Shadow said, "Do I have to wait for something before I can be like this? Does what I wait for also have to wait for something before it can be like this?" (Chap. 2; Watson, *Complete Works*, p. 49)

In classical Chinese, the expression "wait for" could be used to suggest or mean "depend upon." The *Chuang Tzu* also contains reflections on the conditional character of human volition in light of the structure and functioning of the human organism:

The hundred joints, the nine openings, the six organs, all come together and exist here [as my body]. But which part should I feel closest to? ... there must be one I ought to favor more. If not, are all of them servants? But if they are all servants, then how can they keep order among themselves? Or do they take turns being lord and servant? Once a man receives his bodily form, he holds on to it, *waiting for the end*. Sometimes clashing with things, sometimes bending before them, he runs his course like a galloping steed, ... Is he not pathetic? ... utterly exhausting himself and never knowing where to look for rest—can you help pitying him? *I'm not dead yet! he says, but what good is that? His body decays, his mind follows it—can you deny that this is a great sorrow? Man's life has always been a muddle like this.* How could I be the only muddled one, and other men not muddled? (Ibid., p. 38; italics added.)

40. *Waiting for Godot*, p. 44.
41. *Chuang Tzu*, chap. 18; Watson, *Complete Works*, p. 195.
42. Graham, *Chuang Tzu*, pp. 24, 77.
43. Beckett told Harold Pinter: "If you insist on finding form, I'll describe it for you ... I was in a hospital once. There was a man in another ward, dying of throat cancer. In the silence, I could hear his screams continually. That's the only kind of form my work has." (Quoted in Deirdre Bair, *Samuel Beckett: A Biography* [London: Cape, 1978], p. 528.)
44. *Chuang Tzu*, chap. 2; Watson, *Complete Works*, p. 41. See Fung, *A History of Chinese Philosophy*, vol. 1, 2d ed. (Princeton: Princeton University Press, 1952), 1:233–35.
45. "Beckett perceived that those dark and tumultuous aspects of his own personality which he had always 'struggled to keep under' were in reality his most prized possessions. ... he would ... write not about the ... world around him, but rather about the recesses of his own self: 'the within, all that inner space one never sees'" (Graver, *Samuel Beckett*, p. 7).

Special Features of Beckett Performances in Japan

MARIKO HORI TANAKA

When Western culture was introduced on Japanese soil, it was first imitated, then often transformed to make it more suitable to the Japanese sensibility. The same can be said of Samuel Beckett's reception in Japanese theater. There have been at least four different kinds of attempts at performing Beckett plays in Japan: first, the accurate imitation of the original texts; second, radical adaptations by political avant-garde groups; third, collaborations by traditional Japanese theater artists; fourth, arbitrary adaptations by other theater artists.

Those theater groups that first introduced Beckett plays in the 1960s were the Shingeki groups. Shingeki is an important genre in Japanese theater. Its literal meaning is "new drama" and the groups' performance styles began with the direct imitation of the way plays were performed in the West. Some Shingeki groups, using accurate translations, attempted to perform Beckett's works the way they were produced in France and Britain. Their performances, however, did not convey as much to their audience as they had expected, because their understanding of Western performance techniques was often superficial.

Then, in the 1970s, many experiments flourished in the theater under the influence of the radical aspirations of the time. The so-called first generation of underground theater, or the avant-garde theater companies, began to mount Western plays, changing them to fit the radical political stance of the artists. In short, performances were moving away from imitation toward creation. Numerous adaptations of Beckett's plays expressed the radicalism of this generation, though the forms they followed, both in the acting and in the playwriting, were more reactionary than radical: elements of traditional Japanese theater became models for their staging.

It was not only underground theater artists but also Shingeki groups of the time who became interested in performing styles of traditional theaters. Some Shingeki artists experimented by collaborating with traditional theater artists such as Noh actors. In these collaborative works, traditional theater artists adopted their acting techniques to Western plays. Several Beckett plays were performed by them—sometimes alone and sometimes with Shingeki actors. In one particular group traditional actors worked collaboratively with a Western director and Western views of Japan were integrated within Beckett's works. Those efforts gave rise to new perspectives in the performing of Beckett's plays.

This type of performance generally followed the original Beckett script except for small changes made by the directors. In the last two decades, however, hardly any performances using Beckett's original texts have been presented. The successors of the underground theater started to change his works arbitrarily and turned their backs on authenticity. Fortunately, Beckett's eyes did not reach the other side of the earth, and not one Japanese theater practitioner was blocked by Beckett's withholding authorization—an action that prevented certain adaptations of his plays in Western countries. "Freedom of expression" was given to Japanese artists in their being able to work without authorization. They took liberties in changing the original pieces—and the essence of Beckett's plays was lost in the adaptations; the true nature of Beckett was gone. As a result, straight Beckett performances have nearly disappeared.

Since my purpose here is to provide an overview of the history of Beckett performances in Japan and to pinpoint problems posed by them, I will now discuss in greater detail the introduction of Beckett to Japan and the transformation of his plays there.

Although Beckett's first few plays shocked Western audiences in the 1950s, it was some time until they were brought to Japan. It was not until the late 1960s that Beckett's name became familiar to the Japanese and the so-called antitheater movement had critics quoting Ionesco and Beckett. (Minoru Betsuyaku, for one, playwright and Beckett scholar, says that he was frustrated by naturalistic plays and was deeply moved by the use of space and the stark presence of stage and characters when he first read *Waiting for Godot* in translation.)[1]

Since Shingeki's acting method was, in part, based on naturalism, acting Beckett plays was all the more difficult. Interestingly enough, however, Bungakuza, one of the major Shingeki companies, cast Yoshi Oida, who is now known as Peter Brook's leading actor, when it produced *Act Without Words I*. Oida had been trained in the traditional Japanese theater and, already in 1961, he was unique as an actor who knew both Western and Japanese acting techniques. This was suitable casting, for *Act Without Words I* needs more stylized acting than *Waiting for Godot*.

Compared with that mime play, *Waiting for Godot* is not as difficult for Shingeki actors whose acting styles were strongly influenced by naturalistic techniques. This was demonstrated by Michael Rudman's 1987 production of *Waiting for Godot* at the National Theatre in London, in which he started to work on naturalistic acting techniques so that his actors could more easily approach the text.[2] Though their approach to the play may be said to have been a bit awkward, Shingeki productions were fairly successful.

The first production of *Waiting for Godot* was presented by the Bungakuza Company in May 1960. Tadashi Suwa describes the audience's reaction to the production as follows:

> I did not see at this production the enthusiasm with which the Parisian audience at the Théâtre de Babylone had reacted to *Waiting for Godot*. It is not that the Tokyo audience was inferior or insensitive, but that the performance was so comically performed that it did not evoke any feeling in the audience.[3]

Waiting for Godot is full of vaudeville, but there is also the metaphysical question of life and death, a theme that this production did not convey.

A similar critical comment was made about the 1965 Shinbutai Company's production of the same play:

> Both Vladimir and Estragon were enacted as Manzai [of traditional Japanese vaudeville], using superficial gestures and nasal voices. The psychological anxiety caused by the situation of "waiting" did not arise at all.[4]

In spite of the challenge to the acting tradition of Shingeki and the six months' full rehearsal period, Shinbutai's effort did not reach the core of the play.

In comparison with the two productions above, the Mingei Company's production of *Waiting for Godot* in 1965 came closer to the original by expressing the timelessness of "waiting." Hiroko Watanabe, the translator and director of this production, and also the first woman director of Beckett in Japan, explains her intentions in this, her first directorial effort:

> I tried to cut rhetoric from the words in translation. I tried to create an extremely simplified language with no euphemisms and emotional sentiment but with plain and direct expression. Then I did my best to combine the

rhythms of words and sounds. You may find it dull and bland when you read the printed text, but it is enlivened when actors actually speak their lines.[5]

Watanabe also further simplified the set by placing only an abstract tree on the stage and unified it from the gray backdrop to the monochrome costumes, except for Pozzo's brown coat. This extreme simplicity and abstractness rendered the play too tidy, and thus unreal, but the poetic dimension of the play's images, which Martin Esslin has termed the "lyrical poetic avant-garde,"[6] was manifested.

Watanabe's production of *Waiting for Godot* appears to be the most faithful to the original, for productions thereafter more or less compete with one another in novelty and eccentricity. Tokyoza's 1969 production of *Waiting for Godot* drastically changed the text by replacing Lucky's thinking monologue with an argument on sex and by cutting the simple words. The set was only a rope hanging from the ceiling and the backdrop was a bright aluminum board. The idea was to make the play as abstract as possible. But replacing and adding to the sets in Beckett's plays resulted in their being deprived of their original symbolic meanings.

These changes of sets and lines were less radical than those that occurred in later adaptations, which tended to be totally different from the original in both characterization and situation. Numerous adaptations that differed drastically from the originals were staged in the 1970s when an experimental spirit flourished in the theater. This was the time when Western artists such as Peter Brook, Ariane Mnouchkine, and Eugenio Barba began to search for a new experimental spirit in non-Western culture. Modern Japanese "Westernized" theater artists searched for a new spirit not in other cultures but in their own. Though they shared the worldwide radical aspirations of the 1970s, they found their identity in the sensibility and emotions of traditional Japanese culture. The adaptations of this period reflect this trend.

Kohei Tsuka's Kohdan (a popular traditional melodrama) version of *Waiting for Godot* in 1974, entitled *Matsugaura Godot no Imashime* (A lesson of Godot in Matsugaura Town) is a good example of an adaptation by an avant-garde theater. The universal situation of "waiting" in Beckett's play is replaced by a lower-class aspiration for a savior who would save society from a corrupt government. There is a radical agit-prop spirit in the play. Since radical themes appeal only to a minority of the audience, Tsuka makes much use of the convention of Japanese popular theater, which grasps the heart of the apolitical mass audience. This is quite similar to nineteenth-century Western melodrama.

The characters of the play, for instance, fit stock characters of melodrama:

a suffering heroine or hero, a persecuting villain, and a benevolent comic. They are not, however, absurd. They do not experience an identity crisis as Beckett's characters do. Though Beckett keeps the audience from being emotionally involved in the play, Tsuka's audience cannot help sympathizing with Vladimir, who survives with the expectation of Mr. Godot's arrival despite extreme suffering from an illness. By the end of the play a savior, called "Absurd-Man," appears on a motorcycle, just like Superman. While Mr. Godot never appears in the original play, "Absurd-Man" does. The play embodies the playwright's dream of a cure for corrupt society with the arrival of a savior. Tsuka's production, in its text and staging, was provocative.

Many other avant-garde playwrights in the 1970s shared Tsuka's radicalism. Despite their political stance and general radicalism, also common in the Western world, they searched for expressions in their rediscovery of acting styles and aesthetics of traditional culture, which James R. Brandon calls an "intracultural journey."[7]

Not only the underground theater but also Shingeki and traditional theater groups felt the necessity of renewing their philosophy of performance. It was early in the 1970s that a theater group called Mei-no-Kai was formed, a group that consisted of Noh, Kyogen (a comic interlude during a Noh program), and Shingeki actors. All collaborated in performing plays. After producing two Greek plays that they thought more suitable to the stylized acting of the traditional theater, they produced *Waiting for Godot* in 1973. Hisao Kanze, the Noh actor who played the part of Vladimir, explained why Mei-no-Kai was interested in the play: "I regard *Waiting for Godot* as essentially anti-theatrical, different from naturalistic realism. It contrasts strongly with the conventional form of modern drama by ignoring the usual rules. This is what interested me and the other actors."[8] Although Kanze had not thought very seriously about the similarity between Noh techniques and those used in *Waiting for Godot*,[9] he unexpectedly found in rehearsing the play that necessary physical movements resulted naturally from his training in Noh. This production revealed a special feature of Beckett's dramaturgy: as in Noh, there is a stylized and abstract balance in his plays.

Perhaps for similar reasons, Beckett plays kindled other Noh actors' interests. In 1971, Hideo Kanze played the role of Hamm in *Endgame* with Shingeki actors. New dimensions of Hamm emerged from Kanze's performance: for example, his monotonous tone, which probably derived from the delivery of Noh, rendered his monologue, in part, dull, while his rude Kyogen-like turn of expression provided a good comical contrast with Clov's polite but brusque manner of speaking. The success of the production also owed much to the new translation and direction by Shiro Hasegawa. Attracted by Beckett's work, Hideo Kanze later performed the title role in *Krapp's Last Tape* under his own direction in 1976. This play is more stylized and abstract than *Endgame* and is, in that sense, more suitable for a Noh actor to perform. Moreover, Kanze could make greater use of his comical gifts in *Krapp* than in *Endgame*.

In 1975, Mei-no-Kai attempted another Beckett play, *Not I*. This time Kan Hosho, a Noh actor, stood silently under a spotlight while Hiroko Seki, a Shingeki actress, spoke incessantly. Hosho's presence as a priest *[Waki]* in Noh theater, however, made too strong an impression, to the extent that the subtle feeling of the inner insecurity of the man was weakened.

It is true that Beckett's plays, in requiring precise stylized physical movement, resemble traditional Japanese plays. As Leonard Cabell Pronko has written: "Like the Noh actor, Beckett's actor must assume a certain degree of stylization, for each movement stands for something beyond itself."[10] But performances of Noh actors playing Beckett's characters have made clear that, though Beckett demands precision of movement, the actors' movements do not entirely correspond to those of Noh acting styles. Neither naturalistic acting nor ritualistic stylization alone is enough for the portrayal of Beckett's characters. Rather, the best performance lies somewhere between the two.

Beckett plays inspired not only Japanese but also Western theater artists to link with the traditional theater of Japan. Even before Pronko referred to the link in his *Theater East and West*, Eugene Ionesco, visiting Tokyo in 1964, remarked, "At the root of Beckett's works, there is a nihilistic view based on Christianity mixed with Zen Buddhism. The affinity of Beckett's plays to Noh theater comes from it."[11] While superficial aspects of Noh and Beckett plays may seem the same to Westerners, however, they do not correspond on a deeper level. Nevertheless, the similarities seem to draw the attention of Westerners.

Jonah Salz, for example, has been actively directing many Beckett plays in Noh and Kyogen styles since the foundation of the Noho Theater Group in 1981. The core members of the group working together with Salz are Akira Shigeyama and Yasushi Maruishi, both Kyogen actors. Salz's interpretation of Beckett is noteworthy because it aims to keep the original sense, unlike the efforts of contemporary Japanese avant-garde or underground directors and playwrights who use Beckett's works as raw material. He has explained his adaptations as follows:

> With Beckett's approval, I adapted culturally, not just linguistically. So the suicide contemplation in *Act Without Words I*, when the hapless man unbuttons his collar and fingers his neck—didn't make sense in a Japanese tradition

where only women died so cowardly. Instead the man loosens his kimono and holds his *hara* [stomach], thinking about using the point of the blade to stab, not the side to slash. And of course the wires and pullies of the original are replaced by the *kuroko* [a stagehand masked and dressed in black, to be inconspicuous, who assists during the performance], borrowed from the Kabuki stage, to add an air of menace and simplify things. This translation of stage conventions in *Quad I and II* meant using kneeling, back-turned dancers instead of [dancers] disappearing [offstage] as in the televised original. In *Ohio Impromptu* we replaced the hat in the center of the table with a walking stick (Beckett rejected an umbrella). *Krapp's Last Tape* was rather faithful, although all objects except the table and recorder were mimed, and the actor wore a clown-white nose. *Rough for Theatre I* was the most complete translation, where the language of Kansai-ben [Osaka dialect] for the lame, Kyogen-like Muromachiben [Kyoto dialect] for the blind man, added to their character differences. A wheelchair was replaced by the sound "garagaragara," a violin by a "bembembem" of a biwa. *Rockaby* did away with the chair completely; in later versions, the old woman, played by Noh actor Akira Matsui, knelt to the side of a rocker, then danced the final resignation. In sum: some translation is literal, some transposes the scene to Japan, so uses more Japanese stage conventions and cultural themes, and some is a "Creole" of East and West, borrowing freely for effective theater.[12]

These productions, however, were shown only in small theaters and for a limited period of time in Japan. They were received more favorably by Western audiences of their tour productions (both in United Kingdom and the United States), because Jonah Salz directed from a Western point of view. That his understanding of Japanese culture is still that of a Westerner is evident in the fact that the stock image of suicide mentioned above no longer appeals to the Japanese audience and that *kuroko* is not menacing to the Japanese, because it is merely a convention in Kabuki. Nevertheless, Salz has contributed to Japanese traditional theater in opening it to Beckett, and he has contributed to Western theater as well by providing it with new performance perspectives.

Adaptation became the norm in presenting Beckett in the 1980s. More and more directors and producers began to adapt Beckett's plays however they liked. In 1980, Yozo Ogawa produced two different versions of *Waiting for Godot*. One was completely different from the original and the other was only a partial adaptation. The plot of the former was changed somewhat: both Vladimir and Estragon came to the stage on bicycles and spoke in different dialects, and the number of tramps increased as the play progressed. It went in the opposite direction from Beckett, who was interested in decreasing and minimalizing. His motto was "less is more," but the production ended with "more is less." The latter piece of Ogawa was performed by the "Saint Louis" Manzai duo. They cut one-third of the original dialogue and ad-libbed speeches.

Another change is that Pozzo was played by an actress and the boy was played by a puppet. The boy in Japan is often played by an actress whose body shape and voice are suitable only because using a child actor involves the Labor Standards Act. Who, however, had ever thought of an actress playing Pozzo, a character who embodies male authority? It was the director's intention to emphasize the lively presence of Vladimir and Estragon by making the other characters "objects," which would certainly offend the feminists of the time. If the director used an actress to undermine Pozzo's male authority, why did she wear a bald wig and false whiskers? Would it not have been more effective, in choosing to experiment in this way, to leave her as she was?

The same can be said of the 1984 Yasokai Company's all-female version of *Waiting for Godot*, in which actresses pretended to be men. As is well-known, Beckett was very strict about gender and refused to authorize an all-female *Godot* by a Dutch group in 1989. Even after the author's death, a French group had to bring the issue to the court, though they did win and performed *Waiting for Godot* with an all-female cast at the 1991 Avignon Festival.

What is the meaning of females acting male roles? In the most recent production of *Waiting for Godot* (in March 1994) directed by Shoji Koukami, a young underground theater artist, Vladimir and Estragon were performed by actresses. This time, the characters' masculinity was diminished and their language was feminized. (There is a clear gender difference in the use of words in the Japanese language.) According to Koukami, generally speaking, women are used to waiting while men are used to having women wait, and therefore it is fresh and natural that women wait for Godot: "If men say, 'we are waiting for Godot'," explains Koukami, "it sounds unnatural and I fear the whole play loses the reality of life."[13] His Vladimir and Estragon, despite their feminine language, look unisexual, which suits the age of identity or gender crisis. The resistance to gender change has lessened lately and this kind of transgender performance will no doubt increase more and more in the future. It goes without saying that changes of gender at the performance level add changes of meaning to Beckett's original text.

Changes in plot, theme, and characterization (including those of gender) have become common among today's young adapters. In the 1990 production of an adapted piece by Toru Kawasaki and Hana Kino, entitled *Marubatsu-shiki Godot o Machinagara* (The multiple-choice *Waiting for Godot*), extracts of *Waiting for Godot* are combined with parodies of a few original scenes and completely new scenes. The two main characters—a wife and a husband—are waiting for Godot, who is busy frying tempura and thus answers on the telephone that he cannot come. These same characters later play the parts of Vladimir and Estragon in scenes extracted from the original play. Pozzo and Lucky are replaced by an unnamed man and a character from a fairy tale who shrinks to a diminutive size. Other characters are added to create subplots that derive from schoolchildren's frivolous talk. The structure of the play is complicated and bizarre and less substantial than the original. The superficial intricacy is intriguing to today's younger generation. The metaphysical meanings underlying the simplicity of Beckett plays no longer appeal to them.

Even those relatively faithful productions most recently staged represent departures from the original. A group of Beckett enthusiasts who used to work with Tadashi Suzuki, known as "Kyu-Shinkukan," have been actively producing Beckett plays. They have mounted a combined piece of *That Time*, *Play*, and *Come and Go* in 1980, *Waiting for Godot* in 1981, and *Happy Days* in 1989 and in 1992, as well as other less successful adaptations of Beckett's plays. The two-character play *Happy Days* was changed into a monologue articulated by Winnie, with drastic changes made in sets and costumes as well: there was no mound or blazing light. Instead, Winnie, asleep in a wheelchair, was brought onto the stage by Willie in dim light; only then did the lights come up. Winnie was wearing a long Victorian dress, while Willie was wearing a white suit and a white hat. Willie disappeared, leaving Winnie on the stage. Until Willie reappeared at the end of the play, there was no communication between them. Winnie's call for Willie echoed in a vacuum. In the 1989 production, the mellow romantic pastoral picture painted on the backdrop reflected Winnie's happy days of her past. But in the 1992 production, the backdrop was replaced by black cloth and the floor was covered with two black, hard boards. The director was aware of the importance of simplicity in the sets, but in a way different from the playwright. His effort to create a Noh-like effect with the simple black board, which symbolized death, made Winnie's liveliness, fostered by the earth in the original text, virtually disappear in this production. These set changes were made partly because of the spatial limitation of the tiny theater, but mostly because the director found Beckett's description of the sets meaningless and unnecessary with regard to Winnie's language as the sole character. Without physical objects and Willie's presence on the stage, moreover, the focus of the whole play remains within Winnie's mind.

It is necessary for directors to interrogate the text, but is this production of *Happy Days* much better than the more faithful ones done by Shingeki groups in the 1960s? Both the Bungakuza and Mingei companies produced

Happy Days following the original. Michiko Araki, Winnie in the Bungakuza production, "kept the Noh-mask-like blank face during the performance, which strengthened the inner flow of her speech, and made full use of her vocalization, which was effective to express the cheerful liveliness of the heroine."[14] Tomoko Naraoka, the Mingei Company's Winnie, "helped by the simplified translation of Hiroko Watanabe, could keep the rhythms of the play."[15] Both productions seem to have been more successful.

Why have these kinds of faithful productions been discarded in the last two decades? To deconstruct original texts by combining in collages various creative moments with extracts has become so common that nobody seems to be interested in looking straight at the original. Moreover, the devised pieces have lost the social or political themes that the first generation of underground theater had as artistic inspirations. Today's younger generation believes that the function of its theater is to entertain the audience with gags, parodies, gimmicks, spectacular movements, and acrobatics. This reflects the sensibility of contemporary society, where the superficial, the unphilosophical, and the illogical permeate. The loss of something solid has become so strong that one no longer attempts to create something positive. Negativism has become a pose to resist lost feeling and anxiety. Imitating the techniques and styles of the first generation of underground theater artists in Japan, this generation now survives with only superficial techniques, neglecting meanings submerged in the original texts.

From Shingeki to avant-garde theater, from traditional Japanese theater to that of the West, a number of attempts to present Beckett have been explored.[16] Accurate translations and staging imitations by Shingeki groups contributed as an introduction to Beckett, however superficial their understanding may have been. Shingeki and Salz's collaborative stagings with Noh and Kyogen actors showed us that there are common elements in Beckett and Noh (or Kyogen). These helped Japanese theater artists to probe new possibilities of performing Western plays. Various changes made by certain adapters were, in the beginning, attempts to render Beckett plays familiar to Japanese audiences. But as time passed, the adapters' original desire to mount Beckett changed into a desire to use the plays as they liked. It may be true that arbitrary adaptations can attract an audience by their novelty and eccentricity, and thereby give impetus to the creative energy of certain theater artists. But they deprive both theater artists and audiences of their feelings of respect for the original texts. Without respect, the essence of Beckett plays will never be conveyed to Japanese audiences.

Theater artists must retain their respect for the originals by buckling down to the difficult task of presenting Beckett plays rigorously. But at the same time, they must also continue to open up Japanese theater through experimentation with Beckett plays and the discovery of new possibilities for presentation, such as those based on insights by Noh and Kyogen actors in the 1970s, for example. Only then will a more creative energy of Japanese theater artists spring forth to stimulate Japanese audiences to more fully understand Beckett's plays.

Notes

1. Minoru Betusyaku, interview by Yasunari Takahashi, "Beckett-teki Enkan" (Beckettian cycle), *Eureka* 14, no. 11 (November 1982): 76. Translation mine.
2. Michael Rudman, personal interview, 24 February 1992.
3. Tadashi Suwa, "Bungakuza Atelier Kouen: *Godo o Machinagara*" (A studio production of Bungakuza: *Waiting for Godot*), *Shingeki*, no. 84 (July 1960): 25–26. Translation mine.
4. Kiyoshi Seki, "Gekidan Shinbutai Kouen 5: *Godo o Machinagara*" (Shinbutai's fifth production: *Waiting for Godot*), *Teatro*, no. 258 (April 1965): 61. Translation mine.
5. Hiroko Watanabe, "Beckett no Butaika o Tooshite" (On staging Beckett), *Shingeki*, no. 154 (February 1966): 26. Translation mine.
6. Martin Esslin, *The Theatre of the Absurd* (Harmondsworth: Penguin Books, 1980), p. 25.
7. James R. Brandon, "Contemporary Japanese Theatre: Interculturalism and Intraculturalism," in Erika Fischer-Lichte et al., eds., *The Dramatic Touch of Difference: Theatre, Own and Foreign* (Tübingen: Gunter Narr Verlag, 1990), p. 95. According to Brandon,

> Intercultural contacts involve a journey outward from self to a spacially or geographically distant other. That distance may be short or far, but the journey crosses racial, national, ethnic, or group boundaries: Chinese troupes stage Shakespeare, London audiences attend Grand Kabuki. The intracultural journey may also be short or far, but movement is not outward to "other" cultures, it is inward, borrowing within one's culture. It takes the theatre artist back through time in search of once "familiar" modes of thought and behaviour that have, through the passage of generations, become lost, discarded, "foreign." [Shogo] Ohta's use of Noh aesthetics and [Tadashi] Suzuki's appreciation of Kabuki acting are two clear examples of a deliberate return to and use of earlier forms of Japanese theatre. The intracultural journey crosses time boundaries, but stays within racial, national, ethnic, or group boundaries. Suzuki and Ohta are powerful examples of this vertical journey in Japanese contemporary theatre, a journey downward and inward, to rediscover basic ethnic characteristics, as exemplified in traditional theatre. (P. 95)

8. Hisao Kanze, interview, in Poh Sim Plowright, "The Influence of Oriental Theatrical Techniques on the Theory and Practice of Western Drama" (diss., University of London, 1975), p. 191.
9. Ibid., p. 195.
10. Leonard Cabell Pronko, *Theater East and West: Perspectives Toward a Total Theater* (Berkeley: University of California Press, 1967), p. 109.

11. Moriaki Watanabe, "Eugene Ionesco to no Taiwa" (A conversation with Eugene Ionesco), *Shingeki* 11, no. 1 (January 1964): 3. Translation mine.

12. Jonah Salz, letter to the author, February 1992.

13. Shoji Koukami, personal interview, 10 March 1994.

14. Seki, "Bungakuza Atelier No Kai: *Ah, Uruwashi no Hibi*" (Bungakuza's *Happy Days*), *Teatro*, no. 258 (April 1965): 62. Translation mine.

15. Takashi Iwase, "Kouji na Shinjitsu o Mezasu Dokuhaku-Geki" (Monologue plays in search of the higher truth), *Teatro,* no. 311 (May 1969): 32. Translation mine.

16. There are many other productions I did not mention in this essay. Here is a list of major Beckett performances in Japan:

Waiting for Godot	Producing company	Director
1960	Bungakuza	Shinya Ando
1965	Shinbutai	Yoshikane Kanehachi
1965 & 1966	Mingei	Hiroko Watanabe
1969	Tokyoza	Shinichi Inoda
1970	Nihon Geijutsu Gekijo	Masamitsu Koibuchi
1971	Ogawa Yozo Production	Sumio Hayano
1972	Yaokiza	Kazuo Sasaki
	Yokohama Shogekijo*	Kei Suma
	Tsuka Kohei Office Group*	Kohei Tsuka
1973	Mei-no-Kai	Shuji Ishizawa
	Yugei*	Michihiko Adachi
1974	Alpha Kikaku	Kazuo Sasaki
	Tsuka Kohei Office Group*	Kohei Tsuka
1977	Don-Yoku Theater Group	Kiyozo Araya
1978	Shinkukan*	Kenjiro Shin
1979	Kurumiza	Eizo Kitamura
1980	Kyu-Shinkukan*	Kenjiro Shin
	Ogawa Yoga Production*	Tamiya Kuriyama
1980 & 1981	Ogawa Yozo Production	Sumio Hayano
1981	Kyuu-Shinkukan	(collaboration)
1981 & 1983 & 1985	Daisan Butai*	Shoji Koukami
1982	Aoi Tori*	Ichido Rei
	Honda Kikaku*	Shinpei Fujiwara
1984	Yasokai	Sho Nobuse
1985	KSEC*	Kei Shinguji
1987	Theater 2+1	Tatsu Takagi
1990	Mode*	Osamu Matsumoto
	Kiiro Bukidan*	Shigeo Makabe
	Marble*	Hana Kino
1991 (in English)	Compass Theatre Company	Neil Sissons
	Kuro Tent*	Makoto Sato
1992	Yaokiza	Kazuo Sasaki
	La Foret Museum*	Seikou Ito
1994	Daisan Butai	Shoji Koukami

Endgame

1966	Kuro-no-Kai	Inao Nagasaki
1968	Jikken Gekijo	Ikuo Hosoya
1971	Nigatsu Kogyo	Shiro Hasegawa
	Gekidan Shiki	Shiro Hasegawa
	Geki-Kukan Terukeru	Aiko Wada
1973	Beckett Joen Iinkai	Yasu Ohashi
1978	Studio Mugi Group	Hirofumi Yoshida
	Bungakuza*	Shinpei Fujiwara

Krapp's Last Tape

1966	Kuro-no-Kai	Inao Nagasaki
1968	Kurumiza	Tetsuo Kishi
1971	Roman Gekijo	Motoki Tanaka
1972	Kurabu Maarui	Jiro Amano
1974	Engekisha	Takeshi Kabe
1976	Seki Hiroko Kikaku	Hideo Kanze
	I.S. Art Production	Kazuo Sasaki
	En	Motoki Tanaka
	Geijutsu Shogekijo	Hideo Kanze
1978	Kurabu Maarui	Narumichi Sugita
1979	Shishiza	Yoshitaka Okamura
1983	Iteza	Tsutomu Kawashima
1989	Noho Theater Group**	Jonah Salz
1991 (in English)	Compass Theatre Company	Neil Sissons

Happy Days

1965	Bungakuza	Shinya Ando
1969	Mingei	Hiroko Watanabe
1976	Kurumiza	Eizo Kitamura
1979	Shinkukan*	Kenjiro Shin
1989 & 1992	Kyu-Shinkukan	Jun Toyokawa

Play

1964	Haiyu Shogekijo	Tatsuji Iwabuchi
1968	Kurumiza	Toru Ohama
1969	Shingekijo	Junichi Takagi
1972	Engeki Shudan Suna	Nobuyuki Ebata
1980	Kyu-Shinkukan*	Kenjiro Shin

Act Without Words I

1961	Bungakuza	Shinya Ando
1981 & 1982 & 1985	Noho Theater Group**	Jonah Salz

Act Without Words II

1973	Furegaatoza	Michie Kanda

Embers
1970	Maarui Engeki Saron-no-Kai	Jiro Amano
1972	Engeki Shudan Suna	Yasuji Takagi

Not I
1975	Aoi Gekijo	Tsutomu Norifuji
1975	Mei-no-Kai	Jiro Amano

* Completely adapted pieces from Beckett plays. When there are identical producing companies under the same play, it means that they produced different adaptations.

** Noho Theater Group has produced many other Beckett's short pieces such as *Ohio Impromptu, Rockaby, Rough for Theatre I, Footfalls,* and *Quad I & II* under the direction of Jonah Salz and Akira Shigeyama since its foundation in 1981.

The Syntax of Closure:
Beckett's Late Drama

HERSH ZEIFMAN

In early April of 1981—the exact date was 8 April, coincidentally the same date as the opening of the Beckett conference—I shuffled off to Buffalo to attend the world premiere of Samuel Beckett's latest play, *Rockaby*. I had certainly traveled greater distances in my life to see Beckett on stage (Buffalo is less than a two-hour drive from my home in Toronto), though seldom with greater anticipation. For not only was this a new Beckett work, but it was to be performed by Billie Whitelaw, an actor I deeply admire. My expectations that evening were brilliantly fulfilled; despite its brevity (the play's running time is only about fifteen minutes), I found *Rockaby* to be an extraordinarily moving experience. On one level, my response was purely aesthetic: I'm invariably moved by great acting in the theater, and Whitelaw's performance that night was truly sublime. (As one reviewer rhapsodized: "It's possible that you haven't really lived until you've watched Billie Whitelaw die.")[1] The haunting melodic line of her voice—the heartbreaking intonation, for example, she gave to the repeated refrain "another like herself / a little like"—will live with me forever.[2]

I was also moved, however, on a more personal level: the riveting image of a gray-haired woman rocking away what's left of her life strongly evoked in me the memory of my grandmother ravaged by Alzheimer's, a similarly near-mute figure methodically rocking herself to death. "What is she thinking?," I used to wonder as I visited her, hypnotized by that rhythmic rocking to melodies that remained, for me, unheard. Billie Whitelaw, I later discovered, likewise related personally to the character, as she has to all the Beckett women she has portrayed. "Everything [Beckett] writes," she confessed in an interview, "seems to me to be about my life."[3] In the case of *Rockaby*, Whitelaw was reminded specifically of her mother, who in her last five years suffered from Parkinson's: "My mother used to sit in her chair like that, just rocking . . . I used to sit and watch her. I would think, 'Oh, God in heaven, what's going on inside your mind?'. . . How awful it must be to sit there waiting for death."[4]

As I drove back to Toronto after the performance, simultaneously shattered and elated—my usual paradoxical response to a Beckett play—I gradually began to realize that I had been moved by the play on still a third level, and this one perhaps the most profound. "April is the cruellest month," T. S. Eliot begins the first section of *The Waste Land*, "The Burial of the Dead."[5] But though the ending of *Rockaby* seems to me to be about precisely "the burial of the dead," it by no means struck me, that early April evening, as cruel. For the very fact that there *is* an ending to the play, a resolution—even if that resolution signifies death—is in itself a kind of consolation rarely encountered in Beckett's theater. And it is this act of closure that may be, finally, the most moving element of all in Beckett's late drama.

If we consider briefly the history of drama, it is immediately apparent that the vast majority of plays do come to a definite end; though the exact nature of the resolution may be uncertain and open to debate, a strong sense of closure is nevertheless present. Syntactically, these plays are the equivalent of a periodic sentence. When, for instance, Nora slams the door on her charade of a marriage at the end of *A Doll's House*, we may not be able to foresee the precise reverberations of that slam, but the play still comes to a shuddering stop: the slamming of the door is the "period" that completes the "sentence" of Ibsen's play. While such "periodic" plays are by far the norm, however, the syntax of drama occasionally offers up other constructions. Thus a small group of plays—particularly in the modern theater— ends not on a period but on a question mark: the openness of the ending is built into the play's very structure. The play obviously comes to some kind of close, but genuine closure is denied. Probably the most famous modern play with a "question mark" nonending is Ibsen's *Ghosts*. The hopelessly ill Oswald extracts a promise from his mother that, when the time comes, she will save him from the "living death"[6] of a vegetative existence by giving him an overdose of morphine. In the play's final moments the time has spectacularly come, and yet Mrs. Alving is paralyzed by indecision: can she in effect kill her beloved son? The last words we hear her speak in the play are her attempt to answer that question: "No, no, no!—Yes!—no, no!" The interrogative conclusion of *Ghosts* never resolves that "yes/no": the curtain falls on Mrs. Alving frozen in space, staring at her son "*with speechless terror*" (p. 128).

An equally small group of plays manages to defy closure through a different syntactical strategy, by "ending" on the equivalent of a colon: a brief pause before the action circles back on itself. What follows the colon is in effect a restatement of the original subject: syntactically, the play's "sentence" never actually ends. The most audacious use in modern drama of this type of nonending is the act 1 close of David Mamet's *Glengarry Glen Ross*, which ends *literally* on a colon: having cornered his hapless prey in the Chinese restaurant that provides the setting of the entire first act, real-estate salesman Ricky Roma moves in for the kill. "Listen to what I'm going to tell you now:" Roma says, the "now" followed on the page by a colon and on the stage by the curtain.[7] Although on the surface the colon functions simply as a signifier of the particular (undramatized) sales pitch Roma uses to hook his victim, it also points to the circularity of the play's overall structure. For while what follows the colon in act 2 seems to provide closure—the criminals who have broken into the real-estate office and stolen valuable information are duly identified and apprehended—that criminal act is ultimately not the play's primary concern. The police investigation of the break-in occurs significantly offstage, in an inner office we never see; what happens meanwhile *onstage*, front and center, is a different sort of "crime" totally ignored by the police: the oxymoronic crime of American business ethics. The last line of the play, Roma's "I'll be at the restaurant" (p. 108), thus returns us appropriately to the scene of the play's beginning. For the structure of *Glengarry Glen Ross* is circular: the apparently climactic discovery of the crooks in fact resolves nothing, because a gang of far more insidious crooks—the corrupt salesmen—is still at large. That the play circles back specifically to a restaurant is symbolically apt, for *Glengarry* is finally a play about consumption—not of food (we never see the salesmen eating) but of people. The *"Practical Sales Maxim"* chosen by Mamet as the play's epigraph, "ALWAYS BE CLOSING" (p. 13), is therefore highly ironic: in this circular play, closure is never attained.

Perhaps the most subtle examples in modern drama of plays that end figuratively on a colon are those of Chekhov. Things certainly happen in a Chekhov play—decisive things, heartbreaking things, things that alter the course of entire lives—and yet, on some important level, nothing important really changes. Such seemingly earth-shattering events as Treplev's suicide in *The Seagull*, or the attempted murder of Serebryakov in *Uncle Vanya*, or the killing of Tuzenbach in *Three Sisters*, or the selling of the estate in *The Cherry Orchard* always occur offstage, anticlimactically—their potential melodrama often deflected into farce, their significance subsumed within the larger, infinitely more mundane tapestry of daily life. There is, then, no genuine resolution at the end of a Chekhov play. His dramas are thus *emotionally*, if not literally, circular: life simply goes on. Consider the close of *Three Sisters*, for instance, which recapitulates the emotional stasis of the opening: the sisters will continue dreaming of a Moscow that will always remain a dream. Most productions of the play stage the sisters' despair at the end as a kind of still-life triptych, the trio frozen in grief and mourning their fate—a decision in accord with Chekhov's stage direction: *"The three sisters stand close to one another."*[8] When the Czech company Theatre Behind the Gate, however, performed the play in London as part of the 1969 World Theatre Season, director Otomar Krejca made a very different choice: his three sisters expressed their anguish at the end by racing wildly around the stage in what appeared to be a demented frenzy. Almost a quarter of a century later I can still vividly recall those huge circular arcs of despair, those great loops of movement paradoxically going nowhere—an apt description of the structure of the entire play.

It is likewise an apt description, I suggest, of almost all of Beckett's early plays for the theater. The one major exception is *Happy Days*, which subverts closure by means of the alternative syntax: structurally, *Happy Days* has, unusually for Beckett, a "question mark" ending. As Willie attempts to struggle up the mound at the play's close, Winnie is *"Gleeful"*[9]— but "Willie" or won't he ever reach her? In any case, is it indeed Winnie that he wants, or is it rather the revolver *"conspicuous"* by her side (p. 37)? Winnie herself is uncertain:

> Is it me you're after, Willie . . . or is it something else? (Pause.) Do you want to touch my face . . . again? (Pause.) Is it a kiss you're after, Willie . . . or is it something else? (p. 46–47)

Willie's climactic appearance is rendered deliberately ambiguous by Beckett. Attired in *"top hat, morning coat, striped trousers, etc.,"* he could be on his way equally to a wedding or to a funeral—an ambiguity further sustained in Beckett's description of him as *"dressed to kill"* (p. 45). Is it the carnal he seeks, then, or the charnel? Winnie has previously informed us of Willie's intense interest in the gun, of how he had begged her to take it away "before I put myself out of my misery" (p. 26). Willie's final word in the play, "Win" (p. 47), is similarly ambiguous. Is he calling out to his wife by name, or is he instead making a horrific pun, implying that death is the only way to "win" at life? The play refuses to answer: *Happy Days* "ends" with the tableau of husband and wife gazing into each other's eyes, but precisely what they see remains in question.

Happy Days aside, the more typical structure of Beckett's early drama is one of circularity.[10] In the fading moments of *Endgame*, Hamm, that ham actor extraordinaire, sensing that the end is near ("It's the end, Clov, we've come to the end" [p. 79]), decides to recite a little poetry: "You prayed— . . .

You CRIED for night; it comes— . . . It FALLS: now cry in darkness" (p. 83). Despite Hamm's air of spontaneity, the lines, like most of his more lyrical utterances, are not original, though he manages to give them a distinctive twist. The borrowed verse in this instance plucks one of Baudelaire's "fleurs du mal": "Tu réclamais le Soir; il descend; le voici."[11] In Baudelaire the poem is linear, sequential, an answered prayer measured out in semicolons; Hamm's version, significantly, transforms linearity into circularity, the final semicolon now crucially a colon: the lines slither into a tautology, a serpent eating its own tail. "The end is in the beginning," Hamm intuits sorrowfully, "and yet you go on" (p. 69). Like all of Beckett's dramatic characters, the four "pawns" of *Endgame* have indeed cried for "night," for an end to the suffering and wretchedness of their existence. When night finally falls, however, the bitter irony is that nothing has really changed: the longed-for arrival of the end signifies only that there is no "end."

Hamm's rewriting of Baudelaire could stand as an epigraph for the structure of almost all of Beckett's early drama, up to and including *Not I* (1972): to alter slightly the title of Beckett's two mime plays, each of his early plays could have been called "Act Without End." On one level, then, Estragon's summation of the "action" of *Waiting for Godot* is all too cruelly accurate, and not just of that play: "Nothing happens, nobody comes, nobody goes, it's awful"[12]—a cruelty doubled in Vivian Mercier's wicked description of *Godot* as "a play in which nothing happens, *twice*."[13] Beckett's characters wait endlessly, repetitively, for an end that never definitively ends. "Silence and darkness were all I craved," W1 confesses in *Play*;[14] what she craves is in fact what every Beckett character craves: the cessation of words, the cessation of light, the cessation ultimately of *play*. It is also, paradoxically, what they most fear. "[I]t's time it ended," Hamm states near the beginning of *Endgame*. "And yet I hesitate, I hesitate to . . . to end" (p. 3). And when Clov later implores "Let's stop playing!," Hamm replies "Never!" (p. 77). It is the same ambivalence experienced by the central figure in Beckett's late prose piece *Stirrings Still*: "Head on hands half hoping when he disappeared again that he would not reappear again and half fearing that he would not."[15]

In Woody Allen's *Annie Hall*, the stand-up comedian played by Allen opens the film by telling a joke that, stripped of its Jewish trappings, is quintessentially Beckettian:

> There's an old joke. Uh, two elderly women are at a Catskills mountain resort, and one of them says: "Boy, the food at this place is really terrible." The other one says: "Yeah, I know, and such . . . small portions." Well, that's essentially how I feel about life.[16]

That's essentially how Beckett's characters feel about life, too; strange as it may at first sound, Allen and Beckett share—up to a point—a similar comic sensibility. "Nothing is funnier than unhappiness" (p. 18), Nell reminds us in *Endgame* in what is, for Beckett, the most important line in the play.[17] But Allen's black humor becomes infinitely blacker in Beckett, the pain far more deeply felt. For Beckett's characters, life is simultaneously utterly wretched and wretchedly brief; yearning for an end, they nevertheless resent the inevitable end of yearning. As Beckett remarked in *Proust*: "The mortal microcosm cannot forgive the relative immortality of the macrocosm. The whisky bears a grudge against the decanter."[18]

Whether desired or feared, however—or, rather, *both* desired *and* feared—the end, when it finally arrives in Beckett's plays, is never-ending, never final. "I don't seem to be able . . . to depart," Pozzo concludes in the first act of *Godot*; "Such is life," responds Estragon (p. 47). Similarly, while *Endgame* closes with Clov "*dressed for the road*," in the final tableau he remains trapped on the stage, "*impassive and motionless*" (p. 82). "This is what we call making an exit" (p. 81), Clov stated previously as he attempted to depart; in actuality, though, nobody in Beckett's early drama is ever permitted to make a genuine exit. For where is there to go, except back to the very beginning? The circle, by definition, denies closure. In this, as in many other ways (their extensive use of subtext, for example), Beckett's early plays recall Chekhov's: they too "end" on a figurative colon, a pause before the same action—literally or metaphorically—resumes yet again. Structurally, they are the dramatic equivalent of the illuminated Bovril sign described so outrageously in Beckett's short story "A Wet Night": when the seven gaudy phases of the sign's cycle come to an end, the cycle automatically begins once more— *"Da capo."*[19] Beckett's early drama might thus be termed—to coin a suitably Joycean bilingual pun—*palindrames:* plays that "read" the same backwards as forwards. Except, of course, it's never quite the same: the "backwards" reading of a Beckett text is always slightly yet significantly different from the "forwards" reading, precisely because we have previously read it. The fact that nothing happens twice in Beckett's early drama, then, is on one level the something that happens.

The circularity of Beckett's theater, the repeated denial of closure, creates in effect a trap from which there is no escape: as there is no end to the play, so there is no end to the play of human suffering. The show, in a horrifyingly literal sense, must go on. The most relentless example of this circularity in Beckett is his 1963 drama, *Play*. On the surface, the three characters buried in urns appear to be in the same position as Dante's Belacqua, the Antepurgatory figure described by Beckett in *Murphy* as "immune from expiation until he should have dreamed [his life] all through again, . . . from the spermarium to the crematorium, . . . before the toil uphill to Paradise."[20] The significant difference is that Beckett's cosmography lacks a Paradise. The characters of *Play* relive the details of their earthly lives *endlessly*; for them, there is no possibility of "expiation," no possibility of closure. Thus, at the "end" of *Play*, Beckett directs that the entire play should be repeated, and the curtain finally falls on the beginning of yet another repetition: specifically, on M's line: "We were not long together—" (p. 61).[21] The irony here is doubly exquisite: this eternal triangle is in fact doomed to be together *eternally*, and at the same time doomed never to be *together*— the incorporeal "lines" of their triangle never intersect. The impossibility of a climax in Beckett's drama, in any sense of the word, ultimately becomes as frustrating *theatrically* as it would be sexually. The circular structure of Beckett's early theater is therefore profoundly anti-erotic, regardless of its particular subject matter. For endless repetition invariably creates an unbearable tension in the audience—a tension that, lacking closure, can never find release.

Release is similarly denied in Beckett's *Not I*: trapped in the unyielding glare of a circular spotlight, Mouth ends the play still desperately seeking the "right" words to say, words that will "free" her and bring her torment to a close. No such closure is possible, however, because no such words exist: like Lucky's "think," Mouth's monologue is a round dance of futility that could go on indefinitely. Lucky's unpunctuated monologue "ends" solely because he is attacked and physically forced to keep silent (significantly "finishing" on the word "unfinished" [p. 45]); Mouth's logorrhea, also unpunctuated, likewise "ends" solely because the curtain falls and cuts her off (though she continues to speak, unintelligibly, for a further ten seconds, ceasing only when the house lights come up).[22] The circularity of *Not I*, then, once more resists closure. The actor portraying Mouth never actually leaves the stage, but rather the reverse: the stage leaves the actor.

In the quartet of theater plays that immediately follow *Not I*, however, we note a startling stylistic shift: gradually, almost imperceptibly, Beckett's late minimalist drama inches its way towards a kind of closure. All four plays feature a single onstage character (though only one is truly a monologue); all four characters are literally ec-centric, placed deliberately *"off centre."* In *That Time* (1976), the character is Listener, a disembodied face floating ten feet above stage level, listening to a trinity of voices (his own voice split into three) replaying memories of three different stages of his life. The surface similarity to *Not I* is obvious; indeed, Beckett told Patrick Magee, who originated the role of Listener, that he would never allow the two plays to be performed on the same bill: *That Time*, according to Beckett, was too clearly "cut out of the same texture as *Not I*."[23] And yet, despite their similarity, *That Time* provides a brief flicker of hope, a subtle hint of closure, absent from *Not I*. Like all of Beckett's drama, the play attempts to move from "that time" (its opening words) to "no time" (its closing words)—attempts, that is, to attain closure by bridging the gap between them, in effect obliterating time. And like many of Beckett's protagonists, Listener both yearns for this closure and simultaneously fears it: as [Voice] B notes, Listener's "stories" are designed "to keep the void out just another of those old tales to keep the void from pouring in on top of you the shroud." In *That Time*, however—for the first time in Beckett's theater—the "shroud" may actually be allowed to blanket the play's ending; the possibility of dramatic closure seems, this time, finally within reach.

That Time is divided into three brief "acts," each act followed by a ten-second silence in which the voices are momentarily stilled. As the play progresses, the movement towards closure, towards "no time," becomes more and more urgent, culminating in its last speech, a dirge in which [Voice] C mourns the transience of human existence and his own mortality by evoking the words of "the dust":

> what was it it said come and gone was that it something like that come and gone come and gone no one come and gone in no time gone in no time

In the ritualistic silence that ensues, the play's seemingly infinite pattern is suddenly shattered: after three seconds, Listener's eyes open, as usual, but this is followed two seconds later by an inscrutable "*smile*," held for five seconds until the final fade-out and curtain. That smile, though ambiguous—perhaps scornful, perhaps suffused with happiness, perhaps both—brings the play to a dramatic halt, presumably stilling the voices once and for all: the rest is silence. When Beckett directed *That Time* in Berlin, he deliberately slowed down the last speech in each "act," the play's final speech being the slowest of all. "[R]emember the ritardando at the end of Parts I, II and III," he instructed Klaus Herm, who was playing Listener. "Above all," he continued, "at the very end a dramatic effect should be achieved: 'will it go on again.'"[24] In *That Time*, the tension surrounding closure appears to be resolved: mercifully, the play does not go on again. *That Time* finally seems to have embraced "no time": no more words; no more light; no more "play."

In *Footfalls* (1976), the onstage character is May—a character who has not quite been born, who only *may* exist, who wears, according to Beckett, "the costume of a ghost."[25] As the play opens, we see her dimly lit figure obsessively pacing back and forth along a narrow strip at the front of the stage, listening to the sounds of her footfalls, "revolving it all" in her mind. The strip is about the size of a cemetery plot; May is thus, in a sense, pacing her own grave. Significantly, May begins her "revolution" by walking from right to left; as the protagonist of *How It Is* comments, "and death in the west as a rule."[26] Like so many of Beckett's characters, May is embarked on a long day's journey into night: westward, though not necessarily worstward, ho. Is such closure, however, capable of being attained? "Will you never have done . . . revolving it all?," the voice of May's offstage mother muses aloud—the question implicitly asked of all of Beckett's characters. Like *That Time*, *Footfalls* appears to be divided into three brief "acts," each act a diminution, a *cascando*, of the preceding one: the faint chime that opens the acts becomes progressively fainter, the dim light progressively dimmer, May's slow pacing progressively slower. But *Footfalls*, even more than *That Time*, carries a surprising sting in its tail. For there is a *fourth* "act" to this play—a startling "coda" composed equally of "silence and darkness": as the chime sounds a little fainter, the light, likewise a little dimmer, fades up to reveal *"No trace of MAY."* May has simply disappeared—in Billie Whitelaw's words, "spiralling inward, inward." "I said to Sam," Whitelaw further remarked, "that as the light goes he should have only a little pile of fuller's earth. There is nothing left."[27] The "imprisoned" Clov, frozen in the tableau of *Endgame*'s cyclical endlessness, could only dream of the liberation granted the finally absent May: *this* is what we call making an exit![28]

The speaker of Beckett's *A Piece of Monologue* (1979)—*"White hair, white nightgown, white socks"*—is on a similar journey, though he never once moves during the course of the play: a journey from "Birth," the first word in the play, to its last word, "gone," a journey towards closure. Journey's end is signaled in its beginning: "Birth was the death of him," the speaker notes. "Birth" is thus the "rip" word that embodies its own demise: r.i.p. (rest in peace); "the word go" inevitably becomes "The word begone." Yet "silence and darkness," while always hovering at the edge of the frame, seem to lie tantalizingly just outside the speaker's grasp. Thus, when he remembers "Faint sounds" and comments "None now," he immediately corrects himself: "No. No such thing as none"; his parallel conclusion about the "Light dying," "Soon none left to die," is likewise instantly emended: "No. No such thing as no light." Paradoxically, this monologist is not alone on stage: *"Two metres to his left, same level, same height, [is a] standard lamp, skull-sized white globe, faintly lit."* As Mel Gussow has noted, the lamp becomes the speaker's "silent, totemic double. . . . Any second we expect [it] to speak."[29] Thirty seconds before the speaker reaches his last word, "gone," the lamplight begins to go; at play's end, Beckett's stage directions read: *"Lamp out. Silence."* The light slowly fading in that *"skull-sized white globe"* is one of the most haunting images of closure in Beckett's late drama. And yet, *A Piece of Monologue* backtracks slightly from the more definitive closure of *Footfalls*. For the dying of the light does not result in total darkness: the speaker and globe, Beckett notes, are still *"barely visible in diffuse light."* To find the most powerful instance of closure in the Beckett canon, we need instead to turn to Beckett's next stage play, *Rockaby*.

Rockaby (1981) brilliantly encapsulates the central images of the entire quartet of these late Beckett plays: while *"revolving* it all," her chair steadily rocking into and out of the light, W, the play's protagonist, both *listens* to her own recorded voice (V) crooning a lullaby of eternal sleep and occasionally *speaks* two apparently contradictory phrases: "More," repeated four times, and "time she stopped," repeated seven times. The contradiction is only apparent, for W's "More" is in reality "less," a way of propelling herself towards nothingness: we have been on this journey before. The lullaby V croons modulates imperceptibly into a threnody, a rhythmically incantatory verse that begins midsentence without a capital letter and ends, appropriately on the word "off," without a period—"an extended predicate," Jonathan Kalb has noted, "that refuses to resolve."[30] Like most of Beckett's late drama, the play is divided into a number of brief "acts," each preceded by W's imploring "More," each a deeper descent into silence and darkness. Thus the light becomes progressively a little fainter; the voices of both W and V become a little softer; W's eyes gradually begin to close; the rocking chair ultimately comes to a halt.

Defiantly dressed for closure in her "best black"—a lacy, sequined evening gown with "incongruous frivolous headdress"—W sits at play's end blind, mute, completely immobile. Her last words, "rock her off / rock her off," have become both an auditory and visual pun: she is now truly "off her rocker"; the "rocker" is now permanently "off." If "time she stopped" has been the recurrent leitmotif in this lullaby of stopping, we finally comprehend the double meaning of that haunting and ambiguous phrase. For W's decision that it is time to stop is dramatized in the end by her *stopping time:* rock is stilled; voice is silent; there is literally no "More." As the lights fade, we see her head slowly sink and come to rest—the theatrical period noticeably absent from the text as verse narrative. There is no more moving emblem of closure in all of Beckett's late drama.

When I speak of Beckett's late drama ultimately achieving closure, I by no means wish to imply that a Beckett text is thereby somehow "closed," reducible to a single, fixed meaning—the kind of text that Roland Barthes calls "lisible." On the contrary, Beckett's theater is, in Barthes's terminology, remarkably "scriptible": there is always an open play of possibilities in Beckett, a "galaxy of signifiers" that constitutes a genuinely plural significance. Beckett's drama thus embodies what is for Barthes the goal of all literary work: "to make the reader no longer a consumer but a producer of the text."[31] By closure, rather, I mean only this sense of resolution we discover—however we may choose to interpret it—at the end of Beckett's late drama. The *desire* for such closure—"for to end yet again"—is clearly nothing new in Beckett's work: its urgency pulses through his writing from exuberant beginning to weary close. The protagonist of *Stirrings Still*, for example—one of the last pieces Beckett wrote—is engaged in the same age-old quest: "patience till the one true end to time and grief and self and second self his own" (p. 11). The Shakespearean echo in the phrase "second self" clarifies precisely what the protagonist is awaiting: in Sonnet 73, Shakespeare writes of "black night . . . , / Death's second self that seals up all in rest."[32] It is what every Beckett protagonist is awaiting, and simultaneously dreading: the closing of the book.

What is different in Beckett's late drama is thus only a tiny, though momentous, shift of emphasis—the shift from "Little is left to tell," the opening words of *Ohio Impromptu*, to "Nothing is left to tell," the words that bring that play to a close. It is the difference, in short, between "stirrings still"—there is movement yet—and "stirrings still," the cessation of movement; between simple alliteration and profound oxymoron; between the last gasp of life and the first grasp of death. The tenuously precarious balance of a Beckett play has finally tilted, and the tilt is reflected in a change of syntax: abandoning the endless circularity of the colon, Beckett metaphorically puts a period to his writing. All that has really happened is that the shape of a Beckett text has ever so slightly altered—but then, as Beckett reminds us, "It is the shape that matters."[33]

In a much-quoted interview with Tom Driver in 1961, Beckett reportedly remarked:

> If there were only darkness all would be clear. . . . But where we have both dark and light we have also the inexplicable. The key word in my plays is "perhaps."[34]

Perhaps that judgment was valid for Beckett's plays before *Not I*: since then, however, the "yes-no's of yesteryear"—to borrow an outrageous pun from Tom Stoppard's *Travesties*[35]—have long since melted away. In any case, that "perhaps" was always the longest of shots in Beckett's drama, one of its most cruel ironies. Perhaps Godot will eventually come; perhaps the "endgame" will one day progress to "checkmate"; perhaps the spotlight in *Play* will finally go out. As we have seen, the structure of Beckett's early plays consistently denies such closure; if we continued to hope, it was only because to abandon all hope, as Dante reminds us, is to enter hell. And

Beckett's drama, like the Joycean universe he described in his essay in *Our Exagmination*, seemed so obviously "purgatorial" in its "absolute absence of the Absolute."[36]

In his final decade of playwriting, however, Beckett's drama gradually moved closer to an acceptance of the Absolute, or at least its "relative presence." In the now almost unbearably poignant documentary film of the making of *Rockaby*, the late Alan Schneider explained his interpretation of the play to Billie Whitelaw: "It's not about dying. It's not about coming to die. It's about accepting—*accepting* death."[37] Beckett spent almost his entire writing career both acknowledging the inevitability of death and railing against its acceptance. So too did the poet Philip Larkin; in "Aubade," for example, one of Larkin's last, uncollected poems, the dread of dying still "Flashes afresh to hold and horrify":

> Being brave
> Lets no one off the grave.
> Death is no different whined at than withstood.
>
> Slowly light strengthens, and the room takes shape.
> It stands plain as a wardrobe, what we know,
> Have always known, know that we can't escape,
> Yet can't accept.[38]

Ironically, "Aubade" turns out to be a threnody: the light of dawn serves only to make clear the final sunset that must inevitably follow—a sunset from which the poet resolutely turns away. Beckett also wrote aubades that were in reality threnodies—like "Alba" and "Da Tagte Es," poems that appeared in his 1935 collection *Echo's Bones*. But whereas Larkin's poem dates from 1977, less than a decade before his death, Beckett's work by then—in its shift to the syntax of closure—had long since unflinchingly refused to turn away.

On one of my last visits before her death, my grandmother, who for the previous year had talked not at all or only gibberish, suddenly uttered a coherent sentence; speaking to me in Yiddish—or to herself, or perhaps, like W in *Rockaby*, simply to the rocking chair—she whispered: "We make peace with fate." It takes courage to make that peace, especially when our fate, as Vladimir reminds us in *Godot*, is "cruel" (p. 79) and the peace inevitably Pyrrhic. Beckett's writing has always been courageous—the perfect exemplar of Kurt Vonnegut's definition of high art: "Making the most of the raw materials of futility"[39]—but never more so than in his late plays, where futility is at last allowed to triumph. The movement towards closure in Beckett's late drama—even if it denotes a journey into the void, a journey to an "unspeakable home"[40]—thus resolves an enormous tension in both Beckett's characters and his audiences. For if Hamm's repeated summation of human existence is correct—"You're on earth, there's no cure for that!" (pp. 53, 68)—if the light of salvation is indeed "extinguished" (p. 42) or, worse, merely a mocking "trick" of the light—then to achieve total darkness becomes a blessing, a kind of redemption. During rehearsals of *Endgame* in Berlin, Beckett commented to his actors: "Hamm sagt das Nein gegen das Nichts" (Hamm says No to nothingness);[41] courageously, movingly, the woman in *Rockaby* rocks herself to a resounding yes. In Beckett's late plays, the "silence and darkness" his characters so desperately crave, the transition from "that time" to "no time," is finally, mercifully, attained.[42]

Notes

1. Frank Rich, quoted in Barbara Lovenheim, "A Canvas Who Has Lost Her Paintbrush," *New York Times,* 2 September 1990, H5.
2. Because Beckett's late plays tend to be so brief, specific page numbers will not be cited in the text. The late plays from which I quote are all published in *Collected Shorter Plays of Samuel Beckett* (London: Faber & Faber, 1984): *That Time,* pp. 225–35; *Footfalls,* pp. 237–43; *A Piece of Monologue,* pp. 263-69; *Rockaby,* pp. 271–82; and *Ohio Impromptu,* pp. 283–88.
3. Billie Whitelaw interviewed by Linda Ben-Zvi, in Linda Ben-Zvi, ed., *Women in Beckett: Performance and Critical Perspectives* (Urbana: University of Illinois Press, 1990), p. 3.
4. Billie Whitelaw, quoted in David Edelstein, "Rockaby Billie," *Village Voice,* 20 March 1984, 81; and in Mel Gussow, "Billie Whitelaw's Guide to Performing Beckett," *New York Times,* 14 February 1984, 21.
5. T. S. Eliot, *The Waste Land,* in *Selected Poems* (London: Faber, 1962), p. 51.
6. Henrik Ibsen, *Ghosts,* trans. R. Farquharson Sharp, in John Gassner, ed., *Four Great Plays by Ibsen* (New York: Bantam, 1971), p. 108.
7. David Mamet, *Glengarry Glen Ross* (New York: Grove, 1984), p. 51.
8. Anton Chekhov, *Three Sisters,* trans. Ann Dunnigan, in Robert Brustein, ed., *Chekhov: The Major Plays* (New York: Signet, 1964), p. 311.
9. Samuel Beckett, *Happy Days* (London: Faber, 1966), p. 46.
10. On another level, however, *Happy Days* is not really atypical, since it can be argued that the overall structure of the play is indeed circular: act 2 essentially repeats, mutatis mutandis, the "action" of act 1. The mound of earth in which Winnie is progressively buried thus evokes the Zenoist "impossible heap" alluded to in *Endgame,* a heap that can never attain completion. See Samuel Beckett, *Endgame* (New York: Grove, 1958), p. 70.
11. Charles Baudelaire, "Recueillement," in *Les fleurs du mal,* ed. J. Crépet and G. Blin (Paris: Corti, 1942), p. 195.
12. Samuel Beckett, *Waiting for Godot* (London: Faber, 1965), p. 41.

13. Vivian Mercier, *Beckett/Beckett* (New York: Oxford University Press, 1977), p. xii.
14. Samuel Beckett, *Play, Cascando and Other Short Dramatic Pieces* (New York: Grove, 1970), p. 59.
15. Samuel Beckett, *Stirrings Still* (New York: Blue Moon; London: Calder, 1988), p. 4.
16. Woody Allen and Marshall Brickman, *Annie Hall,* in *Four Films of Woody Allen* (London: Faber, 1983), p. 4.
17. See Ruby Cohn, *Just Play: Beckett's Theater* (Princeton: Princeton University Press, 1980), p. 243.
18. Samuel Beckett, *Proust* (London: John Calder, 1965), pp. 21–22.
19. Samuel Beckett, "A Wet Night," in *More Pricks Than Kicks* (New York: Grove, 1970), p. 47.
20. Samuel Beckett, *Murphy* (London: John Calder, 1963), p. 56.
21. When Beckett attended rehearsals for the French production of *Play* (*Comédie*) in 1964, directed by Jean-Marie Serreau, he introduced some variation—specifically, "a slight weakening"—to the exact repetition of the text, thus producing a sense of "falling off . . . , with suggestion of conceivable dark and silence in the end, or of an indefinite approximating towards it. . . ." See Beckett's letter to George Devine, dated 9 March 1964, in John Knowlson, ed., *Samuel Beckett: An Exhibition* (London: Turret, 1971), p. 92.
22. Samuel Beckett, *Not I* (London: Faber, 1973), pp. 15–16.
23. Quoted in Enoch Brater, *Beyond Minimalism: Beckett's Late Style in the Theater* (New York: Oxford University Press, 1987), p. 37. See also Cohn, *Just Play,* p. 30.
24. Quoted in Walter D. Asmus, "Practical Aspects of Theatre, Radio and Television: Rehearsal Notes for the German Premiere of Beckett's *That Time* and *Footfalls* at the Schiller-Theater Werkstatt, Berlin (directed by Beckett)," trans. Helen Watanabe, *Journal of Beckett Studies* 2 (1977): 92, 94.
25. Quoted in ibid., p. 85. When Billie Whitelaw asked Beckett if May was dead, Beckett replied, "Let's just say you're not quite there." Quoted in Jonathan Kalb, *Beckett in Performance* (Cambridge: Cambridge University Press, 1989), p. 235. See also Gussow, "Billie Whitelaw's Guide," p. 21.
26. Samuel Beckett, *How It Is* (London: John Calder, 1964), p. 134.
27. Quoted in Ben-Zvi, *Women in Beckett,* p. 9.
28. See Brater, *Beyond Minimalism,* p. 60.
29. Mel Gussow, "Beckett Distills His Vision," *New York Times,* 31 July 1983, H3.
30. Kalb, *Beckett in Performance,* p. 12.
31. Roland Barthes, *S/Z* (Paris: Editions du Seuil, 1970), pp. 9–12 (my translations).
32. William Shakespeare, *The Sonnets,* in *Shakespeare: The Complete Works,* ed. G. B. Harrison (New York: Harcourt, 1968).
33. Quoted in Harold Hobson, "Samuel Beckett, Dramatist of the Year," in *International Theatre Annual No. 1* (London: John Calder, 1956), p. 153.
34. Tom Driver, "Beckett by the Madeleine," *Columbia University Forum* 4, no. 3 (1961): 23.
35. Tom Stoppard, *Travesties* (London: Faber, 1975), p. 25.
36. Samuel Beckett, "Dante . . . Bruno.Vico . . Joyce," in *Our Exagmination Round his Factification for Incamination of Work in Progress,* 1929, rpt. in Samuel Beckett, *Disjecta: Miscellaneous Writings and a Dramatic Fragment,* ed. Ruby Cohn (New York: Grove, 1984), p. 33.

37. *Rockaby*, directed by D. A. Pennebaker and Chris Hegedus, Pennebaker Associates, 1982.

38. Philip Larkin, "Aubade," *Times Literary Supplement* 23 (December 1977): 1491.

39. Kurt Vonnegut, *Hocus Pocus* (New York: Berkeley, 1991), p. 14.

40. See Beckett's poem "neither," *Journal of Beckett Studies* 4 (1979): v.

41. Quoted in Cohn, *Just Play,* p. 241.

42. Some of the issues raised in this paper were first explored (more briefly and tentatively) in a short paper I delivered at the "Beckett and Beyond" conference, Princess Grace Irish Library, Monaco, May 1991. See also my article "'The Core of the Eddy': *Rockaby and Dramatic Genre*," in Friedman, Rossman, and Sherzer, eds., *Beckett Translating/Translating Beckett* (University Park: Pennsylvania State University Press, 1987), pp. 140–48.

Notes on Contributors

WANDA BALZANO works in a research group at the English Department of the Istituto Universitario Orientale, Naples (Italy). She has written on modernist and postmodernist critical theory, gender, allegory, and Irish postcolonialism.

ANDREAS BJØRNERUD died in 1992 in a tragic accident at the age of twenty-seven. He had been Lecturer in French at the University of Sussex. His articles had appeared in *New Formations*, and *LIT*, and material is forthcoming in *Paragraph*. He earned his doctorate with a dissertation on Beckett and Céline at Oxford University.

MARY BRYDEN is Associate Director of the Beckett International Foundation, University of Reading, U.K. She has published numerous articles and essays on Beckett, and was assistant editor to John Pilling for the recent publication of *The Ideal Core of the Onion: Reading Beckett Archives* (BIF, 1992). Her monograph *Women in the Prose and Drama of Beckett* was published by Macmillan in 1993.

MARIUS BUNING is Senior Lecturer in English at the Free University of Amsterdam. His writings include *T. F. Powys: A Modern Allegorist, The Companion Novels "Mr. Weston's Good Wine" and "Unclay" in the Light of Modern Allegorical Theory* (Rodopi, 1986), and *Beckett in the 1990s*, coedited with Lois Oppenheim (Rodopi, 1993). He is an editor of *D.Q.R. Studies in English Literature* and of *Samuel Beckett Today/Aujourd'hui*. He was director and co-organizer, with Lois Oppenheim, of the 1992 International Beckett Symposium held in The Hague.

DAVID GORDON is Professor of English at Hunter College and the Graduate Center of the City University of New York. His publications include *D. H. Lawrence as a Literary Critic* (Yale University Press, 1966), *Literary Art and the Unconscious* (Louisiana State University Press, 1976), and *Bernard Shaw and the Comic Sublime* (Macmillan/St. Martins Press, 1990). His recently completed book, *Iris Murdoch's Fables of Unselfing*, is forthcoming.

LESLIE HILL is Lecturer in French Studies at the University of Warwick and the author of *Beckett's Fiction: In Different Words* (Cambridge University Press, 1990) and *Marguerite Duras: Apocalyptic Desires* (Routledge, 1993). He is currently at work on a study of the writings of Maurice Blanchot and a book on recent French fiction.

ELIZABETH KLAVER is in the English Department at Southern Illinois University. She has published articles on Beckett and Ionesco and is currently working on a book on contemporary drama and television.

CARLA LOCATELLI, Chair, Department of English, University of Trent (Italy), is author of *La disdetta della parola* and *Unwording the World*, both on Beckett. She has also written on Virginia Woolf, *Il Test dispoegato*; on Swift, *La parola prigioniera nella carne*; on romantic poets and poetics, *Le poetiche romantiche inglesi* and *Per un introduzione al romanticismo inglese. Un analisi di manifesti e documenti*; and on the history of English and American literature, *The Ways of Words* and *Texts and Contexts*.

FRANK MATTON is a research assistant for the Belgian National Research Foundation (N.F.W.O) at Antwerp University, Belgium. He is currently completing a doctoral dissertation entitled "Beckett's Aesthetics of Suffering" at Trinity College, Dublin. His writings on Beckett include a comparative article on Beckett and Sade, "Sad(e)ness," that appeared in the Belgian periodical *Restant*.

GERRY MCCARTHY is Senior Lecturer in the Department of Drama and Theatre Arts at the University of Birmingham, England, where he was Director of Drama from 1987 to 1992. He has directed numerous Beckett productions including *Endgame*, *Krapp's Last Tape*, *Play*, *Not I*, and *Happy Days*. He directed *Not I* a second time for the first International Beckett Symposium at Stirling, Scotland in 1986. His publications include *Edward Albee* (St. Martin's Press, 1987) and articles on Sam Shepard, Molière, and modern French and French-Canadian theater, as well as Beckett.

ANGELA MOORJANI is Professor of French and Associate Vice-President for Academic Affairs at the University of Maryland, Baltimore County. She is the author of numerous articles, principally on psychoaesthetics and the work of Samuel Beckett. Her publications include *Abysmal Games in the Novels of Samuel Beckett* (University of North Carolina Press, 1982) and *The Aesthetics of Lessness* (Macmillan/St. Martins, 1992).

LOIS OPPENHEIM is Associate Professor of French at Montclair State University. She has authored or edited *Intentionality and Intersubjectivity: A Phenomenological Study of Butor's "La Modification"* (French Forum, 1980); *Three Decades of the French New Novel* (University of Illinois Press, 1986); *Directing Beckett* (University of Michigan Press, 1994); *Beckett in the 1990s*, coedited with Marius Buning (Rodopi, 1993); and the annotated volume, Michel Butor's *Transformation of Writing* (forthcoming, University Press of Florida). She is an editor of *The Beckett Circle* and of *New Novel Review* and on the editorial board of Garland Press's bilingual variorum editions of Beckett. She was co-organizer, with Marius Buning, of the 1992 International Beckett Symposium held in The Hague.

DOROTHEE OSTMEIER teaches German at the University of Washington. She has written on the works of Nelly Sachs, Walter Benjamin, Samuel Beckett, and August Stramm.

JOHN PILLING is Professor of English at the University of Reading (U.K.) and Director of the Beckett International Foundation. He is the author of *Samuel Beckett* (Routledge, 1976) and, with James Knowlson, of *Frescoes of the Skull: The Later Prose and Drama of Samuel Beckett* (John Calder, 1979). He has edited *The Cambridge Companion to Beckett* (Cambridge University Press, 1993) and, with Mary Bryden, *The Ideal Core of the Onion: Reading Beckett Archives* (Beckett International Foundation, 1992). He edited the *Journal of Beckett Studies* from 1979 to 1985.

ROBERT SCANLAN is Literary Director of the American Repertory Theatre in Cambridge, Massachusetts, and Lecturer on Dramatic Arts at Harvard University, where he heads the Dramaturgy Program at the Institute for Advanced Theatre Training. He has directed in the People's Republic of China and Eastern Europe. Scanlan has directed (or supervised the production of) all but two of Beckett's plays and he writes frequently about the staging of Beckett's work.

MARIKO HORI TANAKA is Associate Professor of English Language and Drama at Aoyama Gakuin University, Tokyo. Her publications on modern drama focus primarily on aspects of directing and performing.

KIRILL OLE THOMPSON is Associate Professor in the Foreign Languages and Literature Department at National Taiwan University. He has published numerous articles on Chinese philosophy.

LI-LING TSENG teaches in the Department of Foreign Languages and Literatures at National Taiwan University. She has published several articles on Beckett, most notably in *Twentieth Century Literature*, *Chung-Wai Literary Monthly*, *Fu Jen Studies*, and *Studies in Language and Literature*, and her translations into Chinese of four Beckett texts have appeared in *Chung-Wai Literary Monthly*.

JOHANNEKE VAN SLOOTEN is a musician, essayist, television director, and radio programmer. She is currently writing a book on language and music and working on a compilation of her essays both on musical influences in the work of Joyce, Faulkner, Calvino, Proust, and others, and on linguistic qualities in the work of Schönberg, Berio, Janacek, and Stravinsky.

HARRY VANDERVLIST has written on *Watt*, *More Pricks than Kicks*, and *Murphy*. He has also written extensively on topics in comparative literature. Professor Vandervlist teaches English at the University of Calgary.

HERSH ZEIFMAN is Associate Professor of English at York University in Toronto, coeditor of *Modern Drama,* and a former president of the Samuel Beckett Society. In addition to having written many articles on contemporary drama, he is the editor of *David Hare: A Casebook* and the coeditor of *Contemporary British Drama*.

Index

Act Without Words I, 227, 228, 231, 238n
Act Without Words II, 238n
"Alba," 251
All That Fall, 45, 48, 55, 58
A Piece of Monologue, 248, 249, 252n
As The Story Was Told: Uncollected and Late Prose, 43n
"A Wet Night," 45, 245, 253n

Berceuse, 19, 22
Breath, 60

"Calmative, The"/"Le Calmant," 83, 90
Cascando, 49, 50, 55, 119, 253n
Catastrophe, 11, 26n
Collected Poems, 1930–1978, 224n
Collected Shorter Plays, 19, 20, 21, 23, 24, 25, 26n, 159n, 197n, 198n, 252n
Collected Shorter Prose, 64n, 65n, 135, 139
Come and Go, 234
Company, 20, 26n, 53, 55, 132, 137

"Da Tagte Es," 251
Disjecta, 140, 144n, 158n, 210n, 211n, 253n
Dream of Fair to Middling Women, 38, 42n, 64n, 96n, 138

Echo's Bones, 251
Eh Joe, 57, 59
Embers, 45, 52, 55, 119, 239n
En Attendant Godot, 166, 168, 176n
Endgame, 11, 117, 119, 176n, 230, 231, 238n, 243, 244, 245, 248, 252, 252n
"Enough," 8

First Love, 97n, 135
Footfalls, 23, 55, 59, 94, 239n, 247, 248, 249, 252n, 253n
"From An Abandoned Work," 64

Ghost Trio, 49

Happy Days, 11, 23, 41, 59, 119, 234, 235, 238n, 243, 252n
How It Is, 10, 43n, 51, 64, 65n, 102, 103, 104, 105, 106, 107, 108, 109n, 131, 248, 253n

Ill Seen Ill Said/Mal vu mal dit, 93, 94, 97n, 98n, 138, 142

Krapp's Last Tape, 50, 57, 119, 121, 122, 152, 154, 158n, 176n, 188, 192, 196, 197, 197n, 198n, 231, 232, 238n

L'Innommable, 22, 81n, 83, 87

Malone Dies, 65n, 81n, 130, 179, 180, 183, 201. See also *Malone meurt*
Malone meurt, 81n, 179, 180
Mercier et Camier, 21
Molloy, 20, 23, 26n, 57, 65n, 70, 71, 75, 81n, 87, 88, 91, 93, 97n, 133, 136, 167, 169, 179, 180, 183, 185, 200
More Pricks than Kicks, 45, 179, 253n
Murphy, 37, 42n, 48, 65n, 71, 111, 179, 199, 211n, 245, 253n

Nacht und Träume, 48
"neither," 43n, 50, 254n
Not I, 9, 13n, 19, 25, 27, 28, 29, 30, 33, 34

259

Not I (continued):
  52, 53, 55, 57, 60, 153, 155, 156, 157, 161, 231, 239n, 244, 246, 250, 253n
Nouvelles, 61

Ohio Impromptu, 13, 52, 56, 80, 89, 92, 94, 97n, 98n, 232, 239n, 250, 252n
"Old Earth, " 136

Play/Comédie, 36, 56, 59, 121, 122, 123n, 148, 187, 188, 191, 192, 195, 196, 197, 197n, 198n, 234, 238n, 244, 245, 246, 250, 253n
Proust, 39, 40, 43n, 82n, 83, 95n, 178, 179, 199, 209, 210n, 211n, 245, 253n

Quad, 8, 25, 232, 239n

Rockaby, 9, 11, 13n, 19, 20, 21, 22, 23, 24, 25, 26, 57, 94, 95, 98n, 150, 188, 192, 195, 196, 197, 198n, 232, 239n, 240, 241, 249, 251, 252, 252n, 254n. See also *Berceuse*
Rough for Theatre I, 49, 232, 239n

Stirrings Still, 45, 49, 55, 95n, 244, 250, 253n

Texts for Nothing/Textes pour rien, 90

That Time, 51, 52, 53, 56, 59, 234, 246, 247, 248, 252n, 253n
Three Dialogues, 178
Trilogy, 61, 64, 69, 81n, 199, 200, 201, 202, 205, 206, 207, 208, 209, 210, 210n

Unnamable, The, 13n, 19, 22, 38, 41, 42n, 49, 51, 54, 65n, 69, 73, 74, 76, 78, 79, 81n, 83, 87, 89, 103, 111, 112, 115, 116, 129, 130, 131, 135, 137, 139, 140, 141, 143, 172, 180, 181, 182, 183, 184, 185, 207. See also *L'Innommable*

Waiting for Godot, 8, 11, 24, 26n, 36, 59, 62, 111, 112, 115, 116, 117, 118, 119, 120, 139, 166, 167, 168, 169, 173, 175, 214, 215, 217, 218, 222n, 223n, 227, 228, 229, 230, 232, 233, 234, 236n, 237n, 244, 245, 251, 252n. See also *En Attendant Godot; Warten auf Godot*
Warten auf Godot, 166, 168, 169, 176n
Watt, 10, 24, 38, 48, 51, 56, 58, 61, 62, 63, 64, 64n, 65n, 66, 91, 111, 112, 179, 180, 181
What Where, 8, 121, 122, 159n
Words and Music, 49, 50, 51, 54
Worstward Ho, 55, 64, 65n, 121, 129, 132, 134, 139, 141